The Devil Himself

For Joe

Andrew Ponneln

New Narratives in American History

Series Editors
James West Davidson
Michael B. Stoff

Colonial

Southern

Civil War and Reconstruction

20th Century Environmental

African-American

Twentieth-Century U.S. History

The Devil Himself

A Tale of Honor, Insanity,
and the Birth of
Modern America

Andrew Porwancher

New York   Oxford

OXFORD UNIVERSITY PRESS

Oxford University Press is a department of the University of Oxford.
It furthers the University's objective of excellence in research,
scholarship, and education by publishing worldwide.

Oxford   New York
Auckland   Cape Town   Dar es Salaam   Hong Kong   Karachi
Kuala Lumpur   Madrid   Melbourne   Mexico City   Nairobi
New Delhi   Shanghai   Taipei   Toronto

With offices in
Argentina   Austria   Brazil   Chile   Czech Republic   France   Greece
Guatemala   Hungary   Italy   Japan   Poland   Portugal   Singapore
South Korea   Switzerland   Thailand   Turkey   Ukraine   Vietnam

For titles covered by Section 112 of the US Higher Education
Opportunity Act, please visit www.oup.com/us/he for the
latest information about pricing and alternate formats.

Published by Oxford University Press
198 Madison Avenue, New York, New York 10016
http://www.oup.com

Oxford is a registered trademark of Oxford University Press

Library of Congress Cataloging-in-Publication Data

Names: Porwancher, Andrew, author.
Title: The Devil himself : a tale of honor, insanity, and the birth of modern
    America / Andrew Porwancher.
Description: New York : Oxford University Press, 2016. | Series: New
    narratives in American history | Includes bibliographical references.
Identifiers: LCCN 2015049276 | ISBN 9780190210786
Subjects: LCSH: Trials (Murder)--Pennsylvania--Uniontown (Fayette
    County)--History--19th century. | Honor killings--Pennsylvania--Uniontown
    (Fayette County)--History--19th century. | Dukes, N. L. (Nicholas Lyman),
    -1883--Trials, litigation, etc. | Nutt, James--Trials, litigation, etc. |
    Dukes, N. L. (Nicholas Lyman), -1883--Death and burial. | Nutt, Adam,
    1839-1882--Death and burial.
Classification: LCC KF223.D845 P67 2016 | DDC 345.748/02523--dc23 LC record
available at http://lccn.loc.gov/2015049276

Printing number: 9 8 7 6 5 4 3 2 1

Printed in Canada
on acid-free paper

To My Parents

CONTENTS

Contents

FOREWORD

Honor. The word rings with nobility and bespeaks a devotion to high ideals. Yet honor can be freighted with multiple meanings and fraught with danger. Bound by its historical moment, anchored to its cultural context, honor is nonetheless malleable and sometimes perverse in application. It is difficult to measure, harder still to assess, but its power to arouse people is as undeniable as the sacrifices they make and the violence they employ in its defense.

Historians have wrestled with the anomalies of honor and still found it a useful tool to excavate the past. In the able hands of Andrew Porwancher, the devotion to a Victorian code of conduct becomes a way of understanding a moment of dramatic change in late nineteenth century America. A chance encounter with a long-forgotten murder case, one of the most notorious of the nineteenth century, led Porwancher to dig deeper. In the process, he uncovered a tale, in his words, "of forsaken love and outraged honor" that rocked the nation with not one but two murders, two trials, and newspaper headlines that spread as far west as Oregon and as far south as Georgia.

The episode grew from charges of sex out of wedlock and pregnancy leveled against Lizzie Nutt, the daughter of a prominent Civil War veteran, by her onetime fiancé, Nicholas Dukes. In a letter to Captain Adam Nutt, Lizzie's father, Dukes claimed to have discovered the disturbing fact that his betrothed had had sexual relations with several men and was now with child. He admitted to having tested the maiden's virginity himself and found it wanting. Lizzie's transgressions, Dukes explained, forced him to break off the engagement. The allegations—and Dukes's shocking admission—led to a calamitous confrontation between Dukes and Captain Nutt.

Salacious assertions were hardly unknown in late nineteenth century America. Nor was it unusual for them to produce a thirst for blood from men who saw the reputation of a woman, in this case a daughter, soiled by accusations of illicit behavior. Only with the accusations withdrawn or the accuser eliminated could the stain be washed away. Nutt challenged Dukes in an effort to restore the reputation of his daughter and his family.

In the end, the pursuit of honor led to a string of tragedies. A lethal assault prompted a murder trial. More tragedies followed, and another killer pled insanity. It was a particularly modern defense in an episode generated by a traditional method of imposing justice.

Not only the how but the where of the tangled Dukes—Nutt affair caught Porwancher's attention. Historians have usually seen honor killing as a Southern phenomenon, the residual effects of early settlement by the Celts. They brought a culture of honor and its violent defense to the South. But Porwancher's tale of honor involves figures of Anglo rather than Celtic descent in a predominately Anglo town. And where? In the North of all places! The national reaction, largely positive in its support of the dishonored father, illustrated that the premium on honor extended far beyond the confines of the Old South.

Historians have also contended that although the colonial North spawned its share of honor killings, the practice had long since been abandoned above the Mason-Dixon Line. Especially in the decades after the Civil War, industrialization and growing ethnic diversity created a more complex environment in which the rule of law and the court system replaced the older, more socially governed code of honor as a way of rendering justice and maintaining order.

Not so, as Porwancher's painstaking reconstruction of the Dukes—Nutt case demonstrates. Rather than preserving social order, enforcement of a commonly held honor code buttressed an older order against the relentless intrusions of modern life. Communities across the country were losing autonomy in the face of revolutions in transportation, communication, mass-manufacturing, and marketing. Women were claiming their "inalienable right" to vote. An impersonal court system was removing justice from communal hands. Americans North and South pushed back, enlisting honor in a much broader battle to wall out modernity by returning control of crime and punishment to local communities. At such a moment, it is difficult to distinguish, as Porwancher suggests, between devils and angels.

James West Davidson
Michael B. Stoff
Series Editors

ACKNOWLEDGMENTS

I OWE MY FIRST DEBT OF GRATITUDE TO MY SERIES EDITOR, Michael Stoff. From this book's initial stages to its final draft, he was an enthusiastic advocate. I consider myself highly fortunate to have worked with an editor so generous with his time and so encouraging with his words. His thoughtful suggestions for the manuscript have improved it immeasurably. I will always be appreciative to both him and his fellow series editor, James West Davidson, for taking a chance on a first-time author.

In the critical early days of the research, Noah Feldman and Vernon Burton helped me think through the context and implications of my narrative. Dan Gerstle deserves unrelenting praise and probably my royalties for his studious reading of multiple drafts. He has a keen eye for how to craft a smaller story that tells a larger one. From broad themes to minute details, Dan's insight informs every page. My attentive acquisitions editor, Brian Wheel, helped shepherd this book to completion with merciful alacrity. I am also thankful to the anonymous readers for their astute comments.

Acknowledgments

I completed most of this book while on leave as the Alistair Horne Fellow at St. Antony's College at the University of Oxford. The fellowship provided me with not only unobstructed time to write but also a lively community of scholars and graduate students who made that year among the best of my life. I am particularly indebted to the Warden of St. Antony's, Margaret MacMillan, and Sir Alistair himself, who showed me great kindness upon my arrival to England.

A number of archivists and librarians provided me with crucial assistance, foremost among them Maria Sholtis of the Uniontown Public Library. Her diligence in tracking down primary sources is highly appreciated. Suzanne Williams of the Allegheny College Archives dug up a revealing college essay that Adam Nutt wrote in 1861. Carolyn Olsen of the Holton Library in Kansas went to heroic lengths to track down a key newspaper article from 1895. Several members of the Fayette County Historical Society—Christine Buckelew, Tom Buckelew, and Mick Gallis—extended tremendous hospitality to me during my time spent researching in Uniontown.

I am fortunate to have colleagues that make the University of Oklahoma a wonderful place to teach and write history, especially David Anderson, Luis Cortest, David Wrobel, and Wilfred McClay. Kyle Harper deserves special mention. From the time that I first met him in 2010 when I was still a graduate student until the present day, Kyle has been a true mentor and a friend. This project received funding from various bodies at the University of Oklahoma, including the Institute for the American Constitutional Heritage, Department of Classics & Letters, College of Arts & Sciences, Office of the Vice President for Research,

Research Council, and Office of the Senior Vice President and Provost. Rachelle Barteau did a masterful job preparing images for the book. I also thank Ann Laudick, Kelly Goodson, and Amber Dawn Armstrong for their research assistance.

If there is any merit to this book, the foregoing editors, readers, colleagues and librarians are in no small measure responsible; if there are any errors in its pages, they are mine alone.

I would be remiss if I did not mention my oldest friends, who were perennial sources of support in the course of this project, as they are in all my endeavors.

The professor to whom I am most grateful is my sister, Kara. She launched her academic career before I did, and her constant concern has been to share with me the benefits of her experience and to see me thrive. Her encouragement is unwavering. Fortuitously, Kara lives near Uniontown, and her home provided an ideal base for my trips to the archives, all the more so for the company of her husband, Jonathan, as well as my lovely nieces, Abigail and Talia, and of course my nephew, the incomparable Noah.

My greatest expression of gratitude I reserve for my parents. I hope that they see this book as I do—as a testament to their abiding support. From the beginning, they created a home alive with ideas, nurtured my curiosity, commiserated when I failed, cheered when I succeeded, and always asked how they could help. Years ago, as my mother toiled on her dissertation, I expressed doubts about my own ability to formulate an original thesis. In retrospect, my concern was probably premature for a five year old who had not yet learned to read. Yet neither my age nor my illiteracy prevented my parents from voicing at that time supreme faith in my capacity to make a meaningful contribution to scholarship. I leave it to the reader to determine whether their confidence in me was misplaced. What I do know is that this book would not exist without my mother and father. It is to them that I dedicate this work.

Andrew Porwancher
Norman, Oklahoma

UNIONTOWN, PENNSYLVANIA

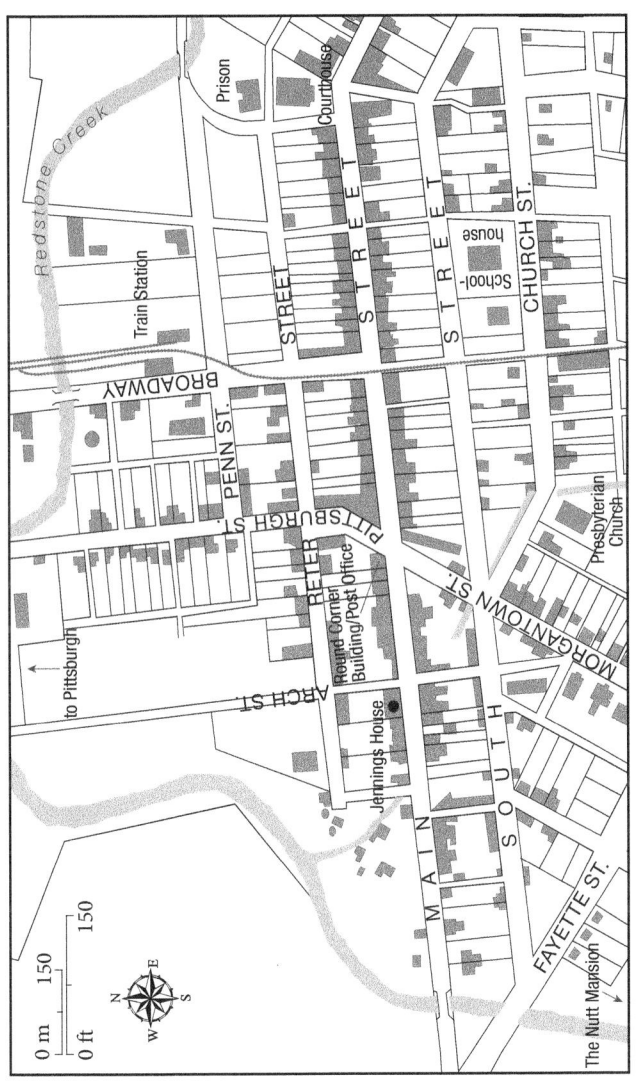

Key Figures

Principal Relatives of Captain Adam Nutt

Mrs. Charlotte Nutt, wife
Lizzie Nutt, eldest daughter
Adam Nutt, eldest son
Clark Breckenridge, nephew
Stephen Nutt, brother
Joseph Nutt, brother
Jim Wells, brother-in-law
Grandma Ann Wells, mother-in-law

Principal Relatives of Nicholas Dukes

Asbury Struble, stepfather
Mrs. Struble, mother
George Struble, half-brother
Lewis Dukes, brother

Key Figures in Uniontown

Sheriff James Hoover

Thomas Searight, court clerk and political patron of Dukes
Reverend N. P. Kerr
Reverend Alexander Milholland, Presbyterian Church
Mr. Henry Jennings, proprietor of the Jennings House
Mrs. Jennings
James Feather, son-in-law of the Jennings
Lewis Williams, porter at the Jennings House
Dr. Smith Fuller, the Nutt family physician
Dr. James Ewing
Officer Frank Pegg, policeman
Officer Lucius Martin, policeman

Key Figures in Harrisburg

State Treasurer Silas Baily (R)
Speaker John Faunce (D)
Representative A. J. Colborn (R)
Representative Jerome Niles (R)
Representative Lemuel Amerman (D)
Representative William Sponsler (R)

Trial 1 (March 1883)

Judge Alpheus Willson

Prosecutors for the Commonwealth of Pennsylvania
District Attorney Isaac Johnson
William Playford
A. D. Boyd

Lawyers for the Defense
Congressman Charles Boyle
S L. Mestrezat
R. H. Lindsey

Trial 2 (January 1884)

Judge Edwin Stowe

Prosecutors for the Commonwealth of Pennsylvania
District Attorney Isaac Johnson
John Boyle, son of Congressman Boyle
David Patterson

Attorneys for the Defense
William Playford
A. D. Boyd
Marshall Swartzwelder
Senator Daniel Voorhees
Major A. M. Brown
General William Blakely

"Revenge is a kind of wild justice."
—Sir Francis Bacon

PROLOGUE

&

Americans of the Gilded Age (1870s–1890s), no less than Americans today, were captivated by trials. Transcripts of especially salacious proceedings were bound and sold for the public's reading pleasure. When I came across the transcript of one such trial from 1883, I found upon turning its pages a tale of forsaken love and outraged honor. The story achieved national prominence in the late nineteenth century but later slipped into obscurity, surviving only as folklore in Uniontown, Pennsylvania, where it began. No one had ever authored a book on the subject, the local historical society informed me. I took off for Uniontown, and there uncovered a tangled web of love letters, court records, and newspaper accounts that amounted to a story even more enticing and revealing than the trial transcript first promised. Every detail in the pages to follow comes directly from the historical record.

Captain Adam Nutt and Nicholas Dukes were two men with much in common. Both were esteemed political figures in Uniontown, both had studied law under the same mentor, and both valued the code of honor above their own lives. After Dukes confessed to seducing Captain Nutt's daughter, the two men dueled on a fateful Christmas Eve. One was slain, the other indicted for murder. The ensuing trial touched a nerve deep in the national psyche and prompted an outpouring of support across the country for honor killing.

Yet historians have long assumed that the honor code was the preserve of Southerners in the late nineteenth century. Never questioning whether the South was distinct in this respect, scholars instead debate why the North and South were supposedly so different. Some point to ethnicity, maintaining that the Celts who settled the South brought with them their traditional culture of honor, whereas the Anglo-Saxons who predominated in the northern United States prized self-restraint. Other historians claim that the North also placed a high premium on honor in the early days of the Republic, but throughout the first half of the nineteenth century, honor lost resonance in an urban-industrial North while enduring in a rural-agrarian South. This line of reasoning holds that as the North grew more ethnically and economically diverse, the rule of law became essential to social stability, effectively superseding the honor code. But the Dukes–Nutt affair suggests that these developments did not render obsolete the tradition of honor in the North. Indeed, it was precisely because urbanization and industrialization proved so bewildering that people in all regions of the nation clung to honor as a bulwark against change.[1]

At the time of the country's founding, America largely comprised what one historian has called "island communities," self-sufficient towns functioning in relative isolation from each other. Villagers understood themselves to govern their labor, their lives, and their fates. By the late nineteenth century, however, this sense of control had come under threat. The kind of institutions to be found in Uniontown in the 1880s—the railroad station, the telegraph office, the factories—embodied the revolutions in transportation, communication, and industry that swept through American society at breakneck pace, eroding the independence of both communities and individuals. Train tracks crisscrossed the continent, collapsing time and distance between far-flung people and places. With the advent of the telegraph, people could now transmit messages without the physical delivery of their dispatches; the newspaper coverage of the Dukes–Nutt scandal offered a striking example of the rapidity and reach of this spreading technology. Whereas the farmers and craftsmen of an earlier era owned their tools and their time, the factory workers of the industrial age controlled neither their means of production nor their schedules of work. The dictatorship of the clock replaced the movement of the sun as the arbiter of the workday. Amid the growing bureaucracies needed to manage an industrialized economy, a new class of white-collar professionals found itself subjected to hierarchy and routine, with little in the way of autonomy. These various transformations compounded one another, subsuming all that was once local into regional, national, and international networks.[2]

Although modernizing trends began before the late nineteenth century, it was in the Gilded Age that their pace vastly accelerated and the center of American gravity shifted from a rural-agrarian society to an urban-industrial order. The town fathers of the self-contained island community had once enjoyed significant control over local affairs. But now, as the outside world intruded on their idyll, this sense of independence deteriorated. Uniontown and countless places like it exhibited deep ambivalence about modern life. Their residents were at once tantalized by the technological wonders of a new era and wary of the challenge to community values that a loss of autonomy portended. As the world of their youth receded behind them and an uncertain future approached with dizzying speed, Americans of the Gilded Age held fast to honor.

The code of honor kept modernization at bay, in large part, by reaffirming the agency of the community. In the nineteenth century, criminal justice, like so many aspects of life, became increasingly professionalized, bureaucratized, and centralized—in other words, remote from the daily lives of ordinary citizens. Honor killing, therefore, was an assertion of local independence, a violent act that championed communal values, a repudiation of the modern justice system's impersonal legalism. When the culture of honor sanctioned killing, the homicide was, in effect, a ritual that reaffirmed the community's prerogative to manage its affairs on its own terms. Vengeance did more than simply restore honor to the aggrieved party. The execution was cathartic for the entire village. Upon death, the victim of an honor killing transformed into a sacrificial lamb offered on the altar of communal mores.[3]

Honor further served as a mainstay against modernization by upholding conventional gender roles at a time when manhood was perceived to be in peril. With no ownership of their businesses and no control over their schedules, most men were robbed by the modern economy of the self-made ideal so central to American masculinity. At the same time, unprecedented numbers of women were entering the workforce, enrolling in college, and demanding voting rights. Women's encroachment on these traditionally male preserves exacerbated a growing feeling of emasculation. The honor code promised an antidote to this crisis of manhood by promoting sharply defined gender roles. For men, the display of masculine courage in the face of disrespect was the ultimate test of one's honor. For women, the code of honor demanded unconditional sexual purity outside of matrimony. These two ideals worked in tandem—there was no greater affront to a man's honor than the seduction of his daughter, wife, or sister.[4]

Victorian notions of sexual restraint thus lay at the heart of the honor code (and at the center of the Dukes–Nutt affair). Middle-class culture in both England and the United States idealized female purity during the Victorian era (1837–1901), which overlapped with the Gilded Age. Yet in a modernizing society rife with temptations, people often failed to practice abstinence outside of marriage. Industrialization moved the locus of work outside the home, creating novel opportunities for interaction between the sexes. Whether a woman stayed home while her male kin left for their places of employment or she herself moved to a burgeoning city in search of work, she found herself removed from the watchful gaze of her father and brothers. It was in the context of this newfound freedom for women that the strident demand for purity came to be seen as necessary. The Victorian premium on chastity was more a reflection of male distress about female independence than a description of actual behavior. By positioning men as the protectors of womanly virtue, the code of honor offered men a reinvigorated sense of masculinity as well as control over female sexuality, or at least the illusion of these things.[5]

This was the world that Nicholas Dukes and Captain Nutt inhabited—one of technological advance, disorienting change, and a desperate struggle to maintain tradition. In fighting against one another to defend their honor, Dukes and Nutt in a sense fought together to defend a conventional society that was quickly fading from view. An anxious nation looked to the murder trial resulting from their duel less as a search for truth than as a test of whether honor could survive amid the uncertain terrain of modern America.

· *One* ·

LETTERS

THE DUKES–NUTT SAGA BEGAN WITH A GLANCE IN A CHURCH. Although the Presbyterian Church in Uniontown was known for its exquisite paintings and stained glass, Nicholas Dukes's gaze was instead drawn to an enchanting young woman across the aisle. With her light hair, large eyes, and slender figure, Lizzie Nutt was hard not to notice. She was the daughter of Captain Adam Clarke Nutt, a revered Civil War veteran who would soon become a high-ranking official at the State Treasury. Dukes had political ambitions of his own, hoping to parlay a successful legal practice into a seat in the Pennsylvania House of Representatives. Before Dukes courted voters, however, he first courted Lizzie. Still in her early twenties, she was ten years his junior, but the difference in age was of little moment to Dukes. Her warmth and beauty captivated him. Not long after he first sighted Lizzie, Dukes asked for her hand in marriage. Lizzie accepted his proposal, undoubtedly with hopes for a lifetime of marital bliss. Yet whatever happiness they enjoyed did not last long. On December 4, 1882, Nicholas Dukes wrote a letter to Captain Nutt that forever severed his ties to Lizzie and the Nutt family.[1]

Lizzie Nutt

Source: Lizzie Nutt's Sad Experience: A Heart Broken, and a Family Plunged in Grief. Wreck and Ruin! (Philadelphia: Barclay, 1886), 32.

Dukes issued an unusual warning at the start of his letter: "Read this in private." He could have little imagined that the contents of his correspondence would soon be reprinted in newspapers across the country. "Dear Sir," Dukes continued, "the matter that I am about to communicate to you is sad, painful and marvellous [*sic*], and if there was any possible way to avoid it I should be only too glad to escape the task that I now impose upon myself." Anticipating that Captain Nutt would meet with incredulity the allegations to follow, Dukes insisted "that what you find herein written is faithful to fact—no exaggerations, no inaccuracies, no false assertions." Still, he hesitated: "This much said I still tremble upon the brink. My message

Nutt and Dukes
Source: Lizzie Nutt's Sad Experience: A Heart Broken, and a Family Plunged in Grief. Wreck and Ruin! (Philadelphia: Barclay, 1886), 24.

is so terribly awful that it is almost impossible to pen it." Dukes was well aware of Captain Nutt's special affection for Lizzie, the eldest of his nine children. "What I have to communicate," Dukes continued, "concerns your daughter, and will almost drive you to madness, because I know how you worship her." The news, terrible as it was, had to be delivered. "Let come what will, the blow must fall; and the sooner, as I take it, the better."[2]

The letter then launched into a lengthy recounting of Dukes's history with Lizzie. Their courtship, Dukes claimed, was marred by indecency from the beginning. He recalled his first visit to the Nutt estate, a three-story mansion on a hill just outside of town with sweeping views of both Uniontown below and the lush Allegheny Mountains ascending in the distance. Dukes had arrived at Lizzie's request, but there was another suitor present, A. C. Hagan, whom Lizzie asked to join her in the next room. There, Lizzie and Hagan passed a half-hour in darkness—a brazen violation of propriety. Exhibiting no trace of shame, she invited Dukes to return several weeks later, and despite her questionable behavior, he acquiesced. Lizzie mentioned that she had burned her hand, and Dukes reached for it to see the damage. He had now made the first move; Lizzie signaled that his modest overture was welcome by making no effort to withdraw from his

Nutt Mansion

The Nutt Mansion stands among the best surviving examples of Queen Anne–style architecture and belongs to the National Register of Historic Places.

Source: Franklin Ellis, *A History of Fayette County, Pennsylvania: With Biographical Sketches of Many of Its Pioneers and Prominent Men* (Philadelphia: Everts, 1882), 298a.

grasp. Heightening the intimacy of the moment, Dukes placed his other hand on hers and leaned in for a kiss, fully expecting her to err on the side of modesty and shy away. He wrote that he was "utterly surprised when, instead of withdrawing her face from me, she absolutely advanced her face to meet me." His desire for Captain Nutt's daughter only grew.[3]

According to Dukes's letter, he returned to the Nutt residence two weeks later to visit his new darling, only to witness an unnerving scene as he passed a window on the front porch—Lizzie was wrapped in Hagan's arms. Now disabused of his interest in her, Dukes kept his distance for some time. His spark, however,

Dukes Peeking
Source: Republican Standard, March 31, 1883, 1.

was reignited when she sent him a note wondering about his conspicuous absence. Dukes began once more to call on Lizzie, but again he was hardly the only one. Several young men of Uniontown boasted alternately that Lizzie had authored an endearing note, squeezed a hand at a dance, or even offered a kiss at a party.[4]

Dukes determined to uncover the truth about Lizzie Nutt, and so he devised a ruse, his letter claimed. He knew that R. P. Kennedy—a fellow member of the bar—also called on Lizzie with some regularity. When Dukes was visiting Lizzie one night, he falsely told her that he had been outside her home on an earlier evening and, peering through the window, found her in Kennedy's embrace. Lizzie denied the charge at first, but Dukes remained adamant and she eventually conceded the incident. At this, Dukes revealed that it had not actually been Kennedy whom he had seen cozying with Lizzie but another man, Frank Hellen. Defeated, Lizzie grew defensive and replied curtly, "Well, I don't care if you did." It was little wonder how she enticed these men. "Her beauty and affectionate manner," Dukes wrote, "would disarm the devil himself." Indeed, Lizzie would soon view her fiancé as evil personified.[5]

When an unnamed source implied to Dukes that Lizzie had gone so far as to engage in sexual intercourse with two other beaus, he decided to subject her to an erotic trial of sorts to see whether she was the kind of woman who committed the egregious sin of fornication. The next time that he called on Lizzie,

> She came up and placed herself on my lap, as usual, and after fondling her for some time, I made a solicitation. To my infinite

astonishment and grief she melted down like wax. Oh, how I pitied her weakness. But where is there a man that could resist the temptation of such beauty and loveliness? You would have done as I did. But what was my horror and heartsickness when I found the signs of her virginity wanting.

Dukes's letter did not say whether they then had sex, only that he confronted Lizzie about this newfound evidence of her promiscuity. She pleaded initially that she was chaste but broke down and confessed that she had indulged in premarital relations.[6]

The litany of indiscretions did not end there. Dukes named yet another of Lizzie's suitors who bragged to his friends that "he had all the favors he wanted from her." For good measure, Dukes also passed along the observation of an unnamed woman who purportedly witnessed Lizzie kissing a well-known local scoundrel. And now came the most incendiary accusation yet: "This brings me to the point to which my foregoing remarks are preliminary and that is this: Unless precautions are duly used she will become a mother. Just when, I am unable to say." Dukes reached an awful conclusion—his fiancée was pregnant by another man. Captain Nutt would not miss Dukes's thinly veiled reference to abortion, a procedure that had been outlawed in Pennsylvania in 1860 and subsequently relegated to a dangerous black market trafficked by disreputable practitioners.[7]

Having finally exhausted his allegations against Lizzie, Dukes dedicated the remainder of the letter to containing the damage his revelations wrought. He exonerated Captain Nutt from any failure to raise his daughter properly. "She has told me that you often cautioned her to kiss no one but you, and that she promised to obey you, and she wondered what you would say if you knew her," Dukes recalled. Mistakenly assuming that Captain Nutt would direct his anger primarily toward Lizzie, Dukes counseled, "Please do not be harsh with her. She loves you." He expressed optimism that Lizzie would find a husband in another if she could rein in her lascivious behavior. "Divest her of her weakness and frailty and she is an angel," affirmed Dukes. "Her sweet, musical voice, her red lips, her white teeth, her pretty face and winning smile are fascinating. Add to this her musical talent, and you have a woman who would be an ornament to any home."[8]

Even Dukes seemed unnerved by what he had written. He admitted as much in closing: "Captain, believe me when I say that this is the hardest thing I ever did in my life. I know this letter seems like stabbing you in the back; but in my humble opinion it is the only means to save both her and you from shameful disgrace. Yours truly, N. L. Dukes." It was a well-established custom that a man who learned his fiancée had had premarital relations was justified in canceling their nuptials. Dukes's implicit message that he would no longer wed Lizzie was too obvious for him to spell out.[9]

He did not mail his letter straightaway—Dukes had a final errand to run. On December 6, two days after writing his message, Dukes visited the Nutt home to see his fiancée. As Lizzie later explained, "he took my [engagement] ring for the purpose, he said, of getting another that would better please him, but his intention was to get the ring out of my hands." Finally, on December 11, Dukes deposited the sixteen-page letter at the Uniontown post office. It arrived that same day in Harrisburg, the state capital where Captain Nutt was now employed as a Treasury official.[10]

We will never know whether there was any veracity to Dukes's charges. And to a man who adhered to a traditional code of Victorian propriety like Nutt, it did not matter. Either Dukes was truthful and indeed seduced Lizzie outside the confines of matrimony or he was a liar who maliciously impugned the reputation of a pure woman to rid himself of his obligation to his betrothed. In either case, Captain Nutt was not the sort of man to suffer lightly an affront to his family's honor. The Nutts ran in social circles that prized middle-class respectability. Rules of courtship were hard and fast where female chastity was concerned. Some mild forms of physical contact—kissing and even petting—might be acceptable in a budding romantic relationship if a wedding was in the offing. But sex was strictly the preserve of marriage.[11]

Dukes's accusations, therefore, were nothing short of astounding. He claimed that Captain Nutt's precious Lizzie engaged in varying degrees of physical intimacy with a startling number of men—seven, including himself. Such a figure was an audacious breach of propriety. More important was the character of these romantic rendezvous. According to Dukes, some of these men did not merely kiss or even fondle Lizzie. They had sex with her. Even if Lizzie had only one sexual partner, in the context of an engagement leading to marriage, such an indiscretion would have offended the central stricture of Victorian culture.

But here Dukes painted a nightmare scenario: he was breaking his engagement because his fiancée was pregnant with another man's child. If true, Captain Nutt's daughter would suffer such damage to her reputation that she could abandon any hope of ever finding a husband. To protect young women from this fate,

Pennsylvania in 1843 became one of the first states to criminalize seduction—legally defined as the persuasion by a man of a female virgin to engage in sex under the false promise that he would later marry her. A conviction for this offense was punishable by three years of hard labor in solitary confinement and a fine of $5,000 (equivalent to $125,000 today).[12]

Nutt initially abstained from responding to Dukes in writing. Rather, he returned to Uniontown from the capital shortly after receiving the letter to confront Dukes. But Dukes was conspicuously absent, and so Nutt, now back in Harrisburg, authored a response on December 17 that inspired the nation when it later became public.

Captain Nutt had bravely risked life and limb to defend the cause of the Union—this challenge to the integrity of his own daughter now demanded nothing less. "You mistake the temper of the man with whom you have to deal," Nutt informed Dukes. He continued:

> You write to me as if you considered me a shameless coward, and even suggest to me the hideous office of the abortionist. I shall convince you that I have the physical courage to espouse my daughter's cause, and defend the honor of myself and family.

Only forty-two years old, Nutt was relatively young, still vigorous, and fully capable of making good on the threat.[13]

All the same, Nutt was perhaps unsure what to believe. On the one hand, he insisted, "your letter is the plea of a quibbler and not the open, sincere, truthful statement of a gentleman and a man of honor. You conceal important facts in the case." On the other hand, however, Captain Nutt never elaborated on what those facts were. And Nutt acknowledged that his initial reaction to the letter was to cast "upon my poor daughter's head a volley of curses." Curiously, he suggested that Dukes should have broken the engagement earlier: "If at any time you discovered she was not the fit companion for you, then was the time to have abandoned her, and your letter and mine need never have been written." Possibly, Nutt was simply speaking hypothetically—or maybe he was admitting that Lizzie's behavior had not been entirely becoming. At no point did Nutt directly deny the charges in Dukes's letter.[14]

In either case, Captain Nutt was outraged by Dukes's contention that even Nutt himself would have failed to restrain his sexual appetite in the presence of a beautiful and willing young woman:

> You say that you have done as I would have done. In this you are a base liar. The daughter or wife of any friend or associate of mine would be safe under any circumstances in my charge. You have no right to suggest that I could possibly be a libertine, or betray a weak, confiding girl. I have always held that when a man invades the sanctity of a home he takes his life in his hands, and under this code I shall act.

He was certain, moreover, that the formal channels of justice would accommodate his code of honor. "It rests with you whether this affair ends in a legal farce," meaning Nutt's acquittal for Dukes's murder, "or a tragedy," that is, Nutt's death at Dukes's hands. He summed up his position pithily: "This Commonwealth is not big enough for both of us."[15]

Captain Nutt planned to return to Uniontown for the Christmas holiday and urged Dukes to come to his mansion on December 23. Anticipating that Dukes might try to evade a fraught encounter with a military hero, Nutt warned, "My return to Uniontown hereafter will not be announced if I fail to meet you this time," adding, "my accidental death will not stop proceedings nor gain you immunity." Nutt well knew that if he fell in defense of his family's honor, another would rise up in his place. He concluded his correspondence with a mix of bluster and courtesy: "You can call this a threat or what you please. Very respectfully, A. C. Nutt."[16]

Dukes received the letter on December 18. With his life—and, more importantly, his honor—now at stake, Dukes wrote a prompt reply the following day. It had hardly escaped Dukes that Captain Nutt failed to address the details of the original letter. "You pass by all the main facts at issue," he protested. And although Nutt had not explicitly afforded Dukes the option of remedying the current predicament by marrying Lizzie, Dukes surmised Nutt's message to imply as much:

> I understand, however, that you offer me the party spoken of or death. I therefore hereby indicate to you that I choose the latter alternative. I cannot accept for a wife the toy of the town, and thus become the butt of the town's mocking derision. Death is far sweeter.[17]

Dukes, a sworn member of the bar, conceded that sometimes circumstances indeed merited extralegal justice. "Had the girl been a chaste woman and I had seduced her," he suggested, "then your anathemas and proposed violence would have been perfectly justifiable." Although Lizzie was too old to fall under the state seduction statute, which only protected women under twenty-one, communal values nevertheless endorsed lethal vengeance against a lothario who seduced a pure woman of any age. Lizzie, however, was hardly a paragon of virtue—at least according to Dukes. "I feel none of the guilt of a seducer, and you know I am not such," he maintained. "She told me herself that you had received an anonymous letter warning you of her erotic conduct." Captain Nutt *was* sent an unsigned letter of that character, but whether Dukes in fact authored it would prove a source of contention in court.[18]

Dukes then sought to rationalize why he had continued to play the part of doting suitor even after learning Lizzie was a jezebel. He explained that she was deeply distressed upon first missing her "monthly sickness" around the previous March. Dukes was confident at the time that she was not actually pregnant, so he decided to delay his inevitable departure and not burden Lizzie until she was at ease that she was not, in fact, with child. (Now ten months later, Lizzie had obviously not given birth, so the current pregnancy scare that Dukes mentioned in his first letter must have been referring to a separate incident).[19]

The remainder of Dukes's reply tried to cast doubt on the legitimacy of Captain Nutt's impending retribution:

You affect horror at the idea of becoming an actor in a peccadillo, yet appoint yourself a murderer and assassin with all the deliberation of a savage or a thug. Your letter would clear me if I should take your life upon sight. But I don't want your blood,

I shall not harm you in any instance. You may murder me if you will. I shall not arm myself. But don't lay to your conscience the flattering unction that the sentiment of the community will sustain you in the assassination. The woman is better known by the community than you know her, and her name is scarcely ever mentioned without a sneer. . . . You want her reputation veneered at my sole expense. You want to blight my life forever for a cheap little cloak. No, sir; my honor is as dear to me as yours is to you, and I prefer to die rather than to live a life of such shame. I could look no man in the face upon the streets.

Whereas Captain Nutt possessed unwavering confidence that a court would legitimate his killing Dukes, the prospective victim—a practicing attorney—was dubious that the justice system would so readily lend its imprimatur to murder.[20]

Nutt had concluded his letter with a demand to meet Dukes in person, and Dukes here expressed his disinclination "to walk into a death-trap." Still, he understood that a confrontation was inevitable and so he acquiesced to Captain Nutt's ultimatum, but only on his own terms, inviting Nutt to visit his office or hotel room. Dukes had lodged for the past eight years at the Jennings House, on the corner of Main Street and Arch Street, just three blocks from the church where he first laid eyes on Lizzie. "Very truly yours," he closed, "N. L. Dukes."[21]

Notwithstanding his assurance to Captain Nutt that he would remain unarmed, Nicholas Dukes bought a gun two days after mailing his reply. He paid a visit to the local hardware store, Z. B. Springer's, in search of a pistol that was, in Dukes's words, "good and sure." William Pickard, the clerk on duty, showed Dukes several handguns, including a single-action firearm that Dukes declined; he wanted a more dependable weapon. While Dukes considered alternatives, two other customers entered Springer's, and Dukes quickly concealed himself in the back of the store behind a showcase. As Pickard later testified, "Dukes said he didn't wish everyone to know his business there." Dukes emerged from hiding when the customers exited and decided on a .32-caliber Smith & Wesson double-acting revolver.[22]

Captain Nutt had no need for such a purchase—he already owned a .38-caliber Colt, a pistol of unusual size and power. On December 23, Nutt set off for Uniontown, unsure whether the journey was his last.[23]

· *Two* ·

BEGINNINGS

REVERED FOR HIS BRAVERY IN BATTLE, RECOGNIZED FOR HIS immense learning, and respected for his high sense of honor, Captain Nutt was accustomed to the esteem of his fellow man. At home, he was a devoted husband and doting father. In Uniontown, he was a civic leader and gregarious socialite. And at the State Treasury, he was a trusted public servant. He had strived for success and social respectability all his life.

Adam Clarke Nutt was born in Jefferson Township, Pennsylvania, to Joseph Nutt, a farmer, and his wife Anna on January 8, 1839. It would have been entirely fitting to name their newborn after the first Democratic president, Andrew Jackson. After all, Joseph was a loyal Democrat, and January 8 was a holiday commemorating the anniversary of Jackson's great military victory during the War of 1812. But Joseph was just as devoted to Methodism as he was to Democratic politics, and he chose for his son the name Adam Clarke in memory of a Methodist theologian. Both sides of Adam Nutt's family were Quakers from New Jersey who had made their way to western Pennsylvania.[1]

Joseph passed away in 1851, when Adam was only twelve years old. After the death of his father, the younger Nutt studied geometry and Latin at a local school, making the six-mile round trip on foot every day. At the age of seventeen, he enrolled in Allegheny College, in the northwestern corner of the state. The college was typical of institutions of higher learning in the mid-nineteenth century. Its curriculum emphasized classical antiquity, its control was in the hands of clergymen, and its student body was small in size, numbering around 100. Although Nutt himself was not especially pious, religion was central to college life. Many students hoped to join the ministry and one's designated seat in the chapel was of no small importance to undergraduates. The real intellectual excitement on campus was found in the student-run literary societies. At weekly gatherings, undergraduates showcased their talents in speech, debate, and writing. Participation was a serious matter, and the societies levied fines against their members for improper decorum during meetings—resting one's head or slouching could result in a 6.5¢ penalty.[2]

Over the course of his five years as an undergraduate, Nutt married a girl from his hometown named Charlotte Wells, and together they had a daughter, Lizzie, whom he adored. Nutt spent the winter months teaching in a grammar school for income. Students at Allegheny College tended to come from modest backgrounds, and it was common for the college to grant leave during the winter trimester to those students who needed to work for tuition money.[3]

Despite his familial and teaching responsibilities, Nutt excelled in his courses. His 1859 essay, "The Western Continent as a Field of Laudable Ambition," won the Philo-Franklin Literary

Society's Woodruff Prize. Nutt's exposition amounted to a celebration of modernization. "In many places, where once stood the wigwams of Savages," he observed, "we now see the mansions of civilized and enlightened men." Yet this progress was far from complete: "Enterprising men are needed to cultivate the prairies of the 'Great West,' and make them contribute their share to the support of the human family." These sentiments were of a piece with popular notions of Manifest Destiny, the belief that fate dictated the United States' development westward across the North American continent. Nutt's essay further lamented that the rivers of Brazil were not open to modernizing forces from other nations. "The shrill whistle of the steamer would be the death knell of the forests that now skirt the river banks," he suggested optimistically. Yet American advances in industry, argued Nutt, had been wisely tempered by tradition in government. "In the Western world were to be founded institutions which should contain the concentrated wisdom of ages, and embody the most conservative elements of civilization." Nutt may have seen great promise in modernity, but at the same time he cherished the conventions of the past. For this twelve-page, handwritten composition, Adam Nutt received a silver medal worth $25 (more than $600 today). In 1861, Nutt earned an even greater accolade—he was named class valedictorian.[4]

Following his graduation, Nutt joined the Union Army. In his prize-winning essay, he had anticipated a future in which "the olive branch of peace shall wave and the rose of affection bloom on every hillside." Now, he was heading for the killing fields of the Civil War.[5]

Nutt enlisted as a private in the 112th Pennsylvania Volunteers. The daily existence of a soldier was a monotonous one. Marches were slow-moving ordeals; numerous wagons, animals, and supplies restricted the pace of movement. When troops set up camp, they endured seemingly endless hours of drilling. Soldiers passed their free time in a variety of activities, from playing baseball and letter-writing to publishing camp newspapers and singing. The army meted out a hard diet of coffee, bacon, and crackers, usually in insufficient rations. Long days of marching and camping were punctuated by the occasional terror of battle, which typically disabused soldiers of whatever romantic notions of warfare they may have entertained before enlistment. Amid the chaos of combat, the senses were overwhelmed by clouds of smoke and a cacophony of artillery shells, drums, and screaming. Even more deadly than battle were the diseases that ran rampant in the camps.[6]

Army life was steeped in the code of honor. Dueling was technically forbidden, but in practice military authorities often condoned duels between officers. For men like Nutt who fashioned themselves gentlemen and aspired to positions of status within the army, the defense of one's honor was of signal importance. Contemporary newspapers regularly referred to the war as a duel—secession constituted nothing less than a Southern affront to Northern honor. In his proclamation first calling for troops in April of 1861, Lincoln himself described the endeavor as an "effort to maintain the honor, the integrity, and the existence of our National Union."[7]

In July of 1863, Nutt was promoted to Captain for the 3rd United States Colored Troops (USCT). It was standard practice for white officers such as Nutt to lead black troops, in part because of racial prejudice and the fact that white soldiers had battlefield experience. Abraham Lincoln had resisted using black soldiers at the war's inception for fear of alienating slave states in the Upper South that had thus far remained loyal to the Union. But as the carnage of the war claimed ever more lives and disease drove the body count higher still, attitudes toward the prospect of black troops began to change. On January 1, 1863, Lincoln issued the Emancipation Proclamation, which included a provision that former slaves would "be received into the armed service of the United States." In reality, several forward-thinking generals had already employed black regiments in Louisiana, Kansas, and South Carolina.[8]

As Captain of Company K in the 3rd USCT, Adam Nutt commanded two musicians, six sergeants, seven lieutenants, eleven corporals, and ninety privates. After its formation, Captain Nutt's regiment was sent directly to South Carolina to partake in the ongoing siege of Fort Wagner, situated at the entrance to Charleston Harbor. Taking the fort would be the crucial first step in reclaiming the city itself. Although outnumbered three to one, Confederates had managed to stave off Union attacks for weeks. The 3rd USCT joined other Union troops in the trenches and by early September Fort Wagner was ceded to the Union.[9]

In February of 1864, the 3rd USCT fought in the Battle of Olustee, a terrible defeat for the Union in what was the deadliest battle of the war in Florida. Through this battle and all others, no member of Captain Nutt's regiment was ever captured alive. These soldiers preferred to die as free men than be taken as prisoners of war. For the remainder of the hostilities, the 3rd USCT manned forts around Jacksonville. From there, groups of soldiers were often dispatched to the countryside to free slaves and ravage Confederate property.[10]

After the Confederacy's surrender, the South remained under the control of the Union Army. Captain Nutt took charge of Lake City, Florida, where he played a role in uncovering the conspiracy behind Lincoln's assassination. On the same night that John Wilkes Booth fired a lethal bullet into the president's brain, a member of the Confederate Secret Service named Lewis Powell made a parallel attack on the life of the secretary of state, William Seward. Powell was admitted to the Seward home under the false pretense that he was delivering medicine for Seward, who was then recovering from a serious carriage accident. After stabbing Seward several times, Powell fled to a boardinghouse, where he was captured. Seward survived; Powell did not. Following a military tribunal, Powell was hanged for treason in July of 1865.[11]

That August, Captain Nutt was sent to the home of Powell's parents in Swanee County, some thirty miles from Lake City. The War Department speculated that Powell had operated under the alias Payne, and Nutt's mission was to investigate whether Payne and Powell were one man. "There is no doubt," Captain Nutt relayed, "that the so-called Lewis Payne, executed for the attempted murder of Secretary Seward, was the same Lewis T. Powell." Although Nutt's faith in the Union cause was unshakeable, still, he could not help but be moved by the anguish of Powell's mother at the loss of her son. The final line of Nutt's report read, "The mother is a woman of fine personal appearance, and of strong maternal feeling, and judging from what I saw, she suffered intense mental agony."[12]

Captain Nutt returned home in late 1865, moving his family to Uniontown soon after. He studied law under a local attorney and joined the bar in 1868. After practicing law for a short time, Nutt became a banker, but he was not without political aspirations. Like many Union Army veterans, Captain Nutt belonged to the Republican Party, which championed its legacy as the "Party of Lincoln" and supported pensions for former soldiers. Republicans enjoyed strongholds in the North and Midwest, whereas the Democratic Party predominated in the South. Neither party stressed ideology—the distance between Republicans and Democrats on most matters of policy was insignificant.[13]

Nutt purchased a stake in a Republican newspaper, the *Harrisburg Telegraph*, and in 1881, he ran on the Republican ticket for the position of county court clerk. Uniontown itself was a Republican community, but it was part of Fayette County, which trended heavily Democratic. Although many Democratic voters broke party ranks and voted for Captain Nutt, the partisan demographics proved in the end too great an obstacle and he lost by a narrow margin. The following year, Nutt assumed a far more substantial role in government than court clerk. The state treasurer, Silas Baily—a fellow Republican, Civil War veteran, and resident of Uniontown—appointed Captain Nutt to a high-ranking post in the Pennsylvania Treasury. Nutt quickly earned a reputation for diligence, taking care to personally deliver large sums to various banks.[14]

Although widely regarded for his business acumen, Captain Nutt enjoyed even greater renown as a man of letters. Nutt's experiences with his literary society at Allegheny College surely nurtured an early interest in intellectual pursuits that he maintained into adulthood. He was particularly well versed in history— both ancient and modern—and took up membership in the Pennsylvania Historical Society. Book collecting was a passion of his, to which his extensive personal library could attest, as could the many public lectures he delivered on a wide range of subjects.[15]

Captain Nutt was also active in the civic life of Uniontown. He served as treasurer of the local school board, secretary of the Uniontown Building and Loan Association, and manager of the Fayette County Mutual Fire Insurance Company. In an era when the threat of flames seemed omnipresent, locals joked that the insurance company exercised such caution it would only insure "a stone ice-house."[16]

Fraternal associations were central to social life in Uniontown and Captain Nutt eagerly took part. He was a founding member of a local post of the Grand Army of the Republic—a veterans group—and he belonged to the Fayette Lodge of Freemasons. Masonic lodges were veiled in secrecy and rich with ritual. Members arriving for a meeting signified their belonging with a clandestine handshake or password. Costume-adorned masons performed cryptic rites. But for all the ceremony, the heart of the lodge was its camaraderie. Participants often retired after a meeting to a nearby tavern to enjoy the true purpose of the gathering. Uniontown was home to eleven masonic lodges or comparable fraternal associations, usually with several dozen members each. Initiation fees might run $40 with annual dues of $4 (not quite $1,000 and $100, respectively, in today's dollars).[17]

In all circles of his life, Nutt won over whomever he encountered with his gregarious disposition and genteel deportment.

He loved to pamper his family and host his friends. But he was more than just a popular character—Captain Nutt was revered as a man of deep dignity and high honor.[18]

None who knew him professionally or personally could have ever imagined that Nutt was embezzling money from the Pennsylvania Treasury. In an era notorious for financial scandals in government, Captain Nutt was not immune to temptation. He quietly withdrew $10,000 from the state coffers to speculate on oil in September of 1882. Then, just after mailing Dukes his ominous letter, Nutt took an additional $32,000 for the same purpose (a total of nearly $1,000,000 today). Undoubtedly, he hoped to earn a profit and replenish the missing funds at the Treasury without detection. But the price of oil declined, and Captain Nutt was drowning in debt. Here was a man who understood the burden of harboring a dark secret—perhaps Nutt suspected that Dukes's allegations about Lizzie were truthful but sympathized with a daughter who, too, was determined to keep a shameful indiscretion from the world.[19]

Nicholas Lyman Dukes had no such professional indiscretions lurking behind his public persona, but shared with Captain Nutt more than a few experiences. Dukes was born in Ohio around 1851 and, like Nutt, lost his father early in life. His mother remarried a wealthy older man, Asbury Struble, who moved Dukes, his mother, and brother to Fayette County. There, the new couple had two more children. As a boy, Dukes suffered from tuberculosis of the joints, known at that time as "white swelling." Such was his condition that he struggled to walk to school of his own volition. One of the larger students in the class, James Hoover, carried Dukes to the schoolhouse every day. Their friendship, forged on Hoover's back, lasted into adulthood.[20]

Dukes enrolled in Washington and Jefferson College, some forty miles from home, before transferring to Princeton. Although Princeton boasted more prestige and students than Captain Nutt's alma mater, both institutions had bucolic settings and religious atmospheres. Princeton's president was a clergyman, attendance at chapel was a daily obligation, and approximately a third of the undergraduates were bound for the ministry. It was a "quiet country college," wrote Woodrow Wilson, who graduated not long after Dukes. That is not say that campus life was entirely staid—student gambling, drinking, and trips to New York were all sources of anxiety for the trustees. During Dukes's time at Princeton, the institution was on the cusp of major changes. The forces of modernization were sweeping American higher education, and Princeton was determined to keep apace, expanding its curricular offerings, developing graduate education, and hiring more faculty. Dukes received his degree with the class of 1873, ranking eleventh of sixty-five.[21]

He returned to Fayette County and apprenticed in Uniontown under the same lawyer who had trained Captain Nutt. Dukes committed himself to a career in law, building a profitable practice. And, like Nutt, he harbored political ambitions, although Dukes was a Democrat. In 1877, he ran for district attorney but withdrew his name when he sensed a lack of support. Three years later, Dukes campaigned again, this time losing in the Democratic primary. He did not, however, abandon his designs on public office and ran once more in November of 1882 as the Democratic nominee for a seat in the Pennsylvania House of Representatives, the lower chamber of the state's bicameral General Assembly.[22]

The 1882 election cycle proved an optimal time to be a Democrat because the Grand Old Party was weakened by internal divisions. "Stalwart" Republicans defended the spoils system, wherein elected officials doled out government jobs to political allies as reward for their loyalty. The competing "Half-Breed" faction of the Republican Party endorsed civil service reform that would fill government posts based on merit. In 1880, Republicans had managed to hang together, with the Half-Breed James Garfield winning the presidency and Stalwart Chester Arthur serving as his vice president to appease the less moderate wing of the party. Four months into the Garfield administration, a crazed office-seeker named Charles Guiteau mortally wounded the president. Garfield slumped to the ground in Washington's Union Station as Guiteau cried out, "I am a Stalwart, and Arthur is president now." In the eyes of the public, the spoils system had cost an American president his life, and by 1882 the demand for reform was emphatic. Arthur was in no way complicit in the assassination that resulted in his ascension to the White House, but suspicions of his involvement abounded and Half-Breeds derisively referred to Arthur's supporters as "Guiteau Stalwarts."[23]

The infighting that plagued the Republican Party nationally also characterized Republicans in Pennsylvania. The Keystone state was run by a political machine typical of Stalwart rule. Instead of rallying behind Stalwart nominees for office in 1882, Pennsylvania Half-Breeds drafted their own candidates, splitting the Republican vote and ensuring Democratic victory. On an election day that saw Democrats nationwide reclaim public offices from the Republican Party, Pennsylvania elected its first Democratic governor since 1861, and Democrats seized control of the state House of Representatives. As for Nicholas Dukes, he was now Representative-elect Dukes from Fayette County. Dukes's electoral success was not solely attributable to larger political trends—among the citizens of Fayette, he earned a greater proportion of the vote than every other successful candidate for state and county office, buoyed by the voters' faith in his strength of character.[24]

Nutt and Dukes diverged in more than just political affiliation. Temperamentally, they were a study in contrasts. A contemporary who knew both men noted that Captain Nutt's affable demeanor stood in sharp contrast to Dukes's retiring manner:

> The character, habits and pursuits of these two men were as essentially different as could be imagined; the one warm, impulsive and excitable, mixing freely with the world—the other cold, dignified and reserved; not shuning [*sic*], but certainly not inviting the approaches of his fellow-men.[25]

Whatever differences existed between them, still, they shared a willingness to spill blood for honor. Theirs was an era when the preservation of one's honor superseded all other obligations. For men, honor comprised the esteem with which one held himself and that he demanded from others. The failure of one man to respect the honor of another was cause enough for violence. Death with honor was far preferable to a life with shame. For women, honor required absolute sexual purity outside of marriage. Honor was a familial affair—cowardly men or impure women were sources of stigma for their relatives. And honor was communal, too, with the actions of individuals reflecting on the honor of their town, their county, and even their state. With so much at stake, the letter of the law had little weight indeed.

The community that Captain Nutt and Nicholas Dukes inhabited was a bustling village of 4,000 souls. It was here in the verdant Allegheny Mountains of southwestern Pennsylvania that two brothers had founded Uniontown, quite coincidentally, on the very date that the nation declared independence, July 4, 1776.[26] In the century to follow, the hamlet transformed from an outpost of civilization into a center of industry. To walk its streets in 1882 was to bear witness to the story of American progress.

Running through the heart of town was Fayette Street, part of the first federal highway in American history. For communities along the highway such as Uniontown, the road in the first half of the nineteenth century had integrated them into a transportation network that invigorated their local economies. Horses needed shoes from blacksmiths, stagecoaches required drivers, and weary travelers depended on innkeepers.[27]

Fayette intersected with Main Street, where the Southwest Pennsylvania Railroad station offered denizens of Uniontown ready access to Pittsburgh and, from there, the world. Yet Uniontown had initially resisted the railroad. For a place long animated by the horse-and-buggy industry of the highway, rail travel threatened to tear apart the fabric of the community. By the early 1850s, however, Uniontown came to understand that the railroad would inevitably undermine the highway, notwithstanding the defiance of a single town in western Pennsylvania.

Citizens resolved to adapt to modern exigencies and began to raise revenue for a Uniontown locomotive branch. In 1859, as the first line to town was nearing completion, an area judge expressed his enthusiasm in the flowery, racialized language of the day:

> Almost within a span of one short lifetime the same hand that grappled the throat of the blood-thirsty savage can now reach forth and stroke the mane of the all-conquering yet tractable iron horse.

Another local resident captured how, for a place such as Uniontown, rail travel meant the difference between isolation and integration. After the first train arrived, he recorded his impression of the town's reaction: "Uniontown felt herself once more in touch with the outside world from which she had been cruelly severed." Still, the excitement for this new era was tempered by concerns about the first train engineer, Billy Songster, whom townspeople discovered was usually intoxicated, or "half seas over," as locals put it. By 1882, Songster had been replaced and Uniontown boasted three lines connecting it to a nationwide transportation system.[28]

Turn left from Main onto Morgantown Street to find the site of the first telegraph office, which opened in 1848. Four years earlier, the professor Samuel Morse had enlisted Anna Ellsworth, daughter of the patent commissioner, to dictate the inaugural message on the electric telegraph. She chose a weighty verse from the Book of Numbers: "What Hath God Wrought." The first missive sent from Uniontown over the wires lacked the gravitas of Miss Elsworth's telegram. The unimaginatively nicknamed "Telegraph Bill" Bart relayed a message from a Uniontown lawyer asking an acquaintance in New Jersey to ship some peaches. That November, residents crowded around the telegraph office for more important news—they learned with unprecedented immediacy that Zachary Taylor would become America's twelfth president.[29]

At the bottom of Broadway, a local cabinetmaker around 1880 had connected the initial telephone in town history from his workshop to his warerooms. It was only a few years prior that Alexander Graham Bell had made the first-ever telephone call, exhorting his assistant with the immortal words: "Mr. Watson— Come here—I want to see you." The cabinetmaker's telephone in Uniontown was decidedly makeshift; he constructed it himself using two boxes and a copper wire. It would be another decade before the Bell Telephone company established a local office.[30]

An industrializing America put ever greater numbers to work in factories, and Uniontown was no exception. On Redstone Creek by the Broadway Bridge was the community's largest factory, where as many as eighty laborers toiled, manufacturing materials for the construction of buildings. Directly across the creek, the Uniontown Gas and Water Company piped gas to local businesses and homes. The two-story Redstone Foundry and Machine-Shop on nearby Pittsburgh Street featured a twenty-horse-power engine and melted 12,000 pounds of metal every week.[31]

Increasingly, the lifeblood of Uniontown's varied economic activity was a booming coke industry in the surrounding area. The coal derivative served as a fuel and smelting agent in reducing iron ore. Uniontown was the seat of Fayette County, part of the Connellsville coke region. By 1880, no state in the nation produced more coke than Pennsylvania, no region in the state generated more coke than Connellsville, and no county in Connellsville yielded more coke than Fayette. Thanks to the high quality of its coke and proximity to highways and railroads, Fayette County alone supplied nearly half of industrial America's insatiable demand.[32]

Uniontown was dotted with department stores, known as "dry goods stores," which embodied the new consumer culture fostered by industrialization and the wealth it created. Hopwood & Miller offered the women of Uniontown "very elegant embroidered cashmere robes," "fancy neckwear," and "merino underwear," according to its advertisements. Competition came from W. & J. K. Beeson's, which—in addition to its enviable selection of silks, gloves, and corsets—also boasted "Cloaks, Dolmans, and Jackets made from the newest New York Patterns." And three doors east of the train station at the Singley & Boyd store, customers of modest means could purchase a handkerchief for as little as 5¢, whereas well-heeled patrons might splurge for a luxuriant one at $2.50 (about $1 and $60, respectively, in today's money).[33]

Yet, despite all these symbols and symptoms of modern life, Uniontown was still a small community tucked away in the mountains. Its 4,000 inhabitants could walk the width of town in fewer than twenty minutes. Unlike larger urban areas, the town had no hospital or university. A handful of leading citizens dominated Uniontown's various institutions—banks, churches, and newspapers. It was the sort of place where someone refitting his horse's wooden leg was worthy of coverage in the local paper.[34]

After a day of bustle and industry, townspeople would congregate by the "Round Corner" building, which housed the post office, and await the arrival of the 7:00 P.M. mail. It was here that they could send a half-ounce parcel for two cents, wire a money order, or even buy a postcard, a novelty introduced in 1873. Many simply went there to mingle—the post office was, in the words of one resident, "the solar plexus of the community" from which "radiates the social and commercial communication of the people."[35]

As twilight turned to darkness, locals could walk streets illuminated by gas lamps to any number of pubs that often doubled as inns. There was the Spotsylvania, which in 1825 hosted Marquis de Lafayette, the French general who aided George Washington during the American Revolution and for whom Fayette County was named. The National Hotel on the corner of Morgantown and Fayette could also lay claim to famous patronage—president-elect James K. Polk passed an evening there en route to his inauguration in 1845. On the western edge of town, what the White Swan lacked in celebrity it compensated for with the size of its portions. Upon entering its whitewashed log interior, visitors would perhaps be greeted by the tavern's vigorous seventy-two-year-old owner, who inherited the pub from his parents and lived in it all his life.[36]

Immersed in the ways of a small town but enthralled by the wonders of a new age, Uniontown of 1882 stood on the threshold between the past and the future. Its residents had little idea that the nation would soon turn to them and watch intently as they tried to forge a place for honor in a world resembling that of their youth less with each passing day.

Three

DUEL

❦

CAPTAIN NUTT ARRIVED IN UNIONTOWN AT 7:00 P.M. ON December 23, 1882. It was a Saturday night. A companion whom he had traveled with invited Nutt to dine at the Spottsylvania House, but Nutt abstained, anxious as he was to see his family. As Nutt made his way to his home on the edge of town, he encountered friends and greeted them as he would on any other day. "None who saw him," a reporter later wrote, "dreamed of the anguish that was then wringing his heart." Nutt passed the evening in the company of his children, the youngest a girl no older than four. Once his sons and daughters were asleep, he slipped into their rooms and kissed each one goodnight.[1]

The following morning, Uniontown was awash in sunlight as Sunday morning bells beckoned the townspeople to church. Nicholas Dukes came downstairs in the Jennings House for breakfast and asked to have his room tidied. Meanwhile, Captain Nutt left his mansion to see his nephew, Clark Breckenridge, in the latter's quarters at the McClelland House in central Uniontown. It was just past 9:00 A.M. and Breckenridge had yet to dress. Nutt wished to deposit $625 (more than $14,000 today) to the credit of his wife. But it was a Sunday and the bank was closed. He needed his nephew, the bank cashier, to facilitate the transaction. Perhaps Nutt feared that he might not survive the morning and wanted to ensure that his wife would have ready access to funds while his estate was sorted.[2]

Breckenridge was set to spend Christmas at his mother's home in Brownsville some fifteen miles away, and he was eager to dispose of this business quickly.[3] Captain Nutt waited for his nephew to dress and, after eating breakfast together, they made their way to the bank. Once there, Nutt revealed his torment of the past two weeks. "I have some trouble on hand," he disclosed, "and as I wish to talk to someone about it, I may as well make a confidant of you. I have lately received two infamous letters from N. L. Dukes which I will show you. I want to see Dukes this morning and have an interview with him." Nutt began to weep and asked Breckenridge to accompany him across the street, where Dukes boarded. Captain Nutt wanted his nephew to relay to Dukes that Nutt desired to speak with him.[4]

Nutt's face was so pallid that he looked ill as the two headed over to the Jennings House. Mr. Jennings, the hotel proprietor, directed the porter, Lewis Williams, to show Breckenridge to Dukes's room on the second floor. Williams regularly brought coal for Dukes's fireplace, so Dukes recognized the knock and opened the door to find Breckenridge standing alongside Williams.

"Good morning. Mr. Breckenridge, come in," said Dukes.

"Captain Nutt wants to see you," Breckenridge replied. With this, Nutt appeared from behind his nephew and pushed his way into Dukes's room. The door slammed shut behind him, with Breckenridge on the outside in the hallway and Williams heading back downstairs. Dukes and Nutt began to fight immediately. As Mrs. Jennings recalled, "The scuffling shook the whole house; it jarred the doors."[5]

What happened next depended on who was telling the story. According to three people—Breckenridge, Williams, and Mr. Jennings's son-in-law James Feather (who lived across the hall)—a muffled voice from inside Dukes's room cried out "Murder!" instantly followed by Captain Nutt yelling, "Clark! Clark!" At that moment, Feather stepped into the hallway and asked Breckenridge, "What is going on in there?" Breckenridge then burst into Dukes's room, with Feather directly behind him. They found Dukes bent over Nutt in a vicious struggle. "Take hold of him," Captain Nutt pleaded. Breckenridge and Feather managed to separate the two men, with Feather and Dukes in one corner and Breckenridge and Nutt in the other. Feather's hands were clutching Dukes's collar.

"Mr. Dukes, what does this all mean?" asked Feather.

"He came in here to whip me," Dukes explained.

Drained, Captain Nutt was resting against the mantel, his hands free of any weapon, his eyes not even on Dukes but looking out the window. Feather assured Dukes, "He can't whip you now."

Meanwhile, Williams, the porter, heard the commotion and ran back upstairs and into Dukes's room. At this moment, Dukes clumsily pulled a gun from his pocket and exclaimed to Nutt, "I'll shoot you." Captain Nutt was only about eight feet away as Nicholas Dukes fired a bullet into his face. Collapsing to the ground, Nutt reached into his overcoat pocket and grasped his .38 Colt but lacked the strength to draw the sizable firearm.

Feather and Dukes wrangled for control of Dukes's gun, and Feather managed to seize it. Breckenridge, Williams, and Feather testified under oath to these facts shortly thereafter.[6]

Because the law prohibited Nicholas Dukes from testifying, his version of events did not surface until several months later. He told a far different tale, one not of needless homicide but rather of justifiable self-defense. Dukes alleged that when Captain Nutt forced his way into the room, "He did not lift his eyes to mine, but hissed through his teeth, 'I want to see you,' and rushed upon me instantly with his cane upraised." Nutt dealt a heavy blow that Dukes absorbed with his arm shielding his face. From there, the two men grappled for control of the cane. Dukes, who had the thick frame of an athlete, realized that he was stronger than Captain Nutt and resolved not to reach for his own gun and shoot Nutt but merely to keep him at bay.[7]

As the two men tussled, Dukes screamed, "Murder! Murder! Murder!" hoping to attract the attention of someone who could put an end to the brawl. Nutt then called out, "Clark! Clark! Clark!" Dukes knew he could stave off his assailant alone, but Captain Nutt and Clark Breckenridge together would surely make good on Nutt's promise to exact lethal revenge. In desperation, Dukes freed the cane from Captain Nutt and swung. Before anyone else had entered the room, recounted Dukes,

> [Nutt] sprang away from me to avoid another stroke from the cane, back toward the mantel, and as he went, he thrust his right hand into his overcoat pocket, and attempted to draw his pistol. It seemed to be entangled. I shall never forget the murderous look in his eyes. The awful moment had come. It was he

or I. In the twinkling of an eye my pistol was drawn from my hip pocket, my right foot and arm advanced, the trigger pressed, a flash, and Capt. Nutt sank down along the wardrobe.

Just after Dukes fired his weapon, Breckenridge, Feather, and Williams stormed in, none having bore witness to the shot. Feather reached for Dukes's gun, and Dukes warned him, "Be careful, be careful, it will go off." Dukes relinquished the revolver without resistance.[8]

Here the competing narratives converged. Having heard the gunfire, Mr. Jennings raced upstairs, two steps at a time, to

Duel

This depiction of the duel, which appeared in a popular booklet about the Dukes–Nutt affair, conforms to neither Dukes's rendition nor that of the alleged witnesses.

Source: Lizzie Nutt's Sad Experience: A Heart Broken, and a Family Plunged in Grief. Wreck and Ruin! (Philadelphia: Barclay, 1886), 48.

Dukes's room. Inside, Feather chastised Dukes, "My God! You've killed him, Dukes. You have made a damned pretty fool of yourself. You have murdered that man when you had no occasion to do it."[9]

But Captain Nutt was still alive. Holding his uncle in his arms, Breckenridge exclaimed, "Oh, my God! Are you hurt badly?" Nutt turned his face but could not speak. The bullet had entered just below the left eye, dislodged the eyeball from the socket, and penetrated the brain. Blood was gushing from his nose and mouth. Breckenridge, with some effort, pried Nutt's fingers from his gun and turned over the weapon to Feather.[10]

"What does this mean?" Mr. Jennings demanded.

"He shot Nutt," responded Feather.

"If I did, I did it in self-defense," Dukes insisted.[11]

Mrs. Jennings dashed upstairs and, seeing Nutt's severe hemorrhage, hurried back out to find a doctor. Fortunately, a local physician, Dr. James Ewing, happened to be passing by. He immediately returned with Mrs. Jennings to the scene of the clash. Nutt was now stretched out on Dukes's bed, gasping for air. The doctor knew straightaway that these labored breaths would be Nutt's last. With blood pouring freely from his face, Captain Nutt slipped into unconsciousness.[12]

Dukes stood there stunned, watching this surreal scene unfold in his bedroom. But after Dr. Ewing arrived, Dukes snapped back to action. He was still in possession of Nutt's cane, which he now handed to Mr. Jennings. Putting on his hat and coat, Dukes walked out and down the stairs. "Mr. Dukes what did you do?" Mrs. Jennings inquired on his way out. As he had with her husband moments before, Dukes maintained that the shooting was in self-defense. "He would have killed me," Dukes pleaded. Passing through the door to the alley, Dukes took a back street to the home of James Hoover, the childhood friend who had carried Dukes on his back to school. James Hoover was now Sheriff Hoover—Nicholas Dukes was there to surrender himself to the law.[13]

At the Jennings House, four additional physicians arrived on the scene. There was little they could do as the life slipped from Captain Nutt's body. Only twenty minutes after the shooting, Adam Clarke Nutt was dead.[14]

As word spread through Uniontown that Dukes had gunned down Nutt, the news was met with skepticism. It simply did not seem believable that two men of such high station, with no known animosity toward each other, would engage in a lethal struggle. Townspeople raced to the Jennings House to see for themselves. "With bated breath and blanched cheeks," a local paper reported, "strong men rushed eagerly to the hotel, to find, alas! the story was too true. There lay the lifeless body of Capt. Nutt, with a bullet-hole in his head." The Jennings House and surrounding streets were soon packed with anxious crowds.[15]

Upon learning of her husband's demise, Mrs. Nutt hurried to the hotel, but was so paralyzed with despair that she could not bring herself to ascend the steps to her husband's deathbed. Two of her children, Annie and "Little Joe," were in tow and overcome with sorrow. Mrs. Nutt was soon escorted back to her home, where she collapsed in convulsions of grief.[16]

Upstairs in Dukes's room, in the presence of Nutt's corpse, the coroner, John Sturgeon, convened an inquest—a judicial procedure to determine the cause of death. He impaneled a jury of six men to hear from witnesses. Dr. Ewing; Mr. and Mrs. Jennings; Feather, their son-in-law; and Williams, the porter, all testified to the events that had just come to pass. But Breckenridge was absent; in the direct aftermath of the shooting, Captain Nutt's nephew suffered from delirium and was taken to the office of a physician. The coroner's jury traveled to the doctor's office to hear the account of a still badly shaken Breckenridge. Consistent with standard inquest procedure, Dukes was afforded no opportunity to go on record. The jurors promptly concluded, "Adam C. Nutt came to his death by a shot fired from a revolver in the hands of N. L. Dukes." The coroner, in turn, formally charged Nicholas Lyman Dukes with the crime of murder.[17]

The indictment was little more than a legal technicality because Dukes had already turned himself in. Although Dukes was officially in the custody of the state, Sheriff Hoover allowed Dukes to stay as a guest in his home rather than confining him to a cell. The mayor went to visit the accused at the sheriff's house.

"How are things down the street?" Dukes asked.

"Bad enough," replied the mayor. "He is dead."

Dukes remained silent but his body trembled. After a visit from his mother, Dukes spent a wakeful night at the sheriff's, not even bothering to undress.[18]

Captain Nutt's corpse was delivered to his home following the inquest while word flashed across the telegraph lines informing his kin of his passing: his siblings at various locales in Pennsylvania and his eldest son, James, away at a commercial school in Rochester, New York. Telegrams from every corner of the Commonwealth asked for further details of Nutt's death. In Harrisburg, the news reached the daily papers around nightfall. The city was soon abuzz, and Nutt's many acquaintances in the state capital flocked to the telegraph office in hopes of learning more about the shooting. Friends of both Nutt and Dukes in Pittsburgh passed their time in newspaper offices waiting for the latest dispatch. By the next afternoon, the Dukes–Nutt affair was national news. "The tragedy became a leading topic of conversation throughout the entire country," one publication observed. Rumors were already spreading about a scandalous exchange of letters that triggered the deadly fight. The press from major cities could not print enough issues to meet demand and instructed their correspondents to spare no details over the wires despite the significant cost of telegraphic communication. Headquarters sent reporters urgent messages such as, "For Heaven's sake get the letters, the letters."[19]

In the days immediately after the killing, newspapers in every corner of the country covered the story. From the villages of New England and the metropolises of the eastern seaboard to the outposts of the Great Plains and the coastal communities of California, headlines broadcast the news of the father slain in defense of his daughter's honor. In the *New York Times*, subscribers read about the "Fatal Impromptu Duel;" in the *Albuquerque Journal*, "The Father of a Ruined Girl Shot Dead by Her Deceiver;" in the *Chicago Daily Tribune*, "A Daughter's Honor;" in the *San Francisco Chronicle*, "A Prominent Pennsylvanian Shot Dead by a Lawyer," and in the *Worcester Daily Spy*, "A Tragedy in High Life."[20]

The scope of the Dukes–Nutt coverage was made possible by the relatively recent development of mass-circulation newspapers. Whereas the typical periodical of the early nineteenth century appeared only weekly and operated primarily as a political organ, the daily press of an urbanizing America in the latter half of the century turned increasingly to salacious topics to lure readers and thus attract advertising dollars. With people concentrating in cities and learning to read in unprecedented numbers, a booming press replaced word of mouth as the principal source of information for many Americans.[21]

The funeral of Captain Nutt was set for 1:00 P.M. on the day following a heartrending Christmas. All morning, people poured in from every corner of the state, traveling by train, wagon, and horseback. Townsfolk from neighboring villages joined high-ranking officials from distant cities. Some had even made the 300-mile journey from Philadelphia. Although it was a Tuesday, every bank and business in Uniontown remained closed.[22]

As the hour of the service approached, mourners ascended the hill to the mansion that Captain Nutt had recently completed for his wife and nine children. The home was soon filled to capacity and hundreds of people were forced to wait outside. The Reverend Alexander Milholland—pastor of the church where Dukes had first seen the daughter of the deceased—read from Scripture, offered prayers, and delivered a concise eulogy. The crowd in the house then parted and pallbearers carried the coffin to the lawn, where mourners were asked to form a line and look upon Captain Nutt one final time.[23]

The impressive black casket was draped in velvet and featured a silver plate bearing Nutt's name. Robert, Willie, and Harry Beeson, whom Nutt had taken into his keeping after the death of their father, placed on the coffin a wreath of white flowers with a card that read, "Our Beloved Guardian." The face of the dead looked surprisingly normal aside from the plaster covering the wound beneath his left eye and some scrapes on his forehead. Following the viewing, the casket was closed and loaded onto the hearse for its journey to Oak Grove Cemetery.[24]

An immense procession began winding its way toward the burial site. At the head was Rutter's cornet band, which in 1876 had proudly represented Uniontown at the Centennial Exhibition in Philadelphia. Behind the band marched Company C of the Tenth Regiment of the National Guard of Pennsylvania, followed by several posts of the Grand Army of the Republic. Members of the bar to which Captain Nutt had been sworn as a young man trailed behind, succeeded directly by the Freemasons. Then came the hearse, accompanied on either side by three pallbearers, with family members in tow. Friends and citizens trailed behind.[25]

Many more people awaited the funeral procession at the graveyard. When the soldiers reached the cemetery gate, they divided into two parallel lines and allowed the long train of mourners to pass through. Lizzie Nutt was too overwhelmed with sorrow to dismount from her carriage at the cemetery. The band played an elegiac hymn as the Freemasons advanced toward the tomb to perform their fraternal rites, with the Reverend N. P. Kerr presiding. In all, some 2,000 people came to pay their respects to Captain Nutt, and their expressions of bereavement were effusive.[26]

Yet one person was notably absent—Mrs. Nutt was still in such dire condition that she could not attend her own husband's funeral. It was feared that she might not survive. By that evening, however, Mrs. Nutt had come back from the brink, and her doctor reported that she would indeed live. Still, she was hardly in a state of mind to manage her husband's estate. Due to collect $18,000 (more than $420,000 today) on Nutt's life insurance policies, Mrs. Nutt formally ceded control of her husband's affairs to his brother, Stephen Nutt, her brother, Jim Wells, and her nephew, Clark Breckenridge. All of these monies would be required to help pay off Nutt's substantial debts. His family learned of his embezzlement and the shortfall resulting from his oil speculation shortly after his death, but the press would remain unaware of the scandal for another three years.[27]

In the days following the funeral, the written exchange between Lizzie's father and her fiancé that prompted their fateful encounter was a source of considerable intrigue. "The correspondence between the murderer and his victim," reported the *Philadelphia Inquirer*, "which would solve the deep mystery shrouding the terrible affair, is studiously kept from the public eye." Dukes believed that Nutt's threatening letter would exonerate him in the eyes of the public and wanted the correspondence released to the press. Although his lawyers balked at that idea, Dukes soon got his wish when unnamed sources who had seen the letters revealed their contents to the papers, which, in turn, printed summaries.[28]

Most likely the leak came from Breckenridge and a gentleman named Bob Hopwood. Nutt had given Dukes's two letters to his wife. Just after the shooting, Mrs. Nutt sent them to

Breckenridge through an intermediary. Breckenridge showed the correspondence to Hopwood before handing the letters to a prosecutor for the Commonwealth of Pennsylvania.[29]

Although the sources who divulged the details of the letters did indeed provide accurate information, the press had no way of verifying their accounts and warned readers against affording the summaries of the letters too much credence. These disclaimers did little. "When the contents of these letters became known there seemed to be almost an instantaneous change of feeling," explained the *Genius of Liberty*, a Uniontown paper. "People who had regarded Mr. Dukes' case as a good one were free to express hatred against him as well as detestation of his crime. . . . Some called him a libertine, others claimed he was a wolf in sheep's clothing."[30]

Many were upset with the special treatment that Sheriff Hoover afforded Dukes, who was still enjoying a bedroom in the sheriff's home instead of a cell. Hoover shrugged off accusations of favoritism, insisting that anyone in his custody of Dukes's high status would enjoy comparable benefits. It became apparent that nothing would be done to relegate Dukes to a cell when Judge Alpheus Willson affirmed that the treatment of a prisoner was the sheriff's exclusive prerogative. In sharp contrast to the general reprobation of Dukes, many members of the community stepped forward to clear Lizzie's name of sexual impropriety. Lizzie herself refuted the allegations in Dukes's letters and, as the press reported, "The statements about Miss Nutt are indignantly denied by those who know her intimately."[31]

Predictions abounded that Dukes might not survive to see his court date. On December 27, the *Philadelphia Inquirer* relayed that in Uniontown, "the excitement still runs high, and there are threats of attempted lynching of Dukes." But those advocating "lynch law," as the practice was called, were still in the minority. After all, formal legal channels offered the prospect of a death sentence. Pennsylvania law mandated capital punishment for anyone found guilty of first-degree murder. Whether comeuppance came in the form of a mob's noose or a jury's verdict, forsaking the honor code was a life-and-death affair.[32]

· *Four* ·

Maneuvers

Shortly after the killing, Nicholas Dukes inquired whether William Playford would represent him. As the most celebrated criminal lawyer in the county, Playford was an obvious choice. He had taken part in a number of high-profile murder trials in his twenty-five years at the bar. And like Dukes, Playford was a Democratic politician, having served in the Pennsylvania House and Senate. What's more, Playford had the kind of formidable presence that won over juries. A Uniontown resident described him as "a large powerful man with a magnificent suit of hair and a very strong voice."[1]

Playford, however, not only rejected Dukes's request to defend him but also signed on to prosecute Dukes for the Commonwealth of Pennsylvania. A close friend of Captain Nutt, Playford had led the Fayette County bar in Nutt's funeral procession. It was not uncommon for lawyers in private practice, as Playford was, to assist the state in trying criminal cases. Playford had solid credentials as a prosecutor—when he was twenty-five years old, he had won election to a three-year term as district attorney.[2]

William Playford

Source: Franklin Ellis, *A History of Fayette County, Pennsylvania: With Biographical Sketches of Many of Its Pioneers and Prominent Men* (Philadelphia: Everts, 1882), 352f.

Joining Playford on the prosecution was his law partner, A. D. Boyd. After studying law under Judge Willson, Boyd was admitted to the county bar in 1869. His impressive speaking skills soon caught the attention of the local Democratic Party, which nominated Boyd for district attorney in 1871. He won election by a comfortable margin and, after his term ended, continued to take part in prominent criminal cases as both a prosecutor and a defense attorney. Boyd possessed an extraordinary memory and could quote case law extemporaneously. Later in life, he would serve in the Pennsylvania Senate and develop a reputation as a mentor for younger lawyers. Rounding out the legal team for the Commonwealth was Isaac Johnson, the current district attorney who had been elected to that position after defeating Dukes in the Democratic primary two years earlier.[3]

To spearhead his defense, Dukes turned to a man with a background strikingly similar to Playford's—Charles Boyle. Boyle, too, enjoyed widespread renown for his legal ability. Although average in his height and smallish in his features, Boyle's penetrating eyes hinted at the man's boundless stamina, intelligence, and moxie.[4] His legendary drive was evident as early as age nine, when he began to work for a local paper. Boyle was so small at the time that he had to stand on a candle box to set the type.[5]

Boyle had succeeded Playford as district attorney early in his career and enjoyed success as a Democratic politician thereafter.

Charles Boyle

Source: Franklin Ellis, *A History of Fayette County, Pennsylvania: With Biographical Sketches of Many of Its Pioneers and Prominent Men* (Philadelphia: Everts, 1882), 352b.

Following a stint in the 1860s as a delegate for Fayette County in the Pennsylvania legislature, Boyle won election to the U.S. House of Representatives the month preceding Nutt's death. He and Playford had more than just a passing familiarity with each other. In the 1870s, they joined with Judge Willson to start a coke manufacturing enterprise that yielded substantial profits. Like Playford, Boyle had been an intimate associate of Captain Nutt, even assisting at Nutt's funeral as a pallbearer. In explanation of Boyle's decision to defend the killer of the man whose coffin he carried, a newspaper relayed, "he said his friendship for the dead could not interfere with his duties to the living."[6]

In his defense of Dukes, Boyle had help from his law partner, S. L. Mestrezat. Mestrezat was a highly skilled lawyer who had graduated first in his class at Washington and Lee, served as district attorney in Fayette County, and would later become a justice on the Supreme Court of Pennsylvania. Boyle and Mestrezat were joined in their defense of Dukes by another talented attorney, R. H. Lindsey, one of the great legal stars of the era in Uniontown.[7]

With Judge Willson soon to depart for three weeks of cases in a neighboring county and Dukes's own busy legal practice requiring the defendant's time, the judge agreed to hold a hearing on December 30 in the district attorney's office to determine Dukes's eligibility for bail. As the dispirited prisoner awaited his bail hearing, several visitors came to see him. Dukes, however, refused to discuss the events surrounding Captain Nutt's death except with his counsel.[8]

On the day of the bail hearing, moments before leaving Sheriff Hoover's home to appear before Judge Willson, Dukes stopped an acquaintance who was walking by. He needed an urgent favor. "Here is my will," said Dukes. "I want you to witness it, for I don't know what may happen." He had hastily written the will on the back of a letter that very morning. A local reporter explained, "He doubtless feared that some one might shoot him as he was going along the street to the hearing." The sidewalks were teeming with onlookers, eager to see Dukes's first public appearance in the six days since the bloody clash. The crowd, for now, was content to let the legal system run its course. With Sheriff Hoover as an escort, Dukes safely made his way to the hearing shortly after 9:00 A.M. The prisoner was freshly shaven, his attire smart but not ostentatious, as was his custom, and he walked with a brisk and determined step. Although the hearing was not open to the public, several friends of both the deceased and the defendant were admitted alongside the lawyers, witnesses, and reporters. Noteworthy among them was Captain Nutt's brother Stephen, as well as Dukes's stepfather, Asbury Struble, an octogenarian known for his great wealth and unusual vitality.[9]

According to the dictates of the state constitution, Dukes would qualify for bail unless the "presumption is great" that he was guilty of first-degree murder. It was for Judge Willson alone to decide whether to set Dukes free on bail while awaiting trial. To this end, the attorneys examined four witnesses at the hearing: Clark Breckenridge, Lewis Williams, James Feather, and Dr. Ewing. These witnesses largely reiterated their observations from the coroner's inquest, albeit in greater detail. Boyle then argued that the offense was at worst manslaughter. Boyd, Playford's law partner, countered that the offense was greater than manslaughter because at the instant of the shooting, the altercation had ceased and Captain Nutt was making no threatening gestures. Throughout these proceedings, Dukes seemed distressed yet resilient. One reporter noted that Dukes "impressed the observer as a man suffering great mental agonies, but who was at the same time determined to bear them bravely."[10]

After two hours of testimony and argument, Judge Willson announced that he did not find the evidence against Dukes compelling enough to deny him bail. The judge asked whether District Attorney Johnson wished to exercise his right to recommend to the court a dollar amount for the defendant's release. After communing with Boyd, Johnson responded that the Commonwealth would defer entirely to the discretion of the bench. Judge Willson fixed bail at $12,000 (more than $280,000 today); large as it was, the sum was well within the means of Dukes's affluent stepfather to post. Nutt sympathizers, meanwhile, were quick to criticize the bail as too low.[11]

Dukes would stand trial in March, and the jury could still find him guilty of first-degree murder, but for now he was a free man. Immediately after the hearing, the defendant met with his lawyers and then retired to his law office in the afternoon to attend to his own practice. He took off the next day for the home of his mother and stepfather in German Township, some eight miles away, where Dukes would quickly have to make an important choice. In just three days, the members of the Pennsylvania General Assembly would gather in Harrisburg, the state capital, for the inauguration. Dukes had to decide whether he would attempt to take his oath of office amid the ongoing public fury.[12]

Harrisburg was nestled on the Susquehanna River, where the rough-hewn mountains of western Pennsylvania melt into the bucolic landscape of the east. Visitors arriving by train would first pass over the glimmering river on the Mulberry Street Bridge. Hugging the Susquehanna's eastern bank was a park where children gathered in temperate weather for hoop rolling and croquet. The park gave way to Front Street, with its stately homes of marble and granite, among them the governor's mansion. Harrisburgers who could not afford real estate with river views would still come down to Front Street at day's end to watch the sunset. From there, the city expanded east into a maze of streets, factories, and residences where more than 30,000 denizens lived and toiled.[13]

Harrisburg

Source: Willard Glazier, *Peculiarities of American Cities* (Philadelphia: Hubbard Brothers, 1886), 200a.

At the heart of the city was its most impressive structure—the State House, home to the General Assembly. Sitting amid a thirteen-acre park, the State House featured a 108-foot dome and a large portico with Greek columns. The building's prized possessions were a telescope once owned by Benjamin Franklin and a Pennsylvania flag seized by Confederate soldiers in the Battle of Gettysburg and later recovered from the luggage of Jefferson Davis.[14]

Both chambers of the legislature had been refurbished in advance of the inauguration. The House of Representatives boasted new carpeting and freshly painted walls. The Senate, meanwhile, featured recently installed granite at each window and four substantial mirrors—a pair bookending each of two fireplaces—which promised to provide "excellent opportunity for speakers to view there [sic] gesticulating anatomy as they warm up in a lengthy debate," related *The Patriot*, a Harrisburg newspaper.[15]

At noon on January 2, 1883, the chief clerk of the House opened the session. A local reverend offered prayers, the election results from the preceding November were read aloud, and roll call commenced. After a judge administered the oath to the delegates, they signed the roll book and officially began their terms of office. Representative Nicholas Lyman Dukes of Fayette County was not present. Perhaps the man standing trial for his life would not, after all, try to assume the office to which he had been duly elected.[16]

Dukes's empty desk, situated toward the back of the chamber, became something of a tourist attraction in the days following the inauguration. Nearly all visitors to the building requested to see it. They "would look at it with amazement, sit in the chair to it and scrutinize it minutely," a Harrisburg paper reported. "Several chairs have been completely ruined by visitors who have been examining the desk." Finally, on January 10, the sergeant-at-arms grew weary of the spectacle and removed Dukes's name from it.[17]

The sergeant-at-arms may have acted too quickly—the next day, to the shock of many, Dukes arrived in the state capital. He came early in the morning and checked into the United States Hotel, where those who recognized Dukes pointed him out. After breakfast, he walked to the State House together with the other delegate from Fayette County. If Dukes were anxious, he did not show it. In the words of one reporter, he appeared to be "in a serene frame of mind."[18]

Dukes met with the Speaker of the House, John Faunce, in the Speaker's private office, where Faunce informed him that there was no legal bar to swearing in a member charged with a capital offense. However, Speaker Faunce would not be able to satisfy Dukes's request to have the oath of office administered in private. Having investigated the precedents, Faunce determined that the law required all members to take the oath at the House bar. He further recommended that Dukes deliberate carefully before making the decision to claim his seat. Dukes left the State House by a back door, never once entering the House chamber. According to the *Harrisburg Telegraph*, some representatives expressed outrage "that Dukes should have the brazen effrontery to show himself at the Capital with Capt. Nutt's blood fresh on his hands."[19]

The papers the following day reported that Dukes would indeed insist on his right to membership in the General Assembly and planned to take the oath three days hence, on

January 15. Several House members began preparations to expel Dukes should he dare serve alongside them. Dukes attempted to discreetly discern the mood of the House and found his fellow representatives openly berating him. Although Dukes could still count on the support of a few fellow Democrats in Uniontown, the animus against him in Harrisburg was bipartisan.[20]

January 15 came and went; Dukes did not appear before the House to take his oath. He was not abandoning his hope of serving in office but merely postponing his fight for his seat until more favorable conditions prevailed. If his trial exonerated him in the eyes of the law and the eyes of the public, surely then Dukes could represent the people of Fayette County without controversy. He returned to Uniontown four days later, leaping off the moving train during its approach to avoid the station. Dukes followed a back street to the Jennings House.[21]

With the fracas over Dukes's legislative career subdued, at least temporarily, and the trial set for March, February proved a quiet month in Uniontown. Prominent families made a point of inviting Lizzie Nutt to their homes as a signal that they afforded no credence to the allegations of her sexual misconduct. On the final Tuesday of February, the Uniontown post of the Grand Army of the Republic closed its term of mourning for Captain Nutt with a memorial service held in the offices of the *Republican Standard*, a local Uniontown paper. Their mourning period had begun two days after the funeral when members of the post had passed a series of resolutions commemorating their fallen comrade. For the next sixty days, they had covered their charter and worn black over their badges in remembrance.[22]

Now they reconvened to offer a final tribute to a fellow soldier who had survived forty battles but not his daughter's engagement. The somber ceremony took place around a table draped with the American flag. Resting on the flag were two crossed swords and an open Bible. After a preliminary song by the choir, a comrade read selected verses from Scripture. All then joined in singing the Lord's Prayer. To the dismay of the post, the Reverend N. P. Kerr, who had played a central role in Nutt's funeral, was unable to attend and address the gathering. Instead, several comrades eulogized Captain Nutt; they bemoaned his untimely death, celebrated his storied military pursuits, and lauded his enduring commitment to education. The service concluded with the singing of a hymn.[23]

For the men of the Grand Army and the people of Uniontown, the time for mourning was coming to an end and the hour for justice readily approaching. Nicholas Dukes had violated the sacred honor of the Nutt family and the community now looked to the legal system to ensure that Captain Nutt's killer followed him to the grave.

· *Five* ·

TRIAL

❧

Oɴ Mᴀʀᴄʜ 10, 1883, ᴛʜᴇ ɴᴀᴛɪᴏɴ ғɪxᴇᴅ ɪᴛs ɢᴀᴢᴇ ᴏɴ Uniontown. An elected member of the state legislature would stand trial, before a court in which he was licensed to practice, for the murder of a man whose daughter he had promised to wed. Newspapers nationwide passed the day awaiting word from their correspondents over the telegraph lines.[1]

The Dukes–Nutt scandal was just one of many sex scandals that captured the Gilded-Age imagination. In 1875, the nation obsessed over the adultery trial of Henry Ward Beecher, minister of the Plymouth Church in Brooklyn and arguably the most renowned clergyman of his day. Beecher had engaged in a sexual relationship with Elizabeth Tilton, the wife of his friend, Theodore Tilton. The Tiltons and Beecher agreed to keep the affair quiet but Victoria Woodhull, a free-love advocate whom Beecher had criticized, caught wind of the minister's indiscretions. In an effort to expose Beecher as a hypocrite, Woodhull went public with news of the infidelity. Theodore Tilton decided that he would not passively suffer damage to his own reputation for Beecher's sake and filed adultery charges against him. Elizabeth Tilton came to Beecher's defense at the trial and denied their affair despite an abundance of incriminating letters that had passed between them. Beecher's congregants also rallied behind their leader and celebrated when a hung jury failed to convict him. Three years later, Elizabeth reversed course and confessed that she had lied during the trial. Beecher, however, continued to maintain his innocence and emerged relatively unscathed from the aftermath of Elizabeth's revelation that she had perjured herself. With Nicholas Dukes standing trial amid a swirl of bawdy accusations, Americans once again looked to the courthouse as a place to indulge their erotic interests under the cover of moral outrage.[2]

The courthouse in Fayette County was an especially impressive structure, eighty-five feet high, in the heart of Uniontown on Main Street. Built thirty-six years earlier, after a fire had scorched its predecessor during a hearing, the courthouse featured a statute of General Lafayette standing atop a belfry.[3]

"Commonwealth against Nicholas Lyman Dukes," Judge Willson began. "Is the counsel on the part of the prosecution ready?"

"Ready," replied William Playford.

With this, Dukes entered the courtroom and sat down at his table, looking poised, rested, and, as always, clean shaven. His legal team—Charles Boyle, S. L. Mestrezat, and R. H. Lindsey—followed shortly thereafter. Boyle's term in the 48th Congress of the United States had begun just six days prior. At the opposing table was Captain Nutt's brother, Stephen, along with William Playford, A. D. Boyd, and District Attorney Isaac Johnson.

Courthouse

Fayette County Courthouse. The statute of General Lafayette stands today in the rotunda of a newer courthouse.

Source: Franklin Ellis, *A History of Fayette County, Pennsylvania: With Biographical Sketches of Many of Its Pioneers and Prominent Men* (Philadelphia: Everts, 1882), 134a.

Court Clerk Thomas Searight then began the proceedings. A prominent Democrat, Searight defeated Nutt for the court clerkship and served as a major political patron of Dukes. When Searight called Dukes's name, the defendant stepped forward and the crowd fell deathly silent. Dukes raised his right hand and, with his head bent forward, stared down as Searight recited the indictment. Searight then asked Dukes to state his plea. The defendant lifted his eyes and stared directly at Searight.[4]

"Not guilty." His voice did not waver.

"How will you be tried?" queried Searight. Dukes failed to respond. His counsel nudged him.

"By God and my country."

"God send you a deliverance," Searight stated with ardor.[5]

The court now began the process of jury selection. Of the sixty jurors called for duty from across the county, fifty-eight answered to their names. All were men—like every other state in the country at the time, Pennsylvania prohibited women from serving on juries. From this panel, a few were excused on account of illness or conscientious objection to the death penalty; many more were challenged for cause as they had already formed a "fixed and deliberate opinion" on the case. The defense had a decided advantage in shaping the jury. It could peremptorily challenge—that is, dismiss without cause—twenty jurors compared to the prosecution's four. Dukes scrawled notes while the twelve men who would decide his fate were gradually chosen.[6]

By 1:00 P.M., the Dukes jury had its dozen men. Roll call began, and the jurors were sworn as a group to render a verdict in accordance with the law and the evidence. Judge Willson informed the gentlemen of the jury that they would be sequestered next door at the Clinton House, where they would remain in the custody of officers of the court. The jurors were to have no conversation with the outside world, and discussion among themselves could not concern the case at hand. Any letters they wished to send would first be subject to the judge's approval. Now a Saturday, court adjourned until Monday morning.[7]

The jurors ranged in age from twenty-seven to fifty-eight and featured three farmers, two blacksmiths, two miners, a laborer, a carpenter, a wagon maker, a distiller, and a horse keeper. None of these men was actually from Uniontown. All were married. And they shared one other trait in common. Like Dukes—and unlike Nutt—every one of them was a Democrat. Although this partisan composition raised suspicion among some Republicans, it was less likely the result of some clandestine conspiracy than the product of two more prosaic realities. For one, Fayette was a Democratic county, so the pool from which the final twelve jurors came was likely to feature more Democrats than Republicans. Additionally, the defense's advantage in having five times the number of peremptory challenges as did the Commonwealth gave Dukes's counsel great ability to dismiss whatever Republicans were present in the original panel of fifty-eight jurors.[8]

Saturday's crowd in court had been limited in size because spectators feared becoming "talesmen," a term for bystanders whom the court inducts into a jury to reach twelve members if the panel is exhausted. But on Monday, March 12—the second day of the trial—with the jurors already selected, a restless throng now amassed outside the courthouse well before the appointed hour in the hopes of gaining admission. When the doors finally opened at 10:00 A.M., the crush of people flooded into the courtroom. Several additional court officers were on hand to manage the horde. Those who could not find an open seat jockeyed for space in the aisles until there was not even standing room available. Disappointed latecomers would have to learn from word of mouth or the newspapers what transpired inside the courthouse.[9]

At the tables for the defense and the Commonwealth were newcomers who had been absent during jury selection. Dukes's stepfather, Asbury Struble, now joined the defendant; Mrs. Nutt and her sister entered the courtroom and walked through a muted crowd toward their seats alongside Captain Nutt's brother and the Commonwealth's lawyers. When Mrs. Nutt passed by Dukes, the hem of her skirt brushed over his shoes. The defendant may have been a paragon of composure on Saturday, but at this moment, wrote a reporter, "a flush crept up over his heavy cheeks and dyed his sensual face to the roots of his hair."[10]

The proceedings began just after 10:00 A.M., with Boyd making the opening argument for the Commonwealth. He first reviewed the facts as given by the witnesses at the coroner's inquest. Boyd's discussion soon went beyond the events immediately surrounding the fatal shot and delved into Dukes's letters that prompted the deadly altercation; the defense objected strenuously to any commentary on the correspondence unless and until the Commonwealth offered the letters into evidence and the court deemed them admissible.[11]

Until this point in time, neither the public nor the jury knew with certainty the true contents of those letters, only rumor and speculation. The Commonwealth well understood that the suppression of Dukes's letters could be detrimental to its case, just as the defense recognized that their admission could be damaging to its own. A showdown would be inevitable. But for now, with the letters not yet offered into evidence, Judge Willson sustained the defense's objection in the main while allowing Boyd to make a passing allusion to the letters in his opening statement. Boyd promised the jurors that the Commonwealth would show how

Dukes lured Nutt to the Jennings House under the false promise that he would remain unarmed and then needlessly committed murder.[12]

The Commonwealth called its first witness, Clark Breckenridge, to the stand. As he had at the coroner's inquest and bail hearing, Nutt's nephew testified that his uncle had no weapon in hand and was not even looking at Dukes when the defendant fired his revolver. In the witness's cross-examination, Congressman Boyle hoped to show that Breckenridge recognized the cry of "Murder!" as belonging to Dukes rather than to Captain Nutt. In other words, Boyle wanted to suggest that Breckenridge heard Dukes shout "Murder!" but did not enter the room because it was Dukes rather than Captain Nutt who was seemingly in danger. Only when Nutt subsequently yelled out "Clark!" did Breckenridge rush in. To this end, Boyle pressed the witness during cross-examination.

"I did not recognize whose voice it was that cried murder," Breckenridge maintained.

"Don't you think it was Dukes' cry?" Boyle suggested.

The witness would not capitulate. "I could not say, as the voice seemed smothered."[13]

After Breckenridge's testimony, court adjourned until 2:00 P.M., when the Commonwealth called to the stand James Feather, the Jennings' son-in-law who lived across the hall from Dukes. Like Breckenridge, Feather swore that Nutt held no firearm in his hand at the time of the shooting. Boyle's aim in his cross-examination of Feather was to cast doubt on the integrity of the testimony by showing that the witness had harbored hostility toward the defendant even before Christmas Eve.

"You have not been on good terms with Mr. Dukes for some time?" asked Boyle.

"Not since this tragedy," Feather explained, blaming their rift on Nutt's death alone. "I was on good terms with him up to this time. I voted for Mr. Dukes."

Boyle pressed the issue: "Did you not say you would not vote for him?"

Playford objected to the question and Judge Willson sustained the Commonwealth. Boyle would have to take another tack.

"Was there not some ill feeling between you and Mr. Dukes before the shooting?"

Ceding no ground, Feather demanded, "Ask your questions pointedly so that I can understand them."

"I am putting them at you as straight as I can," remarked Boyle, eliciting laughter from the courtroom. "Did you not say to Colonel Searight that you would not invite Mr. Dukes to your wedding?"

Again, Playford objected, but this time Judge Willson let the question stand.

"I might have said to Colonel Searight that I would not ask Mr. Dukes to my wedding," Feather conceded.

Boyle turned his questioning to the events of December 24 and Feather, in turn, made clear his aversion to volunteer information. "I evaded all I possibly could at the hearing before Judge Willson," he asserted, "and am doing it to-day too. I'll not tell you anything unless you ask me."[14]

After Boyle dismissed Feather, the Commonwealth recalled Breckenridge to establish Captain Nutt's predilection for traveling with a cane. The Commonwealth's intent was to demonstrate that Nutt had not brought a heavy cane to Dukes's room for the purpose of assaulting the defendant but in fact had carried a cane that morning as a matter of habit. Boyle objected to the question as immaterial and the judge sustained him. Breckenridge was dismissed without answering.[15]

The porter, Lewis Williams, took the witness stand to provide his rendition of the Dukes–Nutt affray. Corroborating Breckenridge and Feather, Williams testified that Nutt had not been holding a revolver when Dukes fired his own. As Mrs. Nutt listened to these witnesses describe the melee that claimed her husband's life, she shook in agony.[16]

Once again, the Commonwealth recalled Breckenridge to speak to Captain Nutt's habit of toting a cane; once again, Boyle objected. But the cane itself had since been admitted into evidence, and so Judge Willson now allowed the witness to respond. "Captain Nutt almost invariably carried a cane," Breckenridge informed the jury. "He had half a dozen at home."[17]

After two physicians who had been present at Nutt's death described his wounds to the jury, the Commonwealth called Mrs. Jennings. Playford sought to prove that the defendant had asked her to tidy his room on Christmas Eve, a rare request from Dukes, indicating that he had expected company. In other words, Dukes had not been taken off guard by Captain Nutt's visit and acted spontaneously in self-defense but had anticipated and prepared for a lethal encounter.

"Did you not swear at the Coroner's inquest that he never before asked to have his room fixed up?" asked Playford.

"I object," Boyle interjected.

The judge sided with Playford but Mrs. Jennings was not much help.

"I don't remember of having sworn at the Coroner's inquest that he never asked his room to be cleaned up," she said.[18]

The Commonwealth called Mrs. Nutt to testify against her husband's killer. She approached the stand dressed entirely in black, as was customary for a widow in full mourning. Just as Playford wanted to illustrate that Captain Nutt's cane was simply an ordinary accessory, so too did he hope to convince the jury that Nutt had not brought a gun to Dukes's room specifically for the occasion but was always armed.

"What was Captain Nutt's habit of carrying a revolver?" Playford inquired.

"He was in the habit of carrying a revolver for twenty-three years," came the reply in low tones from behind a thick veil.[19]

William Pickard then offered a striking account of his gun sale to Dukes at the hardware store just days before the shooting. The fresh-faced witness recollected how the defendant had hidden behind a showcase when other customers entered. Dukes turned crimson during Pickard's testimony. To close the day's proceedings, Coroner Sturgeon and Feather identified Dukes's gun, which was admitted into evidence with the remaining bullets still loaded.[20]

Throughout the session, the dense crowd—composed largely of locals who personally knew both the victim and the defendant—sat in absolute silence. Every word from the witness stand could be heard in the farthest corners of the courtroom. But the concentration of so many bodies had hardly been comfortable. Although the temperature outside was in the thirties, the courtroom itself was sweltering. In the words of the *Harrisburg Telegraph*, "The air was rank almost to suffocation." At 4:30 P.M., Judge Willson complied with Playford's request to adjourn on account of the heat until the following morning.[21]

Discussion on the streets of Uniontown that evening centered on the exclusively Democratic composition of the jury. Many were angered by a comment, attributed alternately to the son of the court clerk or to the clerk himself, that Dukes would be safe in the hands of fellow Democrats. Meanwhile, reports circulated that the young men whom Dukes purportedly identified in his infamous letter as Lizzie's other romantic partners were livid at the accusations and eager to refute them.[22]

Accounts of the day's proceedings spread across telegraph lines to newspaper offices throughout the country, and editors readied the latest headlines. From the *New York Times* to the Sacramento *Record-Union*, the Dukes case was front-page news. Above all, the people of Uniontown and fellow citizens around the nation were eager for what the following morning promised—Judge Willson's ultimate decision on the admission of Dukes's letters. Nothing less than the defendant's life hung in the balance.[23]

When the courthouse opened on Tuesday, March 13, for the third day of the trial, the mob once more jostled its way in. The Commonwealth, finally, directed its energy toward Dukes's correspondence. "Interest had reached a high point," reported a local paper, "for the one feature above all others which held the public ear and eye was the desire to know the contents of these letters." Playford and his team first needed to establish the authenticity of the letters before offering them into evidence. Accordingly, the Commonwealth recalled Mrs. Nutt, who testified that her husband had given her both letters before his death. She had read only the first.

"Didn't you read the second one?" asked Playford.

"No; I tried to, but—" Her voice broke.

Breckenridge retook the stand and described how Mrs. Nutt had delegated a woman to deliver the letters to him on Christmas Eve and how he lent them to Bob Hopwood before turning them over to the Commonwealth. Finally, a bank cashier familiar with Dukes's handwriting was called to verify the defendant's signature.[24]

The Commonwealth was finally prepared to offer the correspondence, and Playford moved to admit Dukes's first letter. But a lawyer of Congressman Boyle's tenacity would hardly allow a character assassination of his client to proceed without a fight.

"What is the purpose of offering this letter?" demanded Boyle.

Playford replied matter-of-factly, "For the purpose of showing the animus of Mr. Dukes in a series of events toward Mr. Nutt which culminated in his death." In a courtroom marked by silence, Boyle examined the letter for several minutes, with the defendant peering over his lawyer's shoulder at the words he himself had penned three months prior. Judge Willson then took the letter and reviewed it before allowing Playford to make the case for admission.[25]

"We contend that this letter led directly to the death of Captain Nutt," affirmed Playford. "It explains why these men met and why Mr. Dukes slew Captain Nutt. We contend it as much evidence in this case as the pistol. These letters show the feelings of Mr. Dukes;

they show why Captain Nutt requested Mr. Breckenridge to seek an interview with Mr. Dukes."

"We have seen but one of the letters," the judge remarked. Playford now produced Dukes's second letter, which Boyle surveyed and objected to as irrelevant. Judge Willson then studied it himself with great care.

Playford asserted, "One letter follows another, and the second refers to the other. They also refer so clearly to the case and show the animus of Mr. Dukes so well that it seems to me they are clearly admissible."

Boyle did not back down. He noted in particular that the first letter contained no threatening language. "Its only effect would be to prejudice the jury against the prisoner," he insisted, "and I submit that it should not be admitted in a case where a man is on trial for his life."

Playford countered that these letters spoke to the very heart of the case. He pleaded for judicial deference to the jury: "The Commonwealth has a right to show the motive of the prisoner, and whether it is the true motive or not, the jury must determine."

Judge Willson had read the letters. He had heard the arguments. And now he had made his decision. "We are of the opinion the evidence is competent," he decreed, "and the objection is therefore overruled." A murmur swept through the crowd and Dukes's face flushed. Amid the eager throng in attendance were attorneys with whom Dukes had practiced law, politicians who had helped Dukes win his seat in the State House, parents whose babies Dukes had kissed on the campaign trail. In just a moment, they would all finally learn the exact content of his graphic allegations about Lizzie Nutt.

And as fast as the telegraph lines could carry the news, so would the nation.[26]

The court first waited for the women present to exit. It would have been highly improper for any lady to hear such lascivious language. Playford personally escorted Mrs. Nutt from the room. One reporter observed that, with the women gone, "there was a momentary rustle as the crowd wriggled itself into a listening attitude." Playford picked up the letters, turned directly to the jury, and began to read. His voice was forceful, his pace steady. The audience was utterly transfixed and leaned forward to absorb every syllable. "They were the morsels for which the packed court room had been patiently waiting," wrote a journalist, "and during the reading of them the silence was so profound that a whisper could have been heard across the room." As Dukes listened to his words recited to a jury of his peers, he stared down, twitching sporadically. A pallid Judge Willson appeared on the verge of tears and turned away from the crowd. Congressman Boyle, for his part, carefully followed Playford's reading with duplicates in hand. Boyle later sneered, "It was read as if it was charged with nitroglycerine, and liable to explode upon touching it." When Playford finally took his seat, spectators exchanged hushed reactions and glared at the defendant in disgust. Amid the throng listening to Dukes's lewd description of Lizzie was her devoted brother, James.[27]

The Commonwealth called Mrs. Nutt back to the stand. Playford wanted to substantiate that Dukes had visited the Nutt home on December 6, the night he retrieved Lizzie's ring. The defense offered an objection on the grounds of irrelevancy, which the bench sustained—a token victory for Dukes after a devastating defeat.[28]

Dukes's second letter had claimed that Captain Nutt possessed prior knowledge of his daughter's indiscretions. "She told me herself that you had received an anonymous letter warning you of her erotic conduct," the letter charged. Playford hoped to show that Dukes himself had written the unsigned letter to create the illusion for Nutt of independent corroborating evidence of his accusations about Lizzie. To that end, the Commonwealth called James Nutt as a witness.[29]

"Did you see Mr. Dukes near your father's residence in October drop an anonymous letter?" Playford asked James.

Boyle objected, but not before the witness blurted out, "I did." Judge Willson sustained the defense. Although Willson directed the stenographer to strike James's response from the record, the judge could not erase the witness's answer from the minds of the jurors. With this, the Commonwealth rested. Indeed, there was little the Commonwealth could do to advance its cause more than Dukes's letters already had. It now fell to the defense to save its client's life.[30]

R. H. Lindsey delivered the defense's opening argument. He well understood his chief aim was to mitigate the damage wrought by Dukes's letters. "Matters have been introduced in this case," Lindsey lamented, "that tend to throw a cloud of dust in your eyes." He admonished the jurors: "Confine yourselves solely to the charge for which the defendant is arraigned." Noting the prejudicial effect of newspaper reports about the coroner's inquest and bail hearing, Lindsey acknowledged, "The testimony has been read by the world and that explains why so many of the jurors declared they had already formed opinions when called before the Court."[31]

Despite the firestorm of scandal surrounding Nutt's death, two timeless principles of law favored the defendant, claimed Lindsey. First, Dukes did not initiate the fatal meeting but had acted in defense of his life. "Self-defense is one of the first laws written in human nature," Lindsey asserted. "It is a principle that impels man to resist all violence and assault. This is not only a law of nature and thus above all laws of society, but is also recognized by the laws of society." Second, the defendant shot his assailant in his own room at the Jennings House. "That was his home and his castle and there no man had a right to come. That is a maxim so old that its origin is lost in the gulf of the dark ages." Here Lindsey was alluding to the castle doctrine, which held that a man's home was his castle, an inviolable space he could defend with impunity. The doctrine had a long-standing basis in the English common law and traced its origins to classical antiquity. Lindsey closed his remarks by questioning the veracity of the three supposed eyewitnesses to the killing and promised that the defense's own evidence would establish that Dukes was an otherwise peaceful man who acted reasonably in response to an unambiguous threat on his life.[32]

The first witness for the defense was Julius Shipley. A civil engineer, Shipley had been commissioned to produce a drawing of Dukes's room, with its various pieces of furniture, as it existed at the time of the shooting. The defense would use this layout to challenge the testimony of Breckenridge, Feather, and Williams in its closing argument. Mrs. Jennings then took the stand. Over Playford's objection, Judge Willson allowed her to testify that

Dukes claimed he had acted in self-defense in the immediate wake of shooting Captain Nutt. The court then adjourned until 2:00 P.M., at which point Mr. Jennings also testified that the defendant insisted he pulled the trigger in defense of his own life.[33]

Boyle had already rigorously cross-examined the trial's most important witnesses a day earlier, so the defense did not require much time to question a succession of peripheral witnesses. There was the waiter at the hotel who heard the commotion upstairs; the woman who saw a blanch-faced Captain Nutt walk to the Jennings House; the cashier at the bank where Nutt once kept his revolver.[34]

Now that Dukes's letters had been read aloud in court, his lawyers' best hope of establishing self-defense and saving him from the gallows was to offer into evidence Captain Nutt's own letter, riddled as it was menacing language. Boyle read aloud Nutt's defiant message. Once again, the throng in the courtroom listened in perfect stillness. But whereas Dukes's letters elicited scorn from the crowd, Nutt's missive prompted applause.[35]

To close its testimony, the defense introduced a parade of character witnesses—forty in total—who depicted Dukes as an upstanding citizen hardly prone to violence. These witnesses included neighbors and old classmates, including Sheriff Hoover, who spoke of Dukes's disposition for peace in the twenty-five years that they had known one another.[36]

The defense had no further evidence. Rules of procedure prohibited Dukes from testifying. He passed the day scribbling, sometimes employing his pencil as a toothpick. His demeanor offered a sharp contrast to that of the teary-eyed Mrs. Nutt, whose sister-in-law sat by her side and comforted the grieving widow. Before dismissing the jury, Judge Willson once again warned the jurors not to discuss the case until both sides made their closing arguments and he himself delivered his charge from the bench. Court adjourned at 5:00 P.M. to resume the following morning.[37]

When the substance of Dukes's letters was first reported in the press in late December, many had turned against him. But not all. The papers had cautioned at the time that the accounts of the letters were based on secondhand information, and at least some people were skeptical that anyone could pen such lewd accusations to a father about his daughter. Now, however, their worst fears had been confirmed. A local reporter described the sudden and final collapse of Dukes's last pillars of support in Uniontown:

> Our people could not believe that the letters were so infamous as reported, and hence some clung to Dukes till the last. . . . When the letters came out, however, and Dukes appeared in his true colors, there was a stampede from him like rats from a sinking ship.

During the trial, newspapers in leading cities reacted to Dukes's letters by affirming Captain Nutt's right to slay his daughter's seducer. Washington, DC's *Evening Critic* described Dukes's first missive as "a letter for which he should have been shot down like a dog." In the same vein, the Chicago *Inter Ocean* maintained that under comparable circumstances, "ninety-nine men in a hundred would have sought the writer out, and, without warning, would have crushed the life out of him."[38]

To make matters worse for the defendant, on this same day, R. P. Kennedy—whom Dukes's letter named as belonging to the sizable cohort of men romantically involved with Lizzie—swore an affidavit on his own volition denying any wrongdoing. "I brand every mention of me by Dukes as villainous and unmerited," Kennedy declared in his notarized statement. "Miss Nutt was always a modest, retiring and proper young lady."[39]

But the trial was not yet over. Court was set to reconvene the next day, when William Playford and Congressman Boyle—two colleagues who shared in reputation, in profits, and in friendship with Captain Nutt—would stand opposite each other and present the most anticipated closing arguments of their careers.

· *Six* ·

VERDICT

On Wednesday, March 14, 1883, the Fayette County courthouse opened for the fourth and final day of the *Commonwealth v. Nicholas Dukes*. The crowd was so tightly packed that one could not exhale without breathing on those around him. Many who were unable to find seats simply knelt on the ground, ready to hold that position for hours on end. Amid the mass of bodies pressed together, the elderly could barely touch their canes to the floor. "It was the spectacle of a lifetime," remarked the *Harrisburg Telegraph*, "to these people to see one of their members of the Legislature tried by a jury of blacksmiths, miners and farmers for the murder of another officer of the State." From on high, a grim-faced Judge Willson surveyed the crush of curiosity seekers; directly above his head, a portrait of a late Pennsylvania chief justice stared down at the teeming horde with comparable solemnity.[1]

When the session opened at 9:00 A.M., R. H. Lindsey for the defense submitted points of law to Judge Willson. Findings of fact belonged to the jury, but it was within the bench's purview to clarify the law for the twelve men sitting in judgment of the accused. To this end, attorneys were free to submit points of law, which the judge in turn could accept, reject, or modify in his instructions to the jurors. The defense put forth as a legal doctrine, "In the consideration of this case it is the imperative duty of the jury to exclude from their minds all public clamor or prejudice. The law and the evidence should be their only guides." Judge Willson would affirm this point.[2]

Congressman Boyle rose to make the defense's closing argument. Turning away from the crowd, he faced the jurors and began to speak in a low voice. He reminded them that their oath had implications in this life and the next: "You swore that as you should answer to God at the great day, you would try this man under the law and under the evidence only." Moreover, Dukes's social status merited neither special consideration nor condemnation because "the law protects and punishes the humblest as well as the highest, and it protects and punishes each to the same extent." Boyle stressed the gravity of the task before them—"You are invested with power over his life and liberty"—and exhorted the jury to limit its concern to the indictment alone and ignore the widespread outrage over the letters.[3]

Boyle then attempted a feat to which even his considerable talents were perhaps unequal; he tried to recast Dukes's correspondence as actually favorable to his client. "I appeal to you if there is any evidence of ill will, of malice, of any purpose on the part of Mr. Dukes to do Captain Nutt any harm!" Boyle exclaimed. "It is full, it is full of the opposite." The Commonwealth had invoked the first letter to establish Dukes's animosity, but, argued Boyle, Dukes was hardly antagonistic to Captain Nutt.

After all, Nutt had done Dukes no wrong. Dukes intended his initial letter, however ill-advised, to aid Nutt in shielding his family from the embarrassment of a daughter pregnant out of wedlock. "See how the letter fades away! The letter is lighter than chaff," Boyle remarked.[4]

Congressman Boyle noted that although Dukes's initial message to Captain Nutt scarcely indicated animosity on the part of the defendant, it did inadvertently provoke deadly hostility from Nutt. Boyle now read Nutt's reply aloud, as he had the day before: "Follow this one, and see who had the ill will, the disposition and purpose to kill." After walking the jury through Nutt's litany of threats, Boyle observed, "In that letter Captain Nutt over and over again avows an unchanging purpose to take the life of Mr. Dukes. . . . I never knew such a fuss, such a sham, made over papers, as has been made over these letters, when in point of fact every line and letter of them makes in favor of this defense."[5]

Still, there were details in the correspondence that weighed against the defendant. In Dukes's second letter, he promised that he would remain unarmed, only to purchase just days later the firearm with which he killed Nutt. Boyle characterized his client's behavior as a reasonable change of mind rather than a premeditated ruse.

Why God himself had invested him with the right to defend himself. Was he to stand and be shot down without attempting to protect himself? You cannot be prevented from carrying a pistol to defend yourself, and Mr. Dukes in the light of this letter of Nutt's had a right to change his mind. . . . Would you not have armed yourselves?

Boyle also questioned the significance of Dukes's request to have his room cleaned the morning of the affray. "What difference did that make to him," asked Boyle, "if he merely wanted Captain Nutt to come into his room so he might kill him? See how insignificant it is—how trifling it is!" Boyle explained that Dukes wanted his room tidied precisely because he planned to cloister himself there in the hopes of avoiding Captain Nutt.[6]

On the subject of Nutt's self-cocking .38 Colt, Boyle insisted that Captain Nutt did not usually carry a firearm of that grade, as alleged by the Commonwealth. "He would no more have thought of arming himself with a weapon like that, and parading the streets of Uniontown with it, than he would have thought of going about without his shoes." Expressing outrage, Boyle added, "That evidence does injustice to his memory." No, Captain Nutt carried that particular gun on Christmas Eve with the intent to kill. Boyle posed a central question:

> Who commenced the struggle? I appeal to twelve sensible men. I speak to you in defense of this man's life, and I ask you in view of the undoubted truth, the undoubted evidence, the undoubted circumstances, who commenced that struggle?

Nutt ascended the steps to Dukes's room seeking not reconciliation but retribution. To justify self-defense, the law did not even require that the danger to Dukes have been real, only apparent. "He is not on trial for seduction, or for writing objectionable letters, but for murder," Boyle reminded the jurors. "If he believed himself in danger, he committed no murder, and you must acquit him."[7]

Because Dukes by law was barred from the witness stand, his counsel had no testimonial evidence on which to base a claim that in fact Nutt reached for his weapon *before* Dukes fired and, what's more, that the three alleged witnesses entered the room *following* the fatal shot. That version of events surfaced only after the trial. In his closing argument, Boyle's strategy was to highlight enough discrepancies in the Commonwealth's case as to raise a reasonable doubt about his client's guilt.

Clark Breckenridge, James Feather, and Lewis Williams had testified on three occasions—at the coroner's inquest, the bail hearing, and now the trial. Although they agreed that Captain Nutt had not been holding his gun when Dukes shot him, they contradicted each other and sometimes their own earlier testimonies on ancillary details. Boyle now pointed out, for example, that Williams stated at the inquest that Captain Nutt held his cane in his left hand prior to the shot yet later swore that it was in his right hand. Breckenridge and Feather, meanwhile, testified that Nutt held no cane at all. Williams also initially maintained that he himself shut the door to Dukes's room, but at trial Williams alleged that Dukes shut his own door. In the same vein, Breckenridge and Feather first testified that Nutt's hands were down when Dukes pulled the trigger but they later vowed that one of Nutt's arms was up, resting on the mantel. Without explicitly denying the presence of these witnesses in Dukes's room, Boyle simply queried, "Can you believe any one of them? And if you doubt as to which tells the truth, how can you convict?"[8]

Boyle also contended that much of what the Commonwealth posited was not physically possible. Williams testified that he saw Dukes's door from the landing on the stairwell, something not permitted by the layout of the hotel. And based on the positioning of the furniture in Dukes's room, Feather would have been directly in the line of fire, thus obstructing a clean shot. Boyle further expressed incredulity that Captain Nutt, having received a mortal wound to his brain, had the wherewithal to reach for his weapon.[9]

In closing his remarks, Boyle sought to steel the jury against the emotional pleas that were sure to follow in the Commonwealth's final argument. "They may be as eloquent as they please about seduction. . . . They may stand aghast at the ruin of a family. God knows it is only too common," he acknowledged. "But the law does not hang a man for that." Legal doctrine provided that good character alone could give rise to a reasonable doubt about a defendant's guilt, and Boyle now alluded to the character witnesses who testified on the defendant's behalf the day before:

> Let his character stand for him now. A man who had won a character like that, ought to have some benefit from it in the hour of trial. When he has fallen into this unfortunate condition, let it come to his assistance. If there be any doubt about his having to defend himself on that awful occasion, throw that character into the scale, and let it preponderate.

As the coda to a performance stretching into its third hour, Boyle reprised his opening note and asked the jurors simply for the rule of law to which their oaths bound them:

> A jury swayed by sympathy, by a man's family relations, or by anything outside the testimony and the law, will go astray. I ask not for mercy, but I ask that you do equal and exact justice between this man and the Commonwealth.

The crowd remained unmoved by Congressman Boyle's appeal to spare the life of the accused, but as Boyle well knew, only a dozen opinions in that courtroom mattered. It was 11:30 A.M., and William Playford did not want the midday recess to break up his highly anticipated speech, so Judge Willson adjourned court until the afternoon.[10]

When the courtroom reopened, eager spectators stormed in to hear the county's greatest criminal lawyer prosecute the state's most notorious legislator. Just after 2:00 P.M., Playford arose, his immense frame looming over the jury. He began his address by considering the profound scale of the tragedy, which Playford described as "so appalling in its character, when all the incidents attending it became known, that the nation was horrified and this community stood aghast." Dukes's slaying of Captain Nutt was "the worst offense that blackens the record of crime in this state since the foundation of it." A few hours earlier, Boyle predicted that the Commonwealth would appeal to the jury's sympathy for the victim's family. Playford wasted little time in proving Boyle right, praising Nutt's widow as "the only one to stand between this wicked world and her little children."[11]

He turned to the infamous letters. Playford scoffed at Boyle's insistence that they advanced the cause of the defense. If that were true, Playford reasoned, then Boyle would not have objected so vehemently to their admission. The letters were the best evidence of the defendant's murderous soul:

A man who could write these letters coolly and deliberately in his office is capable in his heart of committing the highest crime known to the law, because I say in these letters he does worse than that. He deprives a family of its reputation and he destroys its most sacred idol. I say the killing of Captain Nutt was but a trifle in iniquity and enormity.

Playford could have dismissed Dukes's allegations as lies and championed Lizzie's chastity; instead, he accepted Dukes's letters as true and demonized him as a libertine. According to Playford, every womanizer who "debauches his neighbors' daughters" tries to escape responsibility by falsely dividing it with other men, as Dukes did with R. P. Kennedy and several others. Worse still, Dukes ruined Lizzie in Captain Nutt's own home while Nutt was away in Harrisburg, "earning a living with which to feed and clothe his little ones."[12]

In Playford's eyes, Dukes's great failure was that he desecrated the code of honor. The accused may fashion himself a "man of honor," noted Playford, "yet he sits down and writes the most brutal letter ever penned by the hand of a man to the father of the girl whose honor he had destroyed." Referring to Dukes's solicitation of Lizzie to test her purity, Playford asked, "Why would he test her if he was an honorable man?" He read excerpts from the scandalous letter about Lizzie succumbing to Dukes's advances. "Nice talk, nice language from an 'honorable' man," Playford sneered. Whereas Dukes's callous indifference to honor resulted in tragedy, the jury's faithful adherence to honor promised restitution. "You dare not turn him free. I am no more afraid of that than I am this moment of a lighting strike, because I have faith in your intelligence and your honor," Playford assured the twelve men in the jury box. But should the jury fail to convict, there would be consequences. "You dare not let him go," warned Playford. "We'll see you when you do it, and we'll see you after you turn him loose." Here, in a court of law, standing before a judge, a practicing lawyer made a thinly veiled threat to a sitting jury.[13]

Playford went on to justify Nutt's "noble and manly" letter as the only possible response a father who cherished his daughter could have authored: "Captain Nutt's conduct throughout was that of an honorable man." Playford then claimed that Dukes did not interpret Nutt's letter as a threat. Dukes invited Nutt to meet him at his office or hotel room, indicating that the defendant did not, in fact, fear for his life. What's more, Dukes's character witnesses meant little when balanced against his letter openly admitting to his own lecherous behavior. Perhaps the greatest indictment of Dukes's supposedly peaceful character was his promise to remain unarmed and his subsequent purchase of a gun. Clearly, Dukes was "trying to inveigle Captain Nutt into a death trap" where the defendant "stood with his double acting self-cocking, death dealing weapon." Earlier that day in court, Boyle had speculated that once inside Dukes's room, Captain Nutt was probably the one who initiated the brawl; after all, it was Nutt—not Dukes—who felt aggrieved. But Playford here posited an alternate logic: Dukes, who wronged Lizzie in seducing her and wronged her father in writing those letters, was likely responsible for yet another wrong in attacking Nutt.[14]

Playford turned to the testimony of the three eyewitnesses. Although the defense exposed a number of inconsistencies in their stories, Playford stressed that on the material fact—Nutt made no threatening gestures in the moment before Dukes fired—Breckenridge, Feather, and Williams corroborated each other and their earlier testimonies. Playford reminded the jurors that at the coroner's inquest the witnesses offered their recollections immediately following the killing without any opportunity for collusion between them. In fact, noted Playford, Breckenridge went to a doctor's office and gave his account independent of the other witnesses.[15]

Boyle had dwelt on the subject of Nutt's sizable revolver, suggesting that Captain Nutt carried a weapon of that grade on Christmas Eve specifically to kill Dukes rather than as a matter of habit. Instead of challenging that contention, Playford simply lauded honor killing: "I say that Captain Nutt would have been justified, but he had no disposition to do so, in taking a cannon into that room and blowing this defendant into a thousand pieces." Playford also called attention to Feather's testimony that, just prior to the shot, Dukes himself said Nutt came to "whip" him—not *kill* him—proving that Dukes did not believe his life was in danger. Making light of Feather's disinclination to invite Dukes to his wedding, Playford prompted laughter from the courtroom when he joked, "Dukes did not want to go to weddings; he was getting what he wanted without weddings." Playford concluded his remarks by marveling at the audacity of a man who believed that he could needlessly murder an innocent father, employ a skilled legal team to secure his acquittal, and then represent his county in the state legislature.[16]

Over the course of Playford's closing argument, which spanned more than an hour, he spoke with the conviction of a man representing something more than just the government of Pennsylvania. "The indignation that had been swelling up into the court room from every street corner since the letters were made public yesterday was behind him," wrote the *Harrisburg Telegraph*. Many considered the performance the greatest of his already long and distinguished career at the bar. During Playford's castigation, Dukes showed little emotion. As one reporter put it, Playford "showered upon the prisoner a torrent of invectives beneath which any man of human feeling would have bent in shame, but which Dukes withstood with the stoicism of a sphinx."[17]

After Playford finished, Judge Willson—in a voice at once deliberate and dispassionate—began his charge to the jury. He clarified the varying degrees of homicide and discussed the testimony, emphasizing that slight inconsistencies need not discredit the entirety of a witness's statement. On the subject of self-defense, the judge explained that a defendant must believe he had no means of evading his attacker other than by lethal force. The weapons used in self-defense, moreover, could not have been unequal to those employed by the assailant. It was now 4:30 P.M. and, having spoken for over an hour, Judge Willson turned over the case to the jury. The mass in the courthouse watched intently as, one by one, the twelve men charged with determining the fate of the accused retired to the jury room. When the final juror retreated from sight, the mob surged toward the exit.[18]

As twilight approached, the streets of Uniontown were abuzz with condemnation of Dukes. Even the old men shuffled away from their seats by the fire to join the discussion. Murder in the first degree was the only conscionable verdict by all accounts.

But the partisan makeup of the jury gave the townsfolk pause and the air was rife with speculation:

"Will they do it?"

"Dare they acquit him?"

Judge Willson mandated that if the jury reached its verdict by 9:00 P.M., the court officers should ring the courthouse bell, and court would reconvene that evening. And so Uniontown was in a state of constant vigilance because at any moment the chime of the bell could echo through the village.[19]

Meanwhile, under lock and key in the cramped confines of the jury room, a forty-two-year-old juror named Jake Amalong proposed that they pray before discussing the case. The jurors dropped to their knees. One of the four churchgoing members began an appeal to a higher power. Then, after selecting a foreman, the jury turned to the task at hand.[20]

Four possible verdicts confronted them. If Dukes had "reasonable grounds" for believing "he was in danger of death or great bodily harm," the jury was obliged to acquit. If not, Dukes was guilty of some form of homicide. First-degree murder required malice and an "intent to kill;" second-degree murder involved malice and "an intent to do great bodily harm" but no intent to kill; manslaughter applied to cases in which, even if there were an intent to kill, the homicide was characterized by "sufficient provocation" and an absence of malice. In the event that Dukes was found guilty of murder in the first degree and sentenced to die, it would fall to Sheriff Hoover to hang his boyhood friend.[21]

By 7:45 P.M., the jury reached its verdict. A court officer headed to Judge Willson's home on Main Street to alert him in advance of the tolling bell so that the judge could beat the crowd to the courthouse. But when the townspeople caught sight of the officer, they discerned the meaning of his presence, and a frantic dash for the courthouse ensued. Shops were instantly abandoned. Evening newspapers with the most recent accounts of the trial were tossed aside. Diners in the middle of their meals at the hotels ran from their tables, and their waiters sprinted behind them. Even before the first ringing of the bell, the courthouse yard was overflowing. The deputy sheriff tried to hold the crowd at bay at the courthouse doors but he was soon pushed out of the way.[22]

Impossibly, more onlookers than ever before packed into the courtroom. Many found that their collars had been ripped off in the manic rush. The judge, stepping to the bench, speculated, "I am afraid the verdict comes too quickly to be the right one." First entered the jurors, then the lawyers, and finally, the defendant. Dukes knew not whether he would live or die, but he approached his chair with a stoic face and solid step. Roll call for the jurors commenced. As the moment approached when the verdict would be rendered, the defendant stood and turned toward the jury. Thomas Searight, the Court Clerk, began to ask the jury foreman:

"How say you—"

Before Searight could finish, the foreman interrupted with one telling word: "Not—"

"Hold on." Searight continued, "Is the prisoner guilty as he stands indicted or not guilty?"

"Not guilty."[23]

The crowd was shocked. An equally stunned Judge Willson turned to the twelve men who had just set Dukes free and began to criticize them:

> Gentlemen of the jury, I suppose the verdict is one that you thought you should render under your oaths; but it is one that gives dissatisfaction to the Court, because we thought the evidence sufficient to justify a different verdict. If you have committed an error, it is one that we cannot avoid, but can only express our condemnation of it in this mild way. The prisoner is discharged.

Although Judge Willson's language was hardly caustic, that he issued a rebuke at all was extraordinary. Willson was nearing retirement and never before in his tenure on the bench had he denounced a verdict in his courtroom.[24]

Jury

Source: Lizzie Nutt's Sad Experience: A Heart Broken, and a Family Plunged in Grief. Wreck and Ruin! (Philadelphia: Barclay, 1886), 56.

While the townsfolk entertained little doubt that the defendant was guilty of first-degree murder, deep misgivings had surfaced inside the jury room. Dukes's letters, however inappropriate, did not appear to the jurors directly relevant to the question of legal culpability. The jury also recognized that Captain Nutt's letter made an ominous threat on Dukes's life. Discrepancies in the testimony of the Commonwealth's principal witnesses concerned the jurors as well. And even if Captain Nutt had not reached for his gun until after Dukes fired, the jury reasoned that Nutt's cane was weighty enough to be used as an instrument of death and thus prompted a lethal response in self-defense.[25]

On the first ballot, there was not a single vote for murder in the first or second degree; the majority voted for acquittal with some holdouts for manslaughter. By the third ballot, eleven jurors favored acquittal versus one for manslaughter. The lone dissenter continued to cast his vote for manslaughter on the fourth, fifth, and sixth ballots. On the seventh ballot, after three and a half hours of deliberation, the Dukes jury reached a consensus.[26]

When Judge Willson adjourned the court, not a soul congratulated Dukes—not his lawyers, not even his stepfather. The spectators remained paralyzed and made no motion to exit. Eventually, the lights were extinguished, and the throng passed out of the courtroom, cursing the jurors. People lingered about the hallways of the courthouse for a while, hoping to catch a glimpse of Dukes. But he secluded himself in a stairwell away from the crowd. Within a matter of minutes, the streets of Uniontown exploded with rage. Having evaded death at the hands of Captain Nutt and been spared the gallows by the verdict of the jury, Dukes once again found himself in mortal danger.[27]

Seven

MOBS

❧

IN THE IMMEDIATE WAKE OF THE VERDICT, AN EFFIGY OF DUKES was hauled through the streets and, in front of a manic mob, lynched on a tree. By the hundreds, townsfolk sang, "We'll hang Lyman Dukes to a sour-apple tree. The jury will join him on the way." They paired these verses with the melody of a song called "John Brown's Body."[1]

This was a tune chosen with purpose. John Brown was a militant abolitionist who in 1859 seized a federal arsenal at Harper's Ferry, Virginia, with a ragtag militia of twenty men. Brown's ultimate goal was to move southward, swelling his ranks by emancipating slaves and fomenting an uprising large enough to crush the institution of slavery. Yet only thirty-six hours after insurgents took hold of the arsenal, federal troops besieged Brown's men and brought a hasty end to the rebellion. Brown himself was tried and hung for treason, emerging as a hero in death to many Northerners. "John Brown's Body," commemorating his martyrdom, formed the basis of a popular marching song for Union soldiers during the Civil War. As an officer of the

3rd United States Colored Troops, Captain Nutt lived John Brown's unrealized dream of leading free black men into the heart of the South to liberate those still in bondage. Now Nutt had become a martyr as well, and, in a moment suffused with historical symbolism, his supporters selected the melody of "John Brown's Body" to accompany their blood-soaked lyrics.[2]

The members of the jury were terrified by the hysteria. Congressman Boyle assured one of them on the street that the riot would soon subside. But as the jurors moved through the horde, promises of tar and feathers followed them. Groups of angry men congregated on street corners to condemn the verdict. Near the McClelland House, two jurors were appalled as they came upon a swarm of people setting fire to a dummy in Dukes's likeness.[3]

The Harrisburg *Patriot* reported, "There were many threats to lynch Dukes, and if he were to appear on the streets now, his life would not weigh in the estimation of a hair." Dukes successfully made his way into the custody of Sheriff Hoover and waited in the safety of the sheriff's parlor while the frenzy of mock lynchings continued outside. Instead of taking Dukes's life, Sheriff Hoover was saving it.[4]

Uniontown's leading citizens circulated and signed a broadside announcing a meeting to be held the following evening at 7:00 P.M. outside the post office, where "citizens of Fayette county before the civilized world" would "express their indignation at the outrageous verdict of acquittal of the assassin of A. C. Nutt." Word also spread that local attorneys were planning to appeal to the court to have Dukes disbarred. When the frantic mobs dispersed for the night and quiet finally descended on the

Ride Home
Source: Republican Standard,
March 31, 1883, 1.

PECKEA.

AFTER THE VERDICT.
On the Home Stretch From the Jail
to German Township.

town, Nicholas Dukes stole away on horseback with his half-brother and a neighbor in tow. As he fled through the midnight darkness, Dukes rode past the home of the man he had killed.[5]

The following day—Thursday, March 15—Americans read in their local papers the stunning news from Pennsylvania. Headlines were as likely to emphasize the outcry of the public as much as the finding of the jury. "Dukes Acquitted—A Verdict That Amazed the Judge and Infuriated the Community," announced the front page of the *Telegraph and Messenger* in Macon, Georgia. The *San Francisco Chronicle* led its reportage with, "'Not Guilty'—Indignation over the Verdict in the Dukes Murder Case." And in the *Kansas City Star*, simply, "Righteous Indignation." Washington, DC's *Evening Star* noted that the fury in Uniontown was spreading quickly thanks to the trial's ubiquitous news coverage: "Indignation at the acquittal of Dukes, the slayer of Capt. Nutt, is not confined to the village where the murder occurred, or to the state of Pennsylvania. It extends wherever the details of the double and dastardly crime of the ruin of the daughter and murder of the father have been read."[6]

In the aftermath of the trial, the press did not merely report on the public ire but also in many instances promoted it with incendiary editorial commentary about both the verdict and Dukes. The *Washington Post* declared, "Dukes is a human monster whom honest men cannot help loathing." The Philadelphia *Times* considered Dukes's correspondence a graver sin than his slaying of Captain Nutt: "The creature that could deliberately write what he wrote of a girl who had given herself to him, and that to the father of the girl, is worse than a murderer." Perhaps most histrionic was the *Philadelphia Press*'s editorial page:

> The ravening sensualist, whose law is lust . . . may enter any family, corrupt innocence, undermine the teachings of the hearth, prostitute virtue, murder parents, and enter the court assured of indemnity! . . . The history of crime presents no more revolting page; the atrocities of war no crime more cold-blooded, calculating and abhorrent.

Rare indeed was the newspaper that supported Dukes's acquittal.[7]

The morning after the verdict, the notorious dozen men who set Dukes free received their pay for jury duty and hurried for their hometowns in other parts of the county. As they left Uniontown, the jurors saw effigies of themselves hanging from telegraph poles. When locals spotted a departing juror, they shouted:

"Tar and feather him."

"Hit him with a brick."

"Ride him on a rail"—a public shaming ritual in which an object of scorn would be made to sit on a piece of fence that was carried through town.[8]

At the train station, the taunts continued:

"How much did you get?"

"Go home and face your wives."

"Never show your face in Uniontown again."[9]

When the jurors finally escaped, they found the reception was no better elsewhere in Fayette County. The citizens of Brownsville gave one juror five minutes to leave town—he needed fewer. Another juror from Springhill discovered that he would have to depart his hometown as rapidly as he had absconded

Train Depot

Source: Lizzie Nutt's Sad Experience: A Heart Broken, and a Family Plunged in Grief. Wreck and Ruin! (Philadelphia: Barclay, 1886), 64.

from Uniontown. A third juror from Upper Tyrone learned that he had lost his job at a mining company.[10]

At 2:00 P.M. back in Uniontown, one of the oldest and most venerated members of the bar, John Collins, presented Judge Willson with a petition to expel Dukes from legal practice. Collins was intimately familiar with Dukes; they once shared a law office. The petition found Dukes "guilty of a series of acts unbecoming a citizen and member of the bar" and derided him as unworthy of "association with fair and honorable men of the profession." This motion was a bipartisan affair, signed by sixteen Democrats and twelve Republicans—nearly every lawyer in town, including Daniel Kaine, the attorney who had trained Dukes in law. Only Dukes's counsel and two or three friends of his in the legal fraternity refused to endorse the petition. Collins suggested that a hearing be set for early May but one of Dukes's isolated supporters requested that the judge delay any decision until the furor abated. Judge Willson suggested that a May hearing would provide time enough for anger to subside, at which point the court would allow Dukes to defend himself.[11]

That same afternoon, a weary Lizzie Nutt spoke to a journalist in her family's home. "There's not a word of truth in Dukes' letters," she insisted. "His object was to manufacture an excuse for breaking our engagement." Lizzie explained that her father had shown Dukes's letters to her, and she in turn asked Captain Nutt to summon her fiancé to the Nutt mansion so that Dukes would have to make his allegations to her face. Dukes, of course, refused. In her comments to the press, Lizzie questioned Dukes's manhood: "I did not suspect that he wanted the engagement broken. Why didn't he tell me? Such a course would have been manly, and would have commanded my respect." With her father dead and his killer free, Lizzie was bereft of hope. "Oh, that God would only let me die," she pleaded, "for I shall never have any peace this side of the grave." Lizzie's eyes moistened throughout the interview despite her best efforts to keep her composure. At one point, she broke down and sobbed. By Lizzie's side was her mother, whose countenance attested to the depths of her own anguish.[12]

Eleven miles away, at his stepfather's 1,000-acre estate, Dukes was also granting an interview to a newspaper. Pennsylvania law prohibited Dukes from testifying at trial, but sitting by the fire in his family's large brick farmhouse, he told his side of the story at last. Dukes described a far different scene from what the Commonwealth posited: Captain Nutt stormed into his room and immediately began to assault Dukes with a cane. When Dukes seized the cane, Nutt stepped back and reached for his gun, prompting Dukes to fire in self-defense. Clark Breckenridge, James Feather, and Lewis Williams all burst in only after the fatal shot.[13]

Questioned by the journalist about his future, Dukes refused to say whether he would seek induction to the General Assembly or even if he would continue to practice law. He did, however, predict that a snowstorm, which had already begun to envelop the region, would diminish attendance at the imminent indignation meeting.[14]

Dukes's optimism on that count proved ill-founded. In Uniontown that evening, irate citizens persevered with their demonstration. A special train on the Southwest railway delivered people from other points in the county. To stave off the harsh winds and subfreezing temperatures, organizers relocated the gathering from the post office corner to the three-story brick schoolhouse, steps from the church where Dukes first sighted Lizzie. Rutter's band, which led the procession during Captain Nutt's funeral, marched into the assembly hall on the third floor of the school. The bell rang and within ten minutes there was nowhere left to stand; many were turned away at the door. Dr. Smith Fuller, who had been the Nutt family physician for nearly two decades and was present during Captain Nutt's final moments, opened the meeting. Dr. Fuller called on Captain John Bierer, a member of the Grand Army of the Republic, to chair the proceedings. Bierer had eulogized Nutt at the memorial service in February and here again praised the character of his fallen comrade. Unlike William Playford, whose closing argument in court operated on the premise that Lizzie had been ruined, Bierer exalted Nutt's daughter as a paragon of purity. This celebration of Lizzie's chastity brought the crowd to its feet.[15]

The editor of the *Republican Standard*, a Uniontown newspaper, read telegrams sent by other communities. From Wilkes-Barre, Pennsylvania, came a message authored by Henry Palmer, who had just completed a four-year term as state attorney general and would later become a congressman: "The universal sentiment here is that Dukes' acquittal irretrievably disgraces Fayette county and humiliates every Pennsylvanian." From nearby Ursina, "Feelings against Dukes universal, no sympathy for him here." And from Confluence, some twenty-five miles east of Uniontown, "Hang the murderer and penitentiary the jurors." With this, the crowd went wild.[16]

When a local merchant, who advocated killing the acquitted, referred to him as "Mr. Dukes," shouts came from the gathering, "No! Not Mr. Dukes; call him the assassin Dukes." A member of the county bar took the floor. He confessed that for the first time in his career, he felt that "the courts of law are inadequate to mete out justice." He added, vaguely, "We will be driven to take other measures." Once more, the assemblage rose in approval.[17]

The Reverend N. P. Kerr, who had presided over Captain Nutt's burial, began to read aloud a series of resolutions. The preface deplored that "an esteemed citizen has fallen by the hand of the base traducer of the honor of his family." The resolutions that followed accused Dukes and his confederates of "packing and trammeling the jury" and suggested "as the only alternative the bloody arena at the shrine of Judge Lynch," a term of art referring to extralegal justice. Additional resolutions recognized Judge Willson for his fairness while voicing dismay that the prosecution's apt "words were wasted as pearl before swine upon a jury who defied alike the court, the evidence and their oaths before God." The declaration foretold the day "when the detested memory and blood-stained hands of N. L. Dukes have perished from the face of the earth." Throughout the reading of the resolutions, Reverend Kerr paused frequently as the throng interjected boisterous expressions of support.[18]

When the crowd insisted that Reverend Kerr add a speech of his own, he was all too willing to oblige. "Well may parents tremble for their daughters," the Reverend warned, "when twelve men can be found who are so base, so lost to all sense of manhood, decency and honor as to render directly contrary to all the evidence, the verdict which acquitted Lyman Dukes."

The members of the jury were forever condemned to the "black list of Fayette county" and future generations would remember them only with "inexpressible disgust." The acquitted would "go forth to learn, as Cain did, what it is to bear upon his brow the brand of a murderer." The crowd thundered with such fervor that the building shook. To conclude the evening, the gathering groaned three times. Those in attendance left the schoolhouse hoping that news of their indignation meeting would at least partially allay the damage to the county's honor.[19]

The press heightened this sense among locals that the verdict was a sweeping indictment of Uniontown in particular and Fayette County in general. In Somerset, Pennsylvania, the *Herald* suggested, "A horrible state of morals must exist in a community where twelve men can be found willing to disregard their oaths, to save the neck of so depraved a wretch, so foul a murderer, as Dukes was proven to be." The stigma brought upon their proud corner of Pennsylvania was hardly lost on locals. Uniontown's own *Republican Standard* lamented,

> The civilized world is hooting at us, and the press far and wide is pointing to Fayette county in derision. We may protest against it, but we can not blot out the lasting disgrace fastened upon us by twelve perverse and ignorant men who defied the court, their oaths and the sacred claims of justice.

It would take more than an indignation meeting for the citizenry to repair its reputation.[20]

While the schoolhouse in Uniontown swelled with the cries of a raucous crowd, a rumor circulated in Harrisburg that Dukes was en route to the capital on the 11:20 P.M. eastbound train. Word of Dukes's acquittal had reached Harrisburg the previous night, shortly after the jury rendered its verdict. Residents of the capital were furious and comments from members of the General Assembly reflected the widespread anger. An elderly legislator asked, "In God's name, where will this end? No man's daughter is safe, if men like this seducer are permitted to go free." The Speaker of the House decried the acquittal as an "outrage" and a "burlesque on justice." One senator openly advocated reprisal. "After reading those letters," he declared, "I think Dukes ought to be shot or hanged." Members of both sides of the aisle vowed to expel Dukes should he attempt to take his seat. The night after the verdict, with Dukes purportedly headed for the capital, an indignant mob congregated at the Harrisburg train station. Dukes never appeared. Still, the *Harrisburg Telegraph* predicted, "It is very probable that when he does come to Harrisburg he will be involved in a fracas" on account of locals "who were just aching for an opportunity to meet the murderer face to face."[21]

The next day, alongside the interviews with Dukes and Lizzie, the papers featured yet another revelation. With Mrs. Nutt's consent, Playford released to the press two letters that Dukes wrote to Lizzie in the summer of 1882. The letters had not surfaced at trial because they were not directly linked to Captain Nutt's death. Rather, they spoke to something that was never under judicial investigation—the credibility of Dukes's allegations about Lizzie. In his second letter to Nutt, Dukes offered an explanation for why he had not broken off the relationship upon learning of Lizzie's promiscuity: in fact, he *had* resolved to leave Lizzie around March of 1882. However, at that same time, Lizzie failed to menstruate, and she panicked. Confident that this episode was merely a false alarm, Dukes decided to temporarily keep up appearances for Lizzie's sake before leaving her.[22]

The two letters published in Friday's papers raised more doubts about the veracity of Dukes's story. The first was a love letter from Dukes to Lizzie in June of 1882, several months after he supposedly discovered Lizzie's impropriety and determined to leave her. The language seemed far too wistful to come from the pen of a man who was merely playing the part. Lizzie had left for a month's stay in Brownsville and Dukes bemoaned her absence with the kind of effusive language typical of Victorian-era love letters:

> The sun no longer shines brightly, and the birds have closed their sylvan songs since your departure. It's no longer the same place without you, and yet it is not quite a week since you went away, and three long eternal weeks must elapse before your return. Will they ever roll round? It has often been remarked that time flies. I now think it crawls like a lame snail. But I presume you fail to note the long, long days as they drag along. I suppose you are surrounded with gallants and admirers at all times; only don't let some of the country mossbanks carry your heart by storm. . . . Won't you write to me? I am dying to hear from you, and am dead to see you.

The *Republican Standard* wondered, "If he knew then that she was such common property as he alleges, why could he pour forth such gushing and pure love for her?" The second letter that Playford made public was sent from Dukes to Lizzie in August of 1882. In sharp contrast to his yearning message two months earlier, Dukes was now short and cryptic: "Please have the two letters I wrote you while at Brownsville, where you can put your hand on them. I want to see them for a certain purpose." The press speculated that by this point Dukes had contrived his scheme and sought—clearly without success—to retrieve any troublesome letters in advance.[23]

There were more difficulties still for Dukes in the day's media coverage. Affidavits appeared from two other men, Nathaniel Frey and A. C. Hagan, whom Dukes had identified in his letter to Nutt as having had improper relations with Lizzie. "His statements concerning me are all false from beginning to end," swore Fry. He sought to exonerate not only himself but also Lizzie: "I have known Miss Nutt some five or six years, and during all that time I have never regarded her as anything else than a perfect lady." Hagan's statement touched on the same themes. He alleged that Dukes's charges "are without foundation in fact, and are totally and absolutely false." With respect to Lizzie, Hagan described her "as a modest, well-behaved young lady." Hagan was also among those attorneys who signed the petition demanding Dukes's disbarment.[24]

Dukes seemed determine to salvage his public image, giving yet another interview that Friday, this time to the Harrisburg *Patriot*. In the company of his sobbing mother and taciturn stepfather, Dukes remained poised while speaking to the *Patriot* correspondent. Dukes again abstained from comment on whether he would try to claim his seat in the State House but announced that he was preparing a public statement to vindicate himself. "He is determined that if there are to be sacrifices burnt at the altar of innocence, he will not be the only victim," the journalist concluded.[25]

Instead of abating, the ire toward Dukes seemed only to spread. As one paper reported on Friday, "Threats of lynching are heard everywhere." That night, the community of Springfield, also in Fayette County, held an indignation meeting of its own twenty-two miles from Uniontown. There had been some supporters of Dukes in Springfield until the third day of the trial when the infamous letters became known. That scandalous disclosure, coupled with the verdict, enraged local residents. Their only consolation was that their hometown furnished no members of the jury. The people of Springfield crafted effigies of Dukes and the jurors, which they hung and set ablaze.[26]

The *Republican Standard*'s reportage of the Dukes–Nutt tragedy was the most thorough of any newspaper nationwide. As a result, the *Standard* met with unprecedented appetite for its columns. The paper usually was issued on Thursdays, but because the verdict was rendered on a Wednesday evening and the aftermath proved just as provocative as the legal proceedings, the *Standard* delayed publication for two days to gather news. At 3:00 A.M. on Saturday, the paper finally went to press, with editions featuring the headline "Shame! Oh Shame!!" ready for sale by daybreak. Within a few hours, it became evident that the *Standard* would struggle to print enough copies to meet demand. Orders poured in from surrounding towns, counties, and states.[27]

The *Standard*'s type for that issue was set too soon to cover a development that found its way to other papers on Saturday. Yet another man named in Dukes's letter to Captain Nutt, Jesse Bogardus, swore an affidavit denying any wrongdoing with Lizzie and spoke of her as "a virtuous young girl."[28]

Saturday's Harrisburg *Patriot* reported that Dukes would indeed journey to the state capital to take his oath of office, against the advice of Congressman Boyle. The state representative A. J. Colborn, from a county adjacent to Fayette, began formulating a resolution for Monday's session in the House to strip Dukes of his seat. The *Harrisburg Telegraph* explained that the members of the House would "not debase their manhood" by "sitting side by side with the murderer and seducer, Dukes." But even worse than Dukes's bloodshed and womanizing was his correspondence with Nutt. As the Philadelphia *Times* predicted, "The opposition to Dukes on the House floor will probably be based not upon the killing of Captain Nutt, but upon the indecency of the slayer's letters."[29]

On Saturday night, not quite twelve miles from Uniontown, the Fayette County community of Connellsville hosted its own indignation meeting. Sizable contingencies from other towns joined Connellsville citizens in the Newmyer Opera House for a rousing protest against the Dukes verdict. The opera house had opened just two years earlier to much fanfare, featuring as it did a parlor set, a beautiful drop curtain, and a $1,000 piano. Professor M. L. Baer, principal of the school system, served as the meeting's president while several physicians and men bearing military titles acted as vice presidents. After remarks from Professor Baer, a reverend berated the jury, which had claimed among its detested members a Connellsville resident.[30]

A number of telegrams wired from various towns in the county and further afield were then read aloud. Uniontown telegraphed that the two communities stood united "in the condemnation of the verdict and the debaucheries which brought it about." Other messages were more ominous. Ursina cabled, "If you can't hang Devil Dukes, call on us." And from the people of Irwin Station, "Hang N. L. Dukes higher than Haman and tar and feather the jury that acquitted him." Throughout the meeting, various speakers had to pause regularly while the crowd roared its approval. That same evening, 500 incensed citizens assembled in nearby Brownsville for yet another indignation meeting. The Brownsville gathering featured a band from the Grand Army of the Republic and a special guest from Uniontown, Reverend Kerr, who again spoke with fervor about the disgraceful verdict rendered three days earlier.[31]

These expressions of discontent were hardly limited to Fayette County. Throughout the state, towns were hanging Dukes in effigy, and across the country, newspapers called for his lynching. In Massachusetts, the *Worcester Daily Spy* affirmed, "If ever there was a case in which the failure of justice by legal process would excuse a resort to summary methods of exacting the penalty of the basest of crimes and purging the community of a wretch utterly and hopelessly bad, this is one." Michigan's *Jackson Weekly Citizen* suggested that if Dukes were to seek refuge beyond Pennsylvania, his safety would scarcely be ensured. "Dukes had better remain in Pennsylvania," warned the *Citizen*. "Even steady old Michigan would bring out a rope for such a brutal wretch as he has shown himself to be." According to the *Baltimore Day*, the jurors were equally deserving of death at the hands of vigilantes: "There would be more hope for the people of that portion of Pennsylvania if popular fury had manifested itself in lynching Dukes and the base jurors who became accomplices after the fact in his crime by their perjured verdict." One of the more elaborate justifications of extralegal vengeance appeared in New York's *Poughkeepsie Eagle*:

> The law has been trusted to do its duty in protecting society and punishing the criminal and it has failed. But the people are higher and greater than the law, and when it fails it is their province to supply the want. In a case like this we do not say that if Dukes were lynched the act would be merely excusable. We go a great deal further than this, and say we believe his neighbors *ought* to lynch him. It would be a righteous deed, promotive of good order, conduce to good morals. It would clear the atmosphere and improve the tone of the whole community. Human life would be safer after it and the proper and formal administration of law would probably be so improved that it would be worthy of respect which is now impossible.

Some periodicals, without expressly encouraging lynching, suggested that mob action was the natural result of such a brazen miscarriage of justice. Still other papers proposed merely banishing Dukes.[32]

To be sure, there were editorialists, albeit a minority, who protested against violent redress outside the formal channels of the justice system. The *New York Herald* may have conceded that "the verdict is good cause for righteous indignation," but at the same time held, "any attempts at violence would be wholly unjustifiable."[33] Given the political affiliations of Nicholas Dukes and Captain Nutt, it is little surprise that the papers championing lynching were predominantly Republican and those opposed to it Democratic. But the divide was not strictly partisan. Some Democratic journals joined their Republican counterparts in supporting vigilantism—either by retrospectively justifying Nutt's attempted killing of Dukes or by prospectively endorsing mob violence against Dukes. Not one Republican paper called for adherence to the rule of law.[34]

On Monday, March 19, five days after the verdict, a writer for the *Republican Standard* traveled sixteen miles northeast to Bullskin to seek out one of the infamous twelve jurors—George Washington Breakiron. The fifty-two-year-old farmer lived with his family in a part of Bullskin so remote that it seemed forgotten by time. A jagged road carried the reporter past crumbling buildings and unreaped fields to Breakiron's simple log cabin. He was not home but had told his wife Delilah that he dreaded retribution for his verdict. The journalist described in the third person how, as he approached the home, "the wife and children peeped timorously out upon the reporter, as if they feared he was the advance guard of a mob that was hunting for juror Breakiron's blood."

Mrs. Breakiron asked the journalist, "They're making a big stir up there, ain't they?" referring to Uniontown.

"Yes, there's some ugly talk going about these jurors," the correspondent admitted. But he tried to assure Mrs. Breakiron that he personally did not suspect that her husband was guilty of perjury against his oath to render a verdict in accordance with the evidence and the law.

Fixing her bonnet and shawl, Mrs. Breakiron took off for a neighbor's home where she thought her husband might have gone to have his shoes repaired. The interviewer waited inside the cabin, with its unadorned walls, carpetless floors, and spare furnishings. One woman knitted while another breastfed a baby. A boy filled the one-story dwelling with the sounds of his accordion. By the fire, where two bowls of bread were rising, a dog rested, wholly apathetic to the newcomer.

"There he comes," remarked one of the girls. Breakiron, with the aid of a cane, was hurriedly approaching. The journalist stepped outside to greet him and explained to Breakiron that he would do well to tell his story and curb accusations of perjury. The two sat on a log and a frightened Breakiron fought tears as he offered his rendition of what transpired in the jury room.

"What did you think of Dukes' letters?" asked the reporter.

"We thought a man should not write such letters to a father, but we concluded they did not bear directly on the murder, and we passed over them."

"Did you not think a man almost deserved death for writing such letters to a father about a daughter whom he loved so well?"

"They say he did love her powerful," Breakiron replied, evading the question.

Breakiron further described the feeling among the jurors that Captain Nutt's letter did constitute a threat, that Nutt's cane was heavy enough to take a man's life, and that Dukes fired his weapon in self-defense. Inconsistencies in the Commonwealth's testimony also had given the jurors pause.

According to Breakiron, Amalong—who had suggested prayer in the jury room—voted for manslaughter on the initial ballot and thereafter sided with those favoring acquittal. Breakiron himself abstained on the first ballot but then joined Amalong and the majority for a finding of "not guilty." The holdouts for manslaughter eventually gave way as well. The *Republican Standard* speculated in its next edition that Amalong intended to acquit Dukes from the beginning. Amalong had once been a deputy sheriff, and according to the *Republican Standard*'s conspiracy theory, Amalong hoped that setting Dukes free would win him the favor of the Democratic Party, which in turn would reward Amalong by making him a head sheriff. So Amalong feigned religiosity to gain credibility with Breakiron and other naive jurors. He then voted for manslaughter before switching to acquittal to create a false air of momentum toward a not-guilty verdict. In his interview, Breakiron vehemently denied that the jurors accepted bribes or perjured themselves. "I am innocent before God," he insisted.

The correspondent turned to the subject of Breakiron's family. He had seven children, and among his four daughters, three were married.

"You ought to be in a position, Mr. Breakiron, to sympathize with a father who has been wronged as Dukes confesses he wronged Nutt," said the reporter. "Was not your oldest daughter unfortunate?"

Breakiron recoiled at first but then admitted that his daughter had indeed been impregnated out of wedlock. Her seducer, however, had taken her as a wife.

The journalist would not relent. "Hadn't you some further trouble of this kind?"

Breakiron fidgeted uncomfortably and confessed, "They was all three that way, but they got 'em. They are all married to the same fellows as caused the trouble." Breakiron concluded the interview by reasserting his own probity. In the correspondent's article, he suggested that Breakiron had been duped by rather than complicit in any conspiracy.[35]

The same day, a journalist sought out Jake Amalong in his hometown of Bellevernon. Locals had burned Amalong in effigy and heckled him in public. The reporter suspected that Amalong, who was cloistering himself at home, would be hesitant to speak to a member of the press. So the correspondent devised a ruse. Aware that Amalong was a horse keeper, he approached the juror and said, "I would like to see your Clydesdale Stallion, Mr. Amalong." The journalist disarmed Amalong with a discussion of the horse and eventually inquired, as if by happenstance, about the subject that he actually came to discuss:

"By the way, Mr. Amalong, you were one of the Dukes jury?"

"Yes, I was there," Amalong admitted.

"Well they seem to be making a great deal of unnecessary fuss about the verdict."

"Yes, the public makes a great fool of itself sometimes."

The reporter asked whether the rumor were true that the jury had actually reached consensus after twenty minutes but waited several hours to notify the court so as to produce the illusion of considered deliberation. Amalong seemed genuinely surprised by the question and disavowed any deception. Whereas Breakiron claimed that Amalong first voted for manslaughter and then switched to acquittal on subsequent ballots, Amalong suggested that he himself favored acquittal from the start. He was emphatic that he committed no wrong: "So help me God, my verdict in the Dukes trial was rendered according to the evidence and the judge's charge, and I would do the same thing over again to-morrow."[36]

The American people had expected the jury to condemn Dukes to death for his sins against the Nutt family. Yet these twelve jurors, compelled by the evidence in court and the letter of the law, gave him his liberty. The acquittal was an affront to every honor-loving household. Perhaps the only outrage greater than the verdict was the prospect that Dukes might now claim the vaunted title of Representative in the Pennsylvania General Assembly.

· *Eight* ·

Politics

On the evening of March 19 in Harrisburg, an eager crowd gathered in the House of Representatives gallery to see whether Dukes would try to take his oath of office. That day's *Philadelphia Inquirer* seethed at the notion Dukes might collect his salary from the state coffers. "Let a resolution of expulsion be passed to-day," demanded the *Inquirer*, "and save the State from being bled as well as disgraced by this shameless scoundrel." Representative A. J. Colborn intended to advocate summary dismissal of Dukes from the General Assembly without further investigation. The text of Colborn's resolution castigated Dukes's actions as "unbecoming a citizen and member of this house" and "disgraceful to him as a man." Dukes was unfit "for receiving the confidence of men of honor and integrity," and his service in the legislature would bring "disgrace upon the house of representatives and the entire commonwealth of Pennsylvania." Colborn, a Republican, was on the House floor, ready to offer this resolution, but the Democratic Speaker allowed a member of his own party to preempt Colborn with a more cautious measure:

> *Resolved*, That it is the sense of this house that some action should be taken looking to a disposition of the question as to the right of Nicholas L. Dukes, of Fayette county, to hold his title to a seat in the house of representatives.

The House unanimously adopted the resolution and delegated the issue to the Committee on Judiciary General for further inquiry, with instructions that the Committee report back to the House speedily. As one Republican delegate remarked, "We don't want this resolution to go to committee and sleep the sleep that knows no awakening."[1]

The next morning—Tuesday, March 20—the Committee on Judiciary General appointed a five-person subcommittee to address the Dukes question. The three Democrats and two Republicans comprising the subcommittee met later that day. That Dukes would be removed from office was a foregone conclusion, but the representatives debated the means by which to expel him. Two of the Democrats suggested that Dukes be dismissed summarily for having failed to take his oath a full seventy-eight days into the current legislative session. The third Democrat sided with his two Republican colleagues in opposing the measure; before recommending expulsion, they wanted to conduct a thorough inquiry, which would involve calling witnesses and collecting documents. After all, the facts pertaining to Dukes, although notorious, had not been officially established by the House. Representative Colborn, surprisingly, was among those on the subcommittee who now objected to declaring Dukes's seat vacant without due diligence, having sought to do just that the day prior. The other Republican on the subcommittee, Jerome Niles, had convinced Colborn that hasty action would set a risky precedent for the future removal of House members.[2]

Outside the State House, Harrisburg was once again buzzing with word that Dukes was en route. And once again, Dukes failed to appear. Some reports suggested that Dukes remained in German Township with his parents. But according to the conductor of the express train, Dukes did pass through Harrisburg at 4:20 P.M. en route to Philadelphia, supposedly to meet with new legal counsel concerning his seat in the legislature. From under a slouch hat, the ever clean-shaven Dukes purportedly stared through his parlor car window at the elusive capital city that only last November had seemed so firmly in his grasp.[3]

All the while, William Playford had been hard at work formulating new legal justifications for imprisoning Dukes. The Pennsylvania Constitution prohibited double jeopardy, so Dukes could not be tried again for the murder of Captain Nutt. Playford, however, thought that Dukes's letters to Nutt had possibly violated a federal law banning obscene mail. If prosecuted and found guilty, Dukes would face ten years of incarceration.[4]

In Washington, DC, on the same day that the subcommittee was formed in Harrisburg, the assistant attorney general of the United States said that federal obscenity law did not likely apply to letters under seal. This statement seemed to deal a quick death to the prospect of prosecuting Dukes for obscenity, although the assistant attorney general also noted that he had not been formally called on to study the particulars of the Dukes case.[5]

In Harrisburg the following morning, a full week after the verdict, the Committee on Judiciary General issued a report requesting that the House of Representatives grant it the "power to send for persons and papers" to investigate the Dukes affair in greater depth. Notably, the Committee proposed an inquiry not only into Dukes's absence, which was "depriving his constituents and his fellow members of his services without leave," but also into any "immoral and infamous conduct as would render him unfit to occupy his seat." So although the Committee was advocating a considered rather than hasty approach, at the same time, this request indicated the Committee's desire to expand the rationale for Dukes's expulsion beyond the technical grounds of his having failed to take the oath. The Committee was suggesting a broader investigation that would culminate in the House's invalidation of an election on the basis of a member's moral failings.[6]

In the House chamber, one representative responded to the Committee's request by recommending that the legislative body simply remove Dukes without any investigation. The proposition touched off a debate about the very meaning of due process in representative government. The concept of due process—which is central to the rule of law—holds that government proceedings must be fair and deliberative. Having already persuaded Colborn of the merits of a circumspect approach, Representative Niles tried to do the same with the whole House. "This case," Niles declared, "is worth a million Dukes." Representative Lemuel Amerman, a Democrat and fellow participant on the subcommittee, endorsed Niles's position. While affirming that the House could not ultimately allow Dukes to claim his seat, Amerman nevertheless advised that Dukes not "be taken by the neck and heels and pitched out" on the basis of facts not yet officially documented by the House, however infamous they may have been. Amerman presaged future generations of legislators who would exploit a carelessly formulated precedent:

> The day may come when politics may enter in a case such as this. Should unwarranted or arbitrary action be taken now how easy might it be in the future for one party to expel a member of the other side upon imaginary grounds, or an alleged state of facts, and probably thereby make itself the dominant party?

Amerman assured his fellow delegates that the subcommittee could complete its work in a matter of days at most.[7]

The speech that garnered the most interest came from Representative William Sponsler, one of the great legal minds in the Republican caucus. He began by sharing in the general denunciation of Dukes. "Never in the history of this Commonwealth," he contended, "have family, sanctity, Christian character, faith in judicial proceedings or the deepest and most sacred feeling of humanity been so directly insulted." But Sponsler then sounded a note of grave caution. Unlike those legislators who concerned themselves merely with the question of whether to expel Dukes now or following a brief investigation, Sponsler challenged the authority of the House to pronounce itself an arbiter of its members' virtue at all. The Pennsylvania Constitution specified that a member of the General Assembly would lose qualification for office if he were guilty of an "infamous crime," meaning perjury, bribery, or embezzlement. Additionally, a minor or nonresident could not serve in the legislative branch. But Dukes fell under none of these categories and could not, therefore, be barred from the House without doing violence to the law, said Sponsler. In stirring prose, he warned,

> Revolution may hang upon the precedent that we shall now establish. We sit here as the supreme power of the State. In proportion to the dignity and greatness of these houses, so should our action be careful. . . . If this man comes here with even a blacker character than that which he has (and I confess it is hard to imagine one blacker), we cannot, under the Constitution, expel him. Has he been guilty of writing immoral letters, of seduction, of a prostitution of every noble instinct of humanity? He has, but what weight should that have with us in comparison with the Constitution? . . . When you come to the question of moral turpitude, who is to say that this man has been guilty of greater moral turpitude than another man?

That Sponsler was from Dukes's opposing political party threw into high relief the genuine conviction behind his words.[8]

The House voted in the end to allow the Dukes subcommittee to proceed with its investigation. With rumors swirling that Dukes had arrived in the capital from Philadelphia and was camped at a home on nearby State Street, Representative Amerman offered a resolution to prevent him from taking his oath of office until the House rendered a final decision. This measure met with unanimous approval. The Harrisburg *Patriot*, a Democratic organ, praised the Democratic majority for its considered approach to the Dukes question:

> The democrats of the house proved themselves equal to a trying emergency last night by the manner in which the Dukes case

was disposed of. . . . The house is undoubtedly competent to summarily declare the seat vacant in advance of an offer to occupy it, but such action would establish a dangerous precedent and savor strongly of arbitrary action.[9]

That evening in Pittsburgh, the retired statesmen Jeremiah Black granted an interview to a reporter on Dukes's eligibility for office. Black had served variously as chief justice of the Pennsylvania Supreme Court, U.S. attorney general, and U.S. secretary of state. Representative Amerman had claimed during the House debate that "nowhere in all the books in the centuries can we find a case like this," but Black suggested that in fact there was a precedent for excluding Dukes from the General Assembly.[10]

To make his point, Black recounted Thaddeus Stevens's dubious role in the so-called "Buckshot War" of 1838. As a newly elected state senator in Pennsylvania, Stevens schemed to admit to the General Assembly several members of his party whose own election results were contested. The sitting governor, a Stevens ally, directed the state militia to arm itself with buckshot cartridges to quell any mob action amid the political tumult, thus giving the incident its name. In the end, the tide of opinion turned against Stevens, who escaped from an angry mob in the State House by leaping through a window. He sought refuge in Gettysburg for a month and then returned to Harrisburg to take his oath of office, only to find that the legislature had declared his seat vacant.[11]

Although a precedent did exist for expelling Dukes, Black expressed serious doubts about the wisdom of a legislative body substituting its moral judgment for that of the electorate. Black noted that the national legislature had made the same mistake. "Congress, in several cases, have turned men out of their places on the ground that they were improper persons, morally unfit to associate with the members who voted against them," Black recalled. "I think Congress was wrong every time it did this." Still, he recognized the impossibility that the Pennsylvania House would seat a member of Dukes's notoriety. And so Jeremiah Black advocated extralegal action. "If the thing is done lawlessly I would rather see it done outside the house than by the action of the members." Asked the most suitable remedy, Black answered, "It would be better, I think, that somebody meet him at the depot [i.e., train station] and run him out of town."[12]

The next day, March 22, the *Republican Standard* published some of the hundreds of sympathetic letters that Lizzie Nutt had received since the verdict. One such letter expressed a certain fatalism. "It was inevitable," the author concluded about the tragedy. "It was God's plan to teach the nation a sad lesson" to "our weak and confiding girls to avoid every appearance of evil." Another letter to Lizzie saw in Captain Nutt's death a vindication of masculinity—his "manliness could not withstand an ignoble attack upon the character of his beloved daughter." Also appearing in the *Republican Standard* that day was a poem that a woman had written about Dukes entitled, "A Murderer's Horoscope," which included the following verse:

> And tongues of flame
> Shall tell to other lands his name
> And black offense.

> And some dread day
> "Vengeance is mine, I will repay!"
> Shall hurl him hence.[13]

Indeed, vengeance was a principal theme of the countless pieces of mail that flooded the *Republican Standard*'s office on a daily basis. Typical was this violent message from a town in central Pennsylvania: "Don't let your tempers cool but act immediately. Rid the world of the rake and fiend Dukes." Captain Bierer, who had chaired Uniontown's indignation meeting, would have hardly been surprised to learn of these calls for vigilantism; he had been receiving similar messages in his own mail. The Quaker City Bachelor Club of Philadelphia, for instance, reminded Bierer that the stakes were national in character. "The whole country is watching you and is with you," the club wrote. "Don't convene too much: don't resolve too much—act, act, act! Lynch that fiend and tar and feather that jury. You must, you have no right to let that devil escape to prey upon other communities."[14]

In Harrisburg that day, the subcommittee initiated its fact-finding investigation. It drew up a subpoena for the state treasurer Silas Baily because the Commonwealth had entrusted Baily with custody of Dukes's notorious letters after the trial. The subcommittee also called for the chief clerk of the House of Representatives, who could attest that Dukes had not taken his oath of office. Finally, subcommittee members dispatched the sergeant-at-arms to Uniontown. His mission was twofold: to subpoena a local bank cashier for the purpose of verifying Dukes's handwriting on the letters and to deliver a notice to

Dukes informing him that he could appear before the subcommittee at a hearing the following Tuesday. Dukes would then be afforded an opportunity to argue for his right to serve in office, but his presence at the hearing was not made mandatory. At midnight, the sergeant-at-arms departed Harrisburg and traveled west in search of the man whose name he had removed from a seat in the House chamber.[15]

Three days later, on Sunday, March 25, Dukes left German Township and returned to his room in the Jennings House where he had killed Captain Nutt. Word of Dukes's presence quickly spread through Uniontown the following morning. Leading citizens met to discuss a course of action and agreed to serve Dukes with a copy of the resolutions adopted at Uniontown's indignation meeting as well as a written warning that he had twenty-four hours to leave the community. Two townsmen arrived at Dukes's hotel around noon and gave the papers to Mr. Jennings, who passed them on to Dukes. "If he remains after that time it will be at his own peril," wrote the Harrisburg *Patriot*. The *Philadelphia Record*, the highest circulating Democratic paper in the state, suggested that although the demand for Dukes's departure was not strictly legal, he had forfeited any recourse to the law:

> It is useless for him to rail against the illegality and technical injustice of such an imperative injunction, for while men make laws to protect society and demand a universal obedience to them, society sometimes rises superior to the law and executes its own mandate. Dukes will do well not to depend upon the letter of the law.[16]

For the rest of the day, the townsfolk waited outside the Jennings House to see whether Dukes would leave but he stayed in his room. The district attorney, who had worked to persuade a jury to hang Dukes two weeks earlier, now collaborated with local police to prevent an assault on his life. That night, under the cover of darkness, Dukes took flight. Because he had fled Uniontown unseen, the next day it was widely believed that Dukes remained in the Jennings House in violation of his twenty-four-hour notice, but a report eventually surfaced that he had absconded to the countryside.[17]

The day after Dukes left Uniontown, the subcommittee continued its work behind the locked door of Room Twelve in the State House. The hearing was not open to the public, and only eight members of the press were allowed in. The bank cashier who was supposed to authenticate Dukes's handwriting telegraphed to inform the subcommittee that he was detained on account of a train wreck. The sergeant-at-arms was the first witness; he relayed that he had left the notice for Dukes at the Jennings House. After the sergeant-at-arms was dismissed, Representative Amerman asked, "Is Mr. Dukes present or does he appear by counsel?" Silence. Neither Dukes nor a lawyer representing him was present. With this, the chief clerk of the House testified that Dukes had been duly elected to his seat but failed to take his oath of office and had submitted no reason for his absence. The clerk provided the oath book to corroborate his statement.[18]

The last witness of the day was Treasurer Baily, who now supplied Dukes's letters to Captain Nutt, although he acknowledged that he could not verify the handwriting. It had been two weeks earlier to the day that these letters were first read at trial, and once again the correspondence that shocked the nation became part of an official state record. In what one reporter described as a "tragic voice," a legislator on the subcommittee recited Dukes's notorious words. The subcommittee then asked Baily whether he had any other correspondence from Dukes. He paused for a moment.

"Yes, I have another letter."

"Where is it?"

"In the safe in the State Treasurer's office."

Baily explained that Dukes had authored a third letter to Captain Nutt, which Nutt had never seen because he had already departed for Uniontown to confront Dukes before the letter reached Harrisburg. When the subcommittee requested that Baily produce it, he demurred. The Nutt family was aware of this

State Treasurer Silas Baily

Source: Franklin Ellis, *A History of Fayette County, Pennsylvania: With Biographical Sketches of Many of Its Pioneers and Prominent Men* (Philadelphia: Everts, 1882), 354d.

third letter and wanted its details kept from the public. Supposedly, in this mysterious missive, Dukes had compiled excerpts from messages that Lizzie had allegedly written to him. The subcommittee instructed Baily to bring the letter the following morning and agreed to examine it in private.[19]

But the next day, an unexpected announcement brought the Dukes investigation to a sudden halt. The chairman of the Committee on Judiciary General read aloud to the House a message, dated two days earlier, from a defeated Dukes:

Hon. John E Faunce, Speaker House of Representatives, Harrisburg—

Sir: I decline to accept the seat to which I have been elected in the House of Representatives of the Commonwealth for the county of Fayette, and request the House to declare the seat vacant.

Very respectfully yours,
N. L. Dukes,
Fayette County, March 26, 1883

In the words of the *Philadelphia Inquirer*, it appeared that "the pressure of public opinion has penetrated even Dukes' epidermis at last." The House immediately and unanimously voted to issue a writ for a special election to secure a replacement. The Committee members heaved a collective sigh, thankful that they disposed of the Dukes matter without establishing a precedent susceptible to future abuse.[20]

Three days afterward, on March 31, the *Republican Standard* published an alarming story that stoked fears that the Dukes verdict was a product of political machinations. The paper reported that James Feather—the Jennings's son-in-law whose testimony had been so central to the Commonwealth's case—received no fewer than seventeen letters in advance of the trial from local Democratic politicians urging him to contradict Clark Breckenridge's testimony. Feather, himself a Democrat, responded to two of these solicitations, affirming that he would not trade his integrity for partisan gain. The rest he left unanswered. The *Republican Standard* commented that Feather "is entitled to great credit for his manly and straightforward testimony throughout, in spite of the unholy pressure brought to bear upon him by party friends." No hard evidence had surfaced of jury tampering, but this story undoubtedly heightened suspicions.[21]

Donkey
A Democratic donkey kicks over the scales of justice.
Source: Republican Standard, March 31, 1883, 1.

Indeed, some Republican papers in Pennsylvania had already been pointing to Dukes's acquittal as evidence of Democratic corruption. One such periodical charged,

> The influence of Politics has outweighed the influence of Justice, and murder has been legalized in Fayette. . . . The edict has gone forth that a Democrat may invite a Republican to his room and there murder him in cold blood with the full sanction of the law as interpreted by a jury of twelve men of Democratic faith.

Democratic publishers rebuffed this kind of criticism by sharing in the condemnation of the verdict while denying that politics prejudiced the jury. The Democratic *Wheeling Register* disparaged the jurors as "low-grade, under-bred men" of "obtuse moral sense" but insisted that "there is not a scintilla of evidence that any extraneous influences were brought to bear upon them," including those "of a political nature." That the prosecutors were themselves Democrats and that the Democratic judge garnered bipartisan praise for his conduct on the bench undermined Republican allegations that the trial was tainted by politics.[22]

Publications of both political stripes were more likely to view the Dukes–Nutt saga as a cautionary tale about sexual depravity rather than partisan duplicity. According to the *Daily Springfield Republican* of Massachusetts, "The details of the tragedy are of less moment than the instructive revelation to parents and young women of the devilish villainy and method of the man Dukes, who is, by the way, not a rare exception." The press considered the Dukes–Nutt affair as much a challenge to manhood as womanhood because the sacred responsibility of protecting female purity—and punishing transgressors—fell to men. The twelve men who set Dukes free had surely forsaken this sacrosanct obligation. As the Philadelphia *Times* griped, "The jurymen have dishonored their own manhood in holding him guiltless of the blood of Captain Nutt."[23]

The preservation of manhood was a source of intense anxiety for men in these years. From blue-collar laborers subjected to the regimentation of factories to white-collar professionals constrained by bureaucracies, a modern economy left men feeling straightjacketed. The ideal of the rugged, individualistic, self-made man could find no purchase in a world governed by hierarchy, regularity, and efficiency. That women were stepping out of the home into the public sphere exacerbated fears that masculinity was under siege. In 1848, the Seneca Falls Convention chastised men for denying women equality at the voting booth, the workplace, and the church. This seminal gathering of activists catalyzed a women's rights movement that gained momentum during the Gilded Age. Meanwhile, the female proportion of the workforce was steadily growing, and a handful of pioneering women even gained a foothold in the learned professions. The late nineteenth century also saw the proliferation of women's colleges in the east and coeducational state universities in the west. By the 1880s, women comprised nearly one in five undergraduates nationally. Some men embraced these trends but most felt threatened. One newspaper warned of the specter of "a complete gynecocracy." The code of honor—with its celebration of male bravery in defense of female virtue—offered men a means to combat the perceived erosion of their masculinity. When the Dukes jury forsook that vaunted code, disaffected men across the country looked for a hero to defend the sacred honor of Lizzie Nutt and thereby vindicate American manhood.[24]

· Nine ·

VENGEANCE

O<small>N APRIL 10, NEARLY A MONTH AFTER THE VERDICT, D</small>UKES returned to Uniontown, riding in from his stepfather's estate on a horse. He may have relented in the battle over his seat in the legislature, but Dukes would no longer abide threats to leave Uniontown. As he walked the streets, many people turned their backs to him. Dukes took up residence in his old room, a reappearance that upset Mrs. Jennings, who had already seen enough drama unfold at her hotel.[1]

Although no notice to leave would be issued this time, Dukes well knew the danger had not fully subsided. The press speculated that Captain Nutt's eldest son, James, was bent on reprisal. Twenty-year-old James was an impressive physical specimen, tall and well built. Dukes confessed to a friend about James, "That is the only man on earth I fear."[2]

Dukes resumed his law practice, but was seen in public rarely by day and never at night. Many friends advised him to leave town for fear of his safety. Dukes refused, insisting, "I will live here or out in the cemetery." And so he carried on, unsure how many days he would have above ground before an eternity below it. In the words of the *New York Times*, "He suffered the tortures of a living death."[3]

A week after Dukes's return, it was not James but a different member of the Nutt family who created a stir. On April 17, in the early afternoon of a warm spring day, Lizzie and her teenage sister Annie were coming down Main Street when they spotted Dukes walking up the other side of the road. Annie dashed into the street, grabbed a cobblestone, and heaved it at Dukes's head, missing her target. Dukes spun around to see who had launched the stone and then hurried back to the Jennings House. For all the bluster of the men of town in the wake of Dukes's acquittal, it was a young girl who had actually taken action. The *Trenton Times* was not impressed: "The fact that Miss Nutt's fifteen-year-old sister was left to throw stones at Dukes on the street, is discreditable to the big boys of Uniontown."[4]

Dukes was scarcely the only one to live in fear—the dozen men who declared him not guilty were receiving unnerving letters in the post. Some of the messages were merely scornful: "Better things were expected of you" or "Shame on you forever." Others were more menacing. The eldest juror, a fifty-eight-year-old farmer from Dunbar, was warned, "You had better Leave Soon or you may die in your boots." These anonymous threats were often signed "Mollie Maguire," a secret society associated with criminal activity. Drawings of coffins and skulls sometimes accompanied the written text. Dukes himself received disconcerting pieces of mail from across the country, many of which included cartoons of him being hanged.[5]

With the special election set for April 24, more than a dozen aspiring representatives jockeyed for Dukes's vacated seat in the legislature. There was a movement to put Captain Nutt's brother Stephen on the ballot for the Republicans, but when the Democrats nominated someone who was considered "an anti-Dukes Democrat," the Republican Party resolved to run another candidate. With the election no longer tinged by the Dukes–Nutt tragedy, the Democratic candidate coasted to a comfortable victory in predominantly Democratic Fayette County.[6]

April rolled into May, and attention turned to Dukes's disbarment hearing. On May 7, John Collins, who had initially presented the petition to disbar Dukes, returned to Court to argue for Dukes's expulsion from the county bar. Congressman Boyle yet again represented his embattled client, who did not himself appear. "He denies all and singular the facts set forth in said petition," Boyle relayed of Dukes. "He denies that by reason of anything alleged in said petition this Court has the power or ought to grant the prayer of the petitioners." In particular, Boyle took issue with the petition's lack of specificity. Indeed, the petition—hastily crafted in the immediate aftermath of the verdict—amounted to a strident censure of Dukes without any particular allegations of illegality. Judge Willson conceded, "The petition is very general." Still, he would not dismiss the proceedings against Dukes. Instead, the judge directed Collins to draft a more precise petition so that Boyle could know what charges he would need to rebut.[7]

One week later, the lawyers reconvened in the courthouse. Amid Collins's stack of papers was a revised petition clarifying the charges against Dukes. The petition set forth that the notorious letters to Captain Nutt constituted libel against Lizzie as well as several of the men accused of inappropriately consorting with her. Moreover, Dukes had urged Nutt to arrange for an abortion, an outlawed procedure. Although this new petition was specific in its allegations of illicit activity, it hardly abandoned the caustic language that had characterized the first version. As one section now read, "Dukes is grossly immoral and depraved, unfaithful, untruthful, unscrupulous, vile, cruel, heartless and shameless."[8]

Judge Willson appointed a commissioner to take relevant testimony from witnesses over the next several weeks and scheduled another hearing for June, when both sides were to argue the merits of the petition in light of the depositions collected. "It seems that the evidence in the murder case will have to be retold," surmised the *Wheeling Register*. "Dukes will succeed nicely in stirring up the latent indignation of the people against him, if he persists in causing a rehash of the terrible past."[9]

Even if Dukes could somehow emerge from this latest crucible with his license to practice law still intact, there were signs that professional life would be difficult for him. Shortly after Collins offered the amended petition, Dukes was engaged as legal counsel in a case in which the opposing lawyer declined to appear with him before a justice of the peace. That attorney's client ended up presenting his own case—and won.[10]

Wednesday, June 13, 1883, was a day that began as inauspiciously as any other. At the Nutt estate, two uncles were visiting the family—Captain Nutt's brother Stephen, who had sat with the Commonwealth lawyers in court, and Mrs. Nutt's brother,

Jim Wells, one of the executors of the Nutt estate. In the late afternoon, the uncles joined James Nutt in some target practice, using pistols that they fired on a board propped up against the carriage house. Soon the uncles mounted their horses and prepared to leave. A nine-year-old boy, who was then playing with one of Mrs. Nutt's younger children, would later testify that Stephen Nutt, upon departing, called out to James, "Don't fail." Whether this comment was simply a reminder to keep the family's garden free from potato bugs or something far more sinister—indeed, whether Stephen had uttered those words at all—would soon be the subject of much controversy.[11]

At the house, James changed his shoes as he prepared to head into town. Mrs. Nutt's seventy-four-year-old mother, Ann Wells, was in the sitting room; she had moved in with her daughter's family the previous year. James told her on his way out, "Grandma I am going to town, I will be back directly; I am going for the mail."[12]

As dusk settled on Uniontown, James made his way to the so-called "Round Corner" building, which wrapped around the obtuse angle formed by the intersection of Pittsburgh Street and Main Street. The side of the building that fronted Pittsburgh Street housed the post office, and at this hour the street corner attracted the usual large crowd that gathered to collect the 7:00 P.M. mail and socialize. It was the kind of mild evening typical of western Pennsylvania in late spring. On the Main-facing side of the Round Corner building, the space had once been a drugstore but had now been gutted to make way for a bank. The storefront was empty except for wooden posts that held up the second story. The posts were fixed on stone sills about three feet high. James stood atop one of the sills and leaned against a post, chatting with a local farmer's son.[13]

Dukes was just a block west on Main Street outside the Jennings House. These were troubling times for Uniontown's most notorious citizen. In two days, the Fayette County court was scheduled hear the case for his disbarment. And, as Dukes recently confided to Mr. Jennings, he had received anonymous letters informing him that his death was imminent. But for the moment, Dukes seemed to forget the anxieties that plagued him, making conversation and laughing with friends on the street in front of his hotel. He soon began the short walk to the post office, as he typically did at this hour, to collect his mail. As always, Dukes's appearance reflected his patrician upbringing—a dark suit, high collar, skinny cravat, and, in his hand, a rattan cane.[14]

The previous Christmas Eve, the final conscious act of Captain Nutt's life was an attempt to draw his pistol and shoot Dukes. But with a bullet in his brain, Nutt lacked the strength to exact revenge. As Dukes now unassumingly walked past the empty storefront, James pulled out the very pistol that his father had clutched in his death throes and fired the shot that Captain Nutt could not.

The bullet tore into Dukes's back. He looked back and saw James standing on the stone sill no more than six feet behind him, cocking his revolver. Dukes turned to flee. James jumped down while unloading a second round, hitting Dukes within a few inches of the first bullet hole. As Dukes's lungs filled with blood, he began a staggered run around the corner for the post office. Bystanders could see the horror in his face. James gave chase, discharging his pistol a third time when he rounded the corner himself. Dukes started to ascend the steps to the post office and James fired a fourth bullet. One of these latter two shots missed, but the other penetrated Dukes's back near the first two wounds. Dukes was nearly at the post office doorway. As James reached the post office steps himself, he pulled the trigger a fifth and final time. James could feel someone seize his shoulders just as the weapon went off. The shot ricocheted off Dukes's leg and shattered a glass mailbox inside the building. With three bullets in his chest—one lodged in his heart—Dukes collapsed face forward into the post office.[15]

James Nutt's attack

Source: The National Police Gazette: New York, June 30, 1883, 9.

The man who had grabbed James was the policeman Frank Pegg. It was no coincidence that an officer of the law had been close by; the police had been regularly keeping watch over both Dukes and James, fearful that the two would engage in a deadly affray. James struggled momentarily against Pegg's hold until he saw that it was a member of the police force who grabbed him.

"Here, take it," said James, referring to his father's gun, "and take me to jail as quick as you can get me there."

A throng began to amass around Dukes as he struggled to breathe. "Stand back, and give him air," someone shouted. The crowd was unsympathetic.

"He needs no air; let him die."

"He got what he deserved."[16]

A relative of Dukes, E. A. Lingo, was a half-block away. Upon hearing the gunfire, Lingo instinctively cried out, "I'll bet that's Dukes." He headed for the post office and pushed his way through the crush of onlookers to Dukes's side. Dukes had been rolled over onto his back. His anguish was evident in every tortured movement of his face. "Dukes, do you want to say anything?" asked Lingo. Dukes remained silent. Within a moment—on the floor of the very post office where he had mailed his infamous letters to Captain Nutt—Nicholas Lyman Dukes drew his final breath.[17]

The gunshots had echoed throughout the town. Most residents immediately suspected that James and Dukes were involved. By the hundreds, people dashed to the post office, but the burgeoning crowd was kept at bay while Coroner Sturgeon conducted an initial inspection of the body. Dukes was promptly declared dead. The corpse was laid on a board, the arms were bound with a handkerchief, and the body was covered with a coat. Several men carried the deceased down Main Street to the Jennings House, there ascending the same stairwell that Captain Nutt had climbed on Christmas Eve. They laid Dukes on the same bed where Nutt had bled to death.[18]

Meanwhile, Officer Pegg walked with James the few blocks to the county jail.

"Jim, you have done bad work," Pegg said. "You have killed Dukes, and I thought you killed another man."

"For the other fellow I am sorry for it, but for Dukes I couldn't help it," James pleaded. He would soon be relieved to learn that, miraculously, the two stray bullets had not injured, much less killed, any innocent bystander. The postmistress had picked up the bullet that broke the mailbox as a keepsake. Many souvenir seekers would offer to buy the mailbox itself but its owner refused to sell.[19]

When they arrived at the jail, Officer Pegg inquired whether James was in possession of any other firearms. "Yes, here is one, but I want Martin to take it and keep it," James replied, referring to the policeman Lucius Martin, who had once been in Captain Nutt's employ and had known James for years. The prisoner pulled a Forehand & Wadsworth six-shooter from his pocket.[20]

At the Jennings House, Dukes's clothes were removed. They were found to hold his keys, $1.17, a telegram for his stepfather, a dagger, and one last item: the revolver with which he had killed Captain Nutt. It was loaded.[21]

Coroner Sturgeon and his father—a local physician—probed the wounds on Dukes's body, extracting two of the bullets but not the ball embedded in the heart. Dukes's forehead featured a

James Nutt

Source: "James Nutt," *Rome Daily Sentinel* (New York), December 11, 1883, 1.

conspicuous bruise, resulting from his hitting the post office floor headfirst. Just as the coroner had after Nutt's death, he convened a jury of six men at the Jennings House to hear testimony for the inquest. It proved challenging to retrieve witnesses immediately, so Coroner Sturgeon adjourned the proceedings until the next morning. (One of the jurors, George Marshall, had a two-year-old son, George Jr., who became secretary of state in 1947 under Harry Truman and the namesake of the Marshall Plan that rebuilt much of Europe amid the ruins of World War II.)[22]

W. H. Cook, a relative of the Nutts, headed to the family home to inform them that James had mortally wounded Dukes and was in police custody. The first floor of the house was empty, so Cook called up the stairwell to Lizzie, who answered. Mrs. Nutt had gone to bed but not yet fallen asleep. Hearing her daughter's conversation, she asked, "Lizzie, what is the matter now?" and stepped into the hallway. Cook ascended the stairs and encountered Mrs. Nutt, who was gripping the balustrade. He hinted that his news was not good and accompanied Mrs. Nutt back to her room, where she lay on the bed. Lizzie joined them.

"Tell me all," Mrs. Nutt implored her visitor. "My cup of sorrow and grief is so full that a drop or two more will make no difference." Cook proceeded to relay the events of the evening.

"Poor Jim; if he had only waited I would have done it myself," remarked Lizzie.[23]

Meanwhile, word went forth across the Commonwealth and the country that Captain Nutt's son had avenged the death of his father. Reporters from Pittsburgh, Philadelphia, and Baltimore took off for Uniontown on the next available trains. In Harrisburg, the *Patriot* posted the news on its bulletin board. The balmy night air soon filled with sounds of buzzing crowds. The consensus in the capital was that Dukes's death was as inevitable as it was deserved. The former mayor, John Patterson, spoke for many Harrisburgers when he lauded James's lethal assault as "honorable." Treasurer Baily was of similar mind. Someone from the *Patriot* informed Baily of Dukes's death while he was relaxing on a bench outside the State House. "Well, now, that is an honorable act, indeed," Baily cried, springing to his feet. "Come in and tell me all about it." The agent from the paper joined Baily and some other officials inside the State House.[24]

Baily confessed, "I expected it some day, and thought it might have come earlier. The town must be very excited to-night. Does the telegram give you any further particulars?" At that moment, a delivery boy from Western Union hastened down the marble hallway and handed an envelope to Baily. It was a message from Uniontown: "Jim Nutt has just this moment shot and killed Dukes. This disbars him."[25]

In Pittsburgh, crushes of people lined Fifth Avenue and learned from the newspapers' bulletin boards that Nicholas Dukes was no more. The prevailing sentiment on the streets was that justice had finally been served. Throughout the city, the saloons were full of boisterous men toasting James and Lizzie over and over again. The celebration was not limited to Pennsylvania—telegrams began to arrive in Uniontown from across the United States praising James and offering financial support for his legal defense.[26]

William Playford and his law partner, A. D. Boyd, headed to the jail and visited the young man who executed the death sentence that they had failed to secure from the law. Many of James's friends came to see him that evening as well. James was not confined to a cell but permitted to walk the hallway freely. Later that night, Sheriff Hoover had a bed made for James under the stairwell rather than behind bars. Hoover was also afraid that James might injure himself and so he ordered a suicide watch for the prisoner. Although James had killed Sheriff Hoover's childhood friend, Hoover conducted himself with a sense of professional duty, perhaps even compassion.[27]

As the night wore on, two barbers moonlighting as undertakers cleaned Dukes's corpse in the parlor of the Jennings House and outfitted it with fresh clothing. Custom required that the living keep watch over the dead, and so James Feather—in company with a hotel clerk—stayed up late into the night with the remains of the man against whom he had testified.[28]

Dukes's stepfather, Asbury Struble, and half-brother, George, reached the Jennings House at 2:00 A.M. After viewing the corpse, they headed to the telegraph office to relay the news to family in Ohio. Another carriage pulled up to the hotel hours later. Out stepped Dukes's mother, Mrs. Struble, accompanied by her daughter. The mother held her head low and covered her face with a moist handkerchief. Upon reaching the lifeless body of her son, Mrs. Struble fell to her knees and began to kiss his cold flesh. He was her "poor boy," she said, her "dear Nicholas." Nearly two decades earlier, Captain Nutt undertook his mission to identify the alias of the hanged Confederate conspirator Lewis Powell, which brought him to the doorstep of Powell's bereaved mother. Despite Powell's treason against the Union that Nutt loved so dearly, the grief of a mother mourning her son left a deep impression on Nutt. So too would it prove impossible for even those who vilified Nicholas Dukes to display indifference to the suffering of his mother.[29]

As the Strubles awaited a hearse wagon at the Jennings House in the morning, Coroner Sturgeon reconvened the inquest jury in his office. Townspeople eager to hear the testimony crammed in. Nearly a dozen witnesses provided straightforward and consistent accounts of the shooting. Unlike the circumstances surrounding

Nutt's death, the details of Dukes's final moments were never in doubt. The jury soon rendered its verdict: "That deceased, N. L. Dukes, came to his death by pistol wounds, the shots producing said wounds being fired from the hand of one James Nutt."[30]

By midday, the hearse appeared outside the Jennings House, and a walnut coffin containing Dukes's corpse was swiftly loaded for the ride to the Struble farm in Germantown. Two buggies carrying members of the family trailed the wagon. Rounding out the procession on horseback were Asbury Struble and his son, George. The morning trains had delivered immense crowds eager to see the body and they now bore witness to the somber cavalcade. As the cortege left Uniontown and began its eleven-mile journey, Dukes passed the Nutt mansion one final time.[31]

Front-page headlines from Boston to San Francisco announced Dukes's demise, and editorial pages across the country celebrated James Nutt's vengeance. The *New Haven Evening Register* declared, "Nutt not only deserves acquittal at the hands of the jury, but also deserves a handsome tribute of appreciation." Dukes's penning of the infamous letters, rather than his killing of Captain Nutt, constituted the primary offense that justified James's revenge, according to the *Saint Paul Daily Globe*. "Dukes did not deserve to live a moment," the *Globe* maintained, "after giving utterance to the foul, beastly, despicable words." The *Atlanta Constitution* called for even more bloodshed, urging "some member of the Nutt family to continue the good work by picking off the jurymen that acquitted Dukes." That James had not acted within the letter of the law was of little moment to the Cleveland *Plain Dealer*:

> The shooting of Dukes was done agreeably to an unwritten law that the near of kin to a woman who has been seduced may kill her seducer at sight. Were the law to explicitly affirm that a seducer may be killed on the spot, wherever found, by a relative of the wronged woman, we do not know that the act of the avenger would have a higher warrant than it has now with *no actual warrant.*

Hardly a menace to civilization, violence of the kind enacted by James was upheld as a preserver of the social fabric. As the *Pittsburgh Commercial-Gazette* explained, James accomplished "what the law failed to do" and thereby "made society secure from further depredation." Expressions of support came as readily from Democratic organs as from their Republican counterparts. The Dukes–Nutt affair had, by this point, transcended partisan divides.[32]

Some periodicals acknowledged that extralegal killing was troublesome but still made an exception for the newfound hero of Uniontown. The *Trenton Times* conceded that "the act of the avenger was illegal," but found, "it is very hard to view the picture with other than sympathetic eyes toward young Nutt. It is equally hard to refrain from rejoicing."[33]

Editorialists found many culprits aside from James on which to pin Dukes's death. One blamed newspapers that had advocated vigilante justice. Another implicated the handful of Dukes's supporters who had encouraged him to remain in Uniontown. The Philadelphia *Times* suggested that promiscuous women invited the kind of troubles that plagued the Nutt family, insisting of the scandal, "It was once in a woman's power to have suppressed by remembering her self-respect."[34]

Yet in the eyes of most commentators, the truly culpable party was the jury that set Dukes free and left justice unrealized. The Sacramento *Record-Union* spoke for many nationwide when it concluded, "That jury can lay to its soul the fact that its dereliction has caused the taking of human life." But just as the Dukes verdict had brought shame on the Commonwealth, the trial of James Nutt would offer the promise of redemption. The honor of the entire Keystone State was at stake.[35]

The press entertained little doubt that the American people would rally behind James. "'Dukes deserved his fate,' will be the voice of thousands this morning," anticipated the *Wheeling Register*. Given the outcry against Dukes's acquittal just three months earlier, this forecast was far from bold. Newspapers also predicted that widespread public support for James would translate into a favorable verdict in the courtroom. The *New York Times* considered James's acquittal inevitable: "The one thing that can with certainty be predicted concerning the killing of Dukes by young Nutt is that the slayer will not be found guilty of murder or any degree of manslaughter." Only among locals in Fayette County was there anxiety that, just as a jury had done the unthinkable and set Dukes free, perhaps even a sympathetic defendant such as James could meet his demise at the hands of twelve peers.[36]

To be sure, there were a few columnists who criticized James—but even they conceded that they were isolated voices of dissent amid a chorus of approval for his lethal assault. The

Evening Critic, published in the nation's capital, considered James's reprisal an affront to the rule of law: "While it is true that the provocation was great, the law has been none the less outraged." Still, the paper had to acknowledge of James, "He is openly spoken of as a hero instead of being condemned as an assassin."[37]

After Dukes's hearse left for the Struble farm, Clark Brecken-ridge delivered Mrs. Nutt in a carriage to the jail, where they met three of James's uncles. The group was guided into the sheriff's parlor. James was then brought in, and tears began to stream down Mrs. Nutt's cheeks. Since Dukes's acquittal, she had warned James to keep his distance from his father's killer, wor-ried that Dukes might cut short her son's life to prevent James from taking his. James now claimed that Dukes had cackled in his face on the street days earlier and driven him to a violent rage. "Mother, I had to kill him," James insisted. "His laughing scorn almost made me mad." Before leaving, James's uncles urged their nephew to maintain his resolve.[38]

Lizzie, who stayed home to look after her younger siblings, granted an interview to a reporter in which she voiced compunc-tion about not having slain Dukes herself. "The only thing I regret about the shooting, is that I did not do it myself," she main-tained. "I had made up my mind if he remained here to kill him, and would have done so had the opportunity been presented." Lizzie was keenly aware that a woman defending her own honor ran counter to the mainstream view that women should be pas-sive spectators to male vengeance. As she told the journalist, "I know I have surprised you by what I have said, and doubtless others will not understand that so timid a woman could be so revengeful, but it is true." When asked if her brother would plead insanity, Lizzie became incensed. "No, sir," she replied, "there will not be any plea of insanity in this case. His defense is that he defended his sister's honor and avenged his father's death. Would not any brave son have done likewise?"[39]

Lizzie was not the only one holding court with the press in the Nutt mansion that day. Dr. Leon Case, a close friend of Captain Nutt, spoke with a correspondent from the *Pittsburgh Commercial-Gazette* in Nutt's library. In this interview, Dr. Case alleged to have spent weeks organizing an investigation into the veracity of Dukes's accusations against Lizzie, the results of which he had planned to deliver in a statement at Dukes's disbarment hearing. According to Dr. Case, he submitted Dukes's letters for analysis to six of the nation's preeminent experts—logicians and philologists—and conducted his own assessment as well. He also took measurements of the areas of the Nutt home where Dukes claimed to have witnessed Lizzie's indiscretions. Dr. Case further claimed to have had assistance from a detective who surreptitiously collected information by donning a variety of disguises, sometimes assuming the form of a woman. In his final assessment, said Dr. Case, "I have found for a certainty 117 falsehoods and misconstructions of the truth and 58 probable ones." With Dukes now in a coffin, the disbarment hearing never took place, but Dr. Case assured the journalist that his report would still be made public. "This statement," Dr. Case contended, "will fully exonerate Miss Nutt's name and establish beyond a doubt her innocence and purity." No such statement ever appeared. Perhaps Dr. Case was so eager to reassure the public of Lizzie's chastity amid renewed attention to the scandal that he exaggerated or even fabricated his findings when discussing them with the press.[40]

On June 16, three days after the shooting, a large gathering congregated at the Struble farm for the funeral of Nicholas Lyman Dukes. Some attended in sympathy with a Struble family long known and respected; others came to see the latest spectacle in Fayette County's ongoing saga. The Reverend Alexander Milholland, who served as the minister at the church where Dukes first saw Lizzie and had presided over Captain Nutt's funeral, officiated the service together with another clergymen, the Reverend M. C. Baily. While making no direct reference to the series of events culminating in Dukes's death, Reverend Baily recited Psalm 51, which concerns illicit sex and murder. King David prays for forgiveness after fornicating with Uriah's wife and arranging for Uriah's murder: "Free me, free me, O Lord, from blood, guiltiness." Reverend Millholland told the mourners that it was not for them to judge the departed, "but it is always best to leave the matter with God, the All-wise and Omnipotent Judge who alone judgeth man rightly."[41]

After prayers and readings from Scripture, all present were afforded the opportunity to view the corpse. The coffin bore a silver plate with the name "N. L. Dukes" and was surmounted by a cross of immortelles. In addition to Mr. and Mrs. Struble, those present included Dukes's brother Lewis, who bore a resemblance to the deceased, their sister Mary, a half-sister, Anna, and a number of step-uncles from Ohio. Sheriff Hoover also came to bid farewell to a friendship that had spanned nearly all his life. An hour passed before the cortege was organized and ready to leave for Church Hill Cemetery. Stretching over one and a half miles, the cavalcade included 109 carriages and 38 people on horseback.[42]

The procession arrived at the cemetery to find more people awaiting Dukes's interment. Still, the total attendance was only a quarter that of Captain Nutt's funeral. Standing atop the clay that would soon fill the tomb, Reverend Baily declared, "We now commit this body to the grave, to mingle with the dust from which it came, and the soul to its God." As Nicholas Dukes was buried, the profound quiet of the cemetery was broken only by his mother's weeping.[43]

Some were conspicuous by their absence. Dukes belonged to two fraternal associations—the Knights of Pythias and Odd Fellows—and although these groups were obliged to perform their respective funeral rites, both organizations refused to appear at the ceremony. The Fayette County bar likewise did not attend and abstained from issuing the standard tribute normally extended upon the death of one of its members. As the Harrisburg *Patriot* wrote of Dukes and his resting place, "He lies there unhonored."[44]

The following day, a Sunday, churchgoers across the Commonwealth listened to sermons about Dukes that expressed no misgivings about his downfall. Just outside of Philadelphia, for instance, the pastor at the Oak Street Methodist Episcopal Church entitled that week's homily "Divine Retribution and the slaying of N. L. Dukes." Lizzie Nutt was similarly obdurate. She told a reporter in her family's parlor, "I do not see how he will be able to rest in his grave after casting such infamy upon me." With her brother in jail, Lizzie confessed to the journalist that the distress enveloping her life kept her awake at night. Her efforts to distract herself by reading had proved futile. "If my father were only alive I could stand it," she reflected, "because he believed in me." Lizzie did not explicitly discuss the possibility of a death sentence for James, but the prospect of another life sacrificed for the sake of her honor must have weighed heavily on her.[45]

· *Ten* ·

PREPARATIONS

❧

Although Captain Nutt left the family steeped in debt, the Nutts did not have to worry about affording the finest legal counsel for James—they were flooded with donations. Supporters organized public subscription funds for James's defense in Pittsburgh and Middleburgh, Pennsylvania. The Mount Savage Firebrick Company of Maryland pooled together $100. From Philadelphia and Baltimore were many more contributions. Some individuals gave a dollar; others provided upward of $50 (more than $1,200 today). On June 20, one week after the shooting, the *Harrisburg Telegraph* reported that the Nutt estate was bankrupt, although the press and public were still unaware that the family's debt was connected to an embezzlement scheme perpetrated by Captain Nutt. This airing of the Nutts' financial woes may have been a calculated move to encourage even more contributions.[1]

At James's request, William Playford and A. D. Boyd agreed to represent him in court. While these prosecutors from the Dukes trial would now assume the role of criminal defense lawyers, Congressman Boyle rebuffed the requests of Dukes's friends to argue for the Commonwealth against James. R. H. Lindsey, who had assisted Boyle in Dukes's defense, likewise refused to prosecute Captain Nutt's son. With considerable resources at his disposal, Dukes's stepfather, Asbury Struble, looked elsewhere for private prosecutors who could assist District Attorney Isaac Johnson. Mr. Struble ultimately retained the congressman's son, John Boyle, as well as a gifted lawyer from Pittsburgh named David Patterson. With piercing eyes, Patterson exuded a quiet intensity that would provide a sharp contrast to the gregarious showmanship of the defense. [2]

James's legal team did not move to have him discharged on bail before his trial. There was no doubt that James had acted with an intent to kill in the absence of immediate provocation. If James were guilty at all, he was guilty of murder in the first degree. His alleged offense, therefore, did not carry the option of bail. With his trial scheduled for the September court term, James Nutt spent the summer in jail.[3]

In the wake of the shooting, the press showed renewed interest in the mystery at the heart of the affair—if Lizzie were pure, as many believed, then why had Dukes manufactured lies to avoid marrying her? The *Atlanta Constitution* suspected that Dukes discovered Captain Nutt's financial woes. Fearful of the burden of supporting the Nutt family, Dukes fabricated lascivious allegations about Lizzie to justify breaking the engagement. Dr. Case was a vocal proponent of this theory.[4]

Some newspapers conjectured that Dukes had grown enamored of another woman in Uniontown, Miss Mary Beeson. The *Harrisburg Telegraph* suggested that perhaps Dukes was engaged to both Lizzie and Mary at the same time, and cut Lizzie loose to free himself to wed Mary. Mary's friends repudiated rumors that she had had an amorous relationship with Dukes. But according to Lizzie, hearsay about Mary and Dukes had been circulating in Uniontown well before Dukes shot Captain Nutt. As she told the press, "When I was engaged to him, gossip had it that he was paying attention to other ladies also. Miss Beeson's name was mentioned at the time. I told him of what I had heard. He said it was all nonsense, and that there was not a word of truth in it." Whether Dukes had in fact romanced Mary, Lizzie could not say.[5]

When Dukes's will was finally unearthed nearly two weeks after his passing, its contents seemed to verify that Dukes indeed abandoned Lizzie for Mary. It was well known that Dukes, likely fearing an assassination, wrote a will on the morning of his bail hearing. But the substance of the document remained an enigma in the immediate aftermath of his death. The Strubles were unable to find the will at first; it had been written inconspicuously on the back of a letter, and in Mr. Struble's initial review of his stepson's papers, he passed over it. Finally, the will was discovered. In it, Dukes awarded some lands in Ohio to his brother, Lewis, and a portion of the estate to his mother. And then there was the clause that, in the minds of many, held the answer to the riddle of the Dukes–Nutt saga: "My debts and funeral expenses being paid, I give to Mary J. Beeson, the daughter of Jesse Beeson the sum of two thousand dollars" (which amounts to nearly $50,000 today). The *Harrisburg Telegraph* felt vindicated in its earlier speculation, concluding, "In his will Dukes recognizes Miss Beeson in such a way as to leave no further doubt of their engagement."[6]

As the summer wore on, James passed his time in jail reading and playing cards. No one anticipated much news until the trial in September. But in August came a voice from the grave. Dukes had indicated shortly after his acquittal that he would issue a public statement revealing the truth behind Captain Nutt's death. No such revelation appeared in print. In fact, Dukes *did* author an open letter pleading his case to the world but never released it for unknown reasons. With Dukes now dead and his killer about to stand trial, Dukes's supporters submitted the statement to the press, which was reprinted on the front page of the *New York Times*, among many other periodicals nationwide.[7]

The wide-ranging letter began with Dukes's version of the previous Christmas Eve. He reiterated the narrative that he first described in a posttrial interview, recalling how a bloodthirsty Captain Nutt attacked him with a heavy cane, which Dukes managed to wrest from him. Nutt then retreated to the mantle and reached for his gun, forcing Dukes to draw his revolver and fire a lethal shot to save his own life. The alleged witnesses to the killing arrived directly after Dukes pulled the trigger. Having detailed his rendition of events, Dukes's posthumous letter insisted, "No man with a shadow of fairness can resist the conclusion that Capt. Nutt came to my room on the morning of the 24th of December to take my life." The jury had been obliged to forgive the killing on the grounds of self-defense.[8]

As for the infamous letters about Lizzie's sexual history, Dukes accused his prosecutors of needlessly bringing them to light to prejudice the jury against him. Although he expressed contrition for having written them in the first place—"It was the personification of stupidity, and the remorse of a lifetime will not be adequate expiation for the error"—it had been lawyers for the Commonwealth, not Dukes's attorneys, who submitted the letters as evidence and thereby publicized Lizzie's exploits. As a result, "She has been crucified by her own friends, and lifted high on the cross for the insulting stare and mock sympathy of the millions."[9]

Dukes further contended, much as Congressman Boyle had at trial, that he did not kill out of malice. Indeed, he harbored no ill will toward Nutt, a man whom Dukes venerated and whose death he mourned. "The images of the disconsolate widow and the helpless orphan children rise up before me like accusing spirits," Dukes professed, "and if such a thing were possible, gladly would I lay down in this man's grave and restore him to his desolate family." Dukes dismissed as absurd the widespread notion that he contrived an evil plot to desecrate Lizzie and murder her father. The events surrounding Nutt's death were not premeditated; instead, "one thing grew out of another, according to the law of cause and effect, until the homicide was the result of a contest for the survivorship."[10]

Dukes shared his realization that the code of honor for which he had once been willing to kill and die was in reality a dangerous travesty of justice. He confessed, "I foolishly thought I was doing Capt. Nutt a cruel kindness, and taking a stand for the preservation of my own honor. Since this occurrence I have concluded that honor is a delusion and a mockery." Instead, Dukes championed the rule of law. Chastising newspaper editors who encouraged extralegal action, Dukes affirmed, "I, unlike these self-constituted public educators and moral censors, respect the law and will judge and be judged by it, and abide by its decrees." He likewise faulted Nutt for practicing vigilantism: "He should not have taken the law into his own hands against me. If I had wronged him or his, the doors of the Court House were open, and he should have sought redress there." Lizzie was too old to come under the protection of Pennsylvania's seduction statute that criminalized the seduction of a girl under the age of twenty-one, but the common law did allow the father of a seduced daughter to file a civil suit for monetary damages. Dukes continued, "The law that is good enough for other people is certainly sufficient for him. But he rises above the law and demands my life."[11]

Dukes's letter castigated the citizens of Uniontown for initially trying to expel him from their community, which exhibited their disregard for the rule of law. "The law," Dukes reminded his readers,

> gives me my liberty and pronounces me an innocent man, and gives me the same rights as any other citizen of the State or United States. I have the legal right to go when and where I please, and do what I please, within the limits of the law. But there is a gang about Uniontown who defy the behests of the law, and undertake to prescribe the limits of my rights, and give me commands as to what I shall do and what I shall not do.

Dukes was also exasperated by the ubiquitous depiction of himself as a perverse libertine and Lizzie as his naive victim. He had "been held up to the public gaze as destroyer of the reputation of 'an innocent little girl,'" but "the *little girl* is 24 years of age."[12]

There was one paragraph in Dukes's statement that his friends expurgated about Jeremiah Black, the former chief justice of the Pennsylvania Supreme Court, U.S. attorney general, and U.S. secretary of state. As the House of Representatives debated Dukes's fate as a legislator, Black had recommended that if Dukes came to the state capital in an attempt to claim his seat, then someone in Harrisburg should "run him out of town." Dukes was outraged by Black's suggestion and upbraided the elder statesmen in his letter, but Dukes's friends evidently thought that the censure of such a highly regarded jurist would do little to restore Dukes's reputation.[13]

Presumably, Dukes's supporters chose this particular moment to publicize his statement because they hoped to weaken support for James Nutt before his trial. If that were their plan, it backfired. The press nationwide issued a new round of denunciations of Dukes's character. As the *New-York Tribune* concluded about his posthumous declaration, "It contains nothing new, and will not relieve his name from the odium that belongs to one of the meanest of mankind." Rather than mend Dukes's broken image, the open letter further galvanized people behind his killer.[14]

With James's trial set for the first week of September, Mrs. Nutt sought to recruit additional lawyers to team with Playford and Boyd in pleading for her son's life. The Pennsylvania state senator Andrew Jackson Herr was a favored choice on account of his persuasive powers—one of Captain Nutt's brothers and Treasurer Baily joined Mrs. Nutt in appealing to Senator Herr for assistance. But Herr had other commitments that prevented him from participating in the case. On Monday, September 3, with the trial only three days away, Mrs. Nutt entreated the aid of two other lawyers. In an era when telegraphic communication was priced by the word, Mrs. Nutt kept her message to the point, sending the following telegram to both attorneys:

Uniontown, Pa., September 3.

Can you assist in defending my son James? Trial set for Thursday. I need not urge the anxiety of a mother.

Mrs. Nutt[15]

The first recipient was Marshall Swartzwelder, a talented criminal lawyer in Pittsburgh who had served in the General Assembly as a young man in the 1840s but abandoned political office to focus exclusively on his legal career. He earned a stellar reputation at the bar thanks to his encyclopedic knowledge of the law. In the words of one contemporary, Swartzwelder "was a terror, in the criminal court, to all young practitioners." His white hair and whiskers betokened his advanced age and were said to resemble the styling of the German emperor William the First. Swartzwelder agreed to come to James's aid.[16]

The other man whom Mrs. Nutt telegraphed was a criminal defense attorney of such preternatural talent that his home state of Indiana passed a law allowing the prosecution rather than the defense to deliver the final closing argument in the hopes of mitigating his influence over juries. He was U.S. Senator Daniel Voorhees, and he informed Captain Nutt's widow that in three days' time she would find him in the Fayette County courthouse at her son's side.[17]

Nicknamed "The Tall Sycamore of the Wabash," Senator Voorhees was a mountain of a man, at once earnest yet theatrical, impassioned yet good-humored. It was 1859 when a thirty-two-year-old Voorhees gained national renown for his courtroom skill. In a widely publicized trial, Voorhees defended John Cook, one of the insurgents who was captured in connection with John Brown's ill-fated raid on Harper's Ferry. As a proslavery Democrat with Southern sympathies, Voorhees was an unlikely choice to represent a militant abolitionist in a Virginia courtroom. But Cook happened to be the brother-in-law of the Indiana governor, who requested that Voorhees assist with the legal defense. During the trial, Voorhees blamed John Brown for corrupting the impressionable Cook and assured anxious Virginians that the failure of the raid to spark a mass slave revolt was a testament to the staying power of slavery. This defense strategy was not compelling enough to sway the jury—Cook was hanged—but Voorhees managed to avoid alienating fellow proslavery Democrats while earning acclaim for trial oratory.[18]

The following year Voorhees was elected to Congress, where he spent most of the next four decades, first in the House and then in the Senate. All the while, Voorhees maintained a career as a trial lawyer in high-profile cases, especially ones that involved homicide in defense of a woman's honor. In 1865, he defended nineteen-year-old Mary Harris, who made headlines when she gunned down a clerk in the Treasury Department in Washington, DC. The clerk, Mary claimed, had promised to wed her but instead married another woman. Voorhees derided the deceased for his "cowardly betrayal of young, inexperienced

Daniel Voorhees

Source: Daniel Wolsey Voorhees, *Forty Years of Oratory* (Indianapolis and Kansas City: Bowen–Merrill, 1898).

female confidence" and suggested, "Such conduct is more injurious to morality than murder." Although there was no hard evidence that the clerk had ever actually been engaged to Harris, Voorhees's performance elicited from the jury both tears and a favorable verdict for his client.[19]

A trial involving Voorhees in 1871 featured circumstances strikingly similar to those of James Nutt's case. In Cumberland, Maryland, a coal mine superintendent fatally shot his sister's seducer on a public street. "Who can estimate the value of family honor?" Voorhees asked in the course of his three-and-half-hour closing argument. "Who shall lay a price on domestic happiness? Who shall remunerate you for the stolen and defiled members of your household?" When the jury acquitted the defendant, the crowd exploded with such excitement that the courthouse building trembled.[20]

Four months before Mrs. Nutt solicited Senator Voorhees's help, he had appeared as counsel in yet another prominent case of honor-bound bloodshed. Walter Davis, a political patron of the congressman "Little Phil" Thompson of Kentucky, betrayed the congressman by inebriating and seducing his wife. Unaware that Congressman Thompson had learned of his treachery, Davis approached Thompson on a train and asked casually, "How are you Phil?" Thompson seethed, "You damned son of a bitch. Do you dare speak to me after debauching my wife?" Davis turned to flee but Thompson drew his firearm and lodged a bullet in the back of Davis's head. In court, Senator Voorhees delivered what one Kentucky paper called a "brilliant invocation" in defense of "virtue and purity." Once again, Voorhees's client walked free.[21]

The day after Mrs. Nutt telegraphed Voorhees and Swartzwelder, the defendant's local counsel petitioned Judge Willson to delay the trial until the court's December term. Clark Breckenridge, one of the defense's principal witnesses, was ill with typhoid, and the defense presented Judge Willson with a physician's certificate verifying that Breckenridge was unable to appear in court. Lawyers for the Commonwealth in turn asked that the doctor testify in person as to Breckenridge's medical status. The next day the doctor did just that and, without any further objection from the Commonwealth, Judge Willson postponed the trial.[22]

Although James Nutt would be confined to jail for another three months, this delay appeared at the time to be a strategic boon for the defense. Only forty-eight jurors had been drawn for the September trial, a relatively small number. Both sides would of course challenge off jurors, and the panel was unlikely to yield the total twelve men required for the jury box. Sheriff Hoover would then be empowered to round out the jury with bystanders; given Hoover's friendship with Dukes, he could hardly be expected to seek men who were sympathetic to James. By way of contrast, fully eighty names would be drawn for the December trial, presumably reducing the chances that Sheriff Hoover would play a role in selecting any jurors.[23]

The postponement had the additional benefit of bringing another sharp lawyer to the defense team—Major A. M. Brown of Pittsburgh, an average-size man with dark eyes, lengthy black hair, and well-defined features. His services had been solicited over the summer, but Major Brown declined on account of a scheduling conflict with the September court term. With the new trial date set for December, Major Brown would be available to join the already impressive defense team of Playford, Boyd, Swartzwelder, and Senator Voorhees.[24]

Efforts were made to bolster the Commonwealth as well by requesting the aid of the former New York judge, George M. Curtis. Judge Curtis mistakenly assumed that the telegram asking for his assistance was from the defense and he agreed to help. When Curtis discovered that it was the Commonwealth that wanted his support, he quickly reneged. "Under no circumstances would I join in the prosecution of the boy," he relayed to a representative for the Commonwealth. "Money cannot tempt me. I believe he did right. You or I would have done the same." Judge Curtis, theoretically dedicated by profession to the rule of law, joined the long list of prominent citizens endorsing honor killing.[25]

The Philadelphia *Times* considered Curtis an index of the general mood. Although conceding that "the killing was deliberate and premeditated," the *Times* insisted, "ninety-nine men out of every hundred, however, believe it was justifiable and echo the sentiments of Curtis." Even the Commonwealth did not seem to think that the prisoner merited a harsh sentence, if any at all. As one of the prosecutors admitted, "We are not anxious to see young Nutt punished much, but should like to convict him, and then, if the Pardon Board and Governor want to pardon him, we don't care."[26]

In the weeks leading up to the trial, James's lawyers offered no public comment on how they planned to defend a client who had deliberately, openly, and maliciously taken life. Prosecutors anticipated that the prisoner would plead insanity when they learned that the defense was issuing subpoenas to witnesses who could speak to James's mental state. Meanwhile, James was visited daily by his mother, invariably escorted by Lizzie or Clark Breckenridge. Strangers, too, called on James in his cell to shake hands with the celebrated defender of honor. The Wilbur Opera Company even offered to serenade him, but the sheriff would not allow it. The only performance that mattered to James was the one his attorneys were preparing to make in defense of his life.[27]

· Eleven ·

PROSECUTION

❧

THE DUKES–NUTT AFFAIR WAS POISED TO RECAPTURE THE
nation's attention on Wednesday, December 5, 1883, when the
Commonwealth v. James Nutt commenced. The day prior marked
one year since Dukes penned his first scandalous letter to Captain
Nutt. At 9:00 A.M., the courthouse bell began to toll, marking
the start of the trial. But the bell's clapper broke off before it
finished chiming, a harbinger that the court's proceedings that
day would be curtailed unexpectedly.[1]

The defendant was brought into the same packed courtroom
where his father's killer had been set free. He sat with his mother,
his legal team, and the two uncles who had joined him in target
practice just before Dukes's death. Dukes's brother, Lewis, and
his stepfather, Asbury Struble, sat with the Commonwealth.[2]

At the side of the venerable Judge Willson was another jurist
who would soon replace him on the bench—this December term
would be Willson's last. After the attorneys from outside the
county were admitted to the local bar, Thomas Searight, the
court clerk, recited the charge against James. Searight, who was

active in Democratic politics, had considered Dukes his protégé and was distraught over his death.

"How say you, are you guilty or not guilty of the felony and murder charged in the indictment?" asked Searight.

"Not guilty," came the response from the defendant, his right arm raised.

"How will you be tried?"

"By God and my country."

"May God send you a deliverance."

The first juror, William Stewart from George Township, was called. "Juror look upon the prisoner," instructed Searight, "prisoner look upon the juror." Searight ran through the preliminary questions to determine the juror's qualifications.

"Are you a citizen of the United States?"

"Are you related to the prisoner at bar?"

Under questioning, Stewart acknowledged that he had formed an opinion in the case but would attempt to render a verdict in accordance with the evidence. Judge Willson here established a rule that no man with a preexisting opinion about the case at hand would be admitted to the jury box. Stewart, accordingly, was dismissed for bias.[3]

The next juror, a rugged blacksmith, proved even less promising when he admitted that not only did he favor James but also no evidence could alter his opinion. Then came a carpenter whom the Commonwealth challenged peremptorily because he hailed from the same corner of Fayette County where Captain Nutt once lived. Counsel for the defense subsequently used one of its own peremptory challenges to dismiss an elderly farmer from Dunbar.[4]

So it continued, with juror after juror released from duty, sometimes for bias, other times by peremptory challenge, and occasionally for opposition to the death penalty. William Playford flashed a grin to opposing counsel when the defense challenged off Christopher Bosley, a rock-ribbed Democrat from the Searight–Dukes wing of the party. After twenty-seven dismissals, a juror named William A. McDowell stepped forward. He was a Yale alumnus, a former editor of the *Genius of Liberty*, and, although a Democrat, not of the Searight–Dukes variety. Both the Commonwealth and the defense consented to his admission. By 1:00 P.M., when court adjourned for lunch, fifty-eight jurors had been exhausted. McDowell sat alone in the jury box.[5]

During the questioning of jurors, the task of objections fell largely to Marshall Swartzwelder, who intermittently chewed tobacco. Senator Voorhees and Major Brown remained quiet. Mrs. Nutt, for her part, regularly exchanged hushed words with her son, her lengthy mourning veil brushing against his knees when she leaned over.[6]

The whole scene was, in many respects, the inverse of the Dukes trial. The chair where the stout and stoic Nicholas Dukes had once sat was now occupied by a less portly and more restless James Nutt. Playford and his partner, A. D. Boyd, previously at the table for the Commonwealth, held their places on the defense's side of the room. Meanwhile, District Attorney Isaac Johnson prepared to make his case against a man who took the very life that Johnson himself had asked a jury to extinguish the previous March.[7]

After the court's recess, the remaining twenty-two jurors were questioned, two of whom passed through to the jury box.

With the panel exhausted and the jury far from complete, Playford moved for a change of venue. Senator Voorhees and Major Brown both spoke in favor of the motion. "Five hundred jurors must be summoned before we can get a jury at this rate," Major Brown calculated. "It is manifest we cannot get a trial in this county." Judge Willson conceded that the struggle to find a dozen impartial men proved to be more onerous than he had anticipated and granted the motion.[8]

The question now presented itself of which county Judge Willson would assign to host the trial. The defense advocated the Allegheny County courthouse in Pittsburgh. Although prosecutors posed no objection to a change of venue in the abstract, they vehemently opposed Pittsburgh as the new site for the trial. David Patterson, speaking for the Commonwealth, argued that if the press had prejudiced the public in Fayette County in James's favor, then all the more so in Pittsburgh. It would be "jumping out of the frying pan into the fire." Patterson recommended four other counties in southwest Pennsylvania. Judge Willson was unpersuaded. He noted that newspaper coverage of the case had been disseminated throughout every county and settled on Pittsburgh as the site of the trial because it was readily accessible. The crowd had listened to the lawyers' exchange in perfect silence, but when the judge rendered his decision, a murmur swept through the courtroom.[9]

After court adjourned, Senator Voorhees clutched the hand of Mrs. Nutt and assured her, "We will send your boy back to you a free man." Her eyes began to well with tears of joy. That evening, Rutter's band, which had played at Captain Nutt's funeral and Uniontown's indignation meeting, staged a performance for the visiting lawyers; Senator Voorhees, Swartzwelder, and Patterson returned the favor with short speeches. With James's trial now set for January in a city that embraced his honor killing and donations for the defense still pouring in, his supporters were more hopeful than ever.[10]

On December 26—the anniversary of Captain Nutt's burial—the Philadelphia *Times* reported disturbing news about Clark Breckenridge. The paper divulged that Breckenridge had received an anonymous death threat in writing just before James's trial in Uniontown commenced. Several weeks later, a note in the same handwriting was left at the home of the president of the bank where Breckenridge worked, warning: "Clark Breckenridge will be shot down at his desk. This is your first and last warning." On the day the story broke, Major Brown informed a journalist that similar threats had been issued to several of James's supporters. Breckenridge remained unshaken.[11]

By the new year, James Hoover's tenure as sheriff had come to an end. His replacement, Sheriff Sterling, now had responsibility for transporting America's most celebrated prisoner to Pittsburgh. Assuming that Sterling would have him handcuffed for the journey, James inquired in advance, "Sheriff, had not you better take the measure of my wrists, you have no hand-cuffs large enough for me." Sheriff Sterling assured James that he could ride to Pittsburgh unshackled.[12]

Known as the "Iron City," Gilded-Age Pittsburgh was a gritty portrait of industrialization. It had once been a scene of considerable natural beauty, lying at the nexus of three rivers and surrounded by sloping hills. Mills, foundries, and factories now

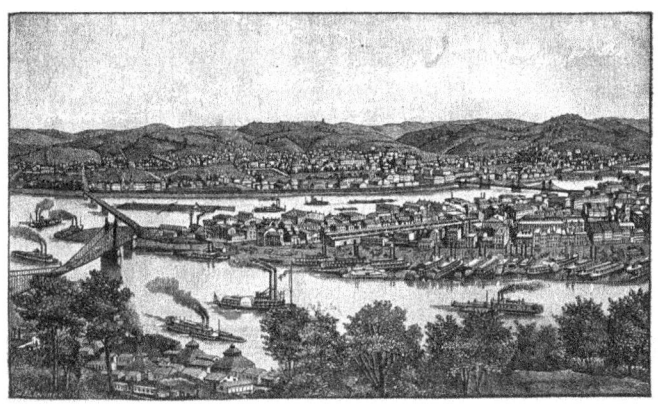

Pittsburgh

Source: Willard Glazier, *Peculiarities of American Cities* (Philadelphia: Hubbard Brothers, 1886), 336a.

lined the water, churning out iron nails, glass bottles, and steel train tracks. Barges clustered at the wharves to load these commodities before setting off for various points across the country. Pittsburgh's industries developed an insatiable appetite for coal, plundered liberally from the city's once verdant landscape.[13]

Perhaps Pittsburgh's most conspicuous feature was the insufferable cloud of pollution that emanated from factory chimneys and enveloped its 160,000 inhabitants. The streets were so darkened with smog that the gas lamps were left on during the day. One visitor to the city recalled, "The buildings, whatever their original material and color, are smoked to a uniform, dirty drab; the smoke sinks, and mingling with the moisture in the air, becomes of a consistency which may almost be felt as well as seen." Immigrant laborers from Southern and Eastern Europe crammed into shantytowns alongside the factories where they endured the din of railroads and stench of horse manure. For these souls, a beer at a tavern or the occasional picnic sponsored by a local ethnic society offered temporary respite from a life of drudgery. An *Atlantic Monthly* contributor described Pittsburgh as "hell with the lid taken off." Even more dramatic was the British philosopher Herbert Spencer, who told Pittsburgh oligarch Andrew Carnegie, "Six months' residence here would justify suicide."[14]

Industrial growth had also created new wealth, largely concentrated in the hands of native-born, white-collar professionals who staffed the business offices downtown. As a result, Pittsburgh featured the institutions of an emerging American metropolis not to be found in a village like Uniontown, such as universities and hospitals. The city's affluent set took advantage of horse-drawn streetcars to retreat to suburbs where they enjoyed a quieter, more lush, less congested existence. Modern amenities—including sewers, clean water, and waste disposal—were slow to come to Pittsburgh's poorer quarters but commonplace in the high-status suburban communities. For leisure, wealthier Pittsburghers patronized the city's Opera House and theaters. Sometimes a murder trial even served as a spectacle worthy of attendance.[15]

On Saturday, January 12, 1884, after 213 days of confinement, an emaciated James Nutt boarded a train for Pittsburgh, escorted by Sheriff Sterling and his deputies. They arrived at 10:00 A.M., whereupon the prisoner was promptly conveyed to his new cell in the Allegheny County jail. With the trial set to begin on

Monday, James passed much of the weekend reading. He had company for two hours that Sunday—a pair of physicians, both veterans of the nearby Dixmont Insane Asylum, who assessed his state of mind. This visit was widely reported in the press, and James's legal team confirmed that it would in fact mount a temporary insanity defense. As Major Brown for the defense set forth in an interview, "There are cases where grief and sorrow, anger and passion take away reason and impel persons to commit deeds, after committing which and when the cause of anger is removed they sometimes become rational again."[16]

The first highly publicized plea of temporary insanity in an American courtroom came twenty-five years earlier—and was employed to condone an honor killing. In 1859, the congressman Daniel Sickles discovered that Philip Barton Key (son of "The Star-Spangled Banner" author Francis Scott Key) was having relations with Sickles's wife. Sickles confronted Key in the shadow of the White House and declared, "Key, you scoundrel, you have dishonored my house—you must die!" Congressman Sickles then mortally wounded his wife's lover. One of Sickles's defense attorneys, John Graham, awkwardly paired temporary insanity and honor in his opening argument. "The condition of his mind at the time of the commission of the act in question as such would leave him legally unaccountable," contended Graham. Yet Graham also proclaimed, "If it be a crime for a husband to defend his humble family altar and death is visited on him for defending it, then the highest honor which can be conferred on any man is to compel him to die such a death." The jury acquitted Congressman Sickles in a widely hailed verdict.[17]

By the time of James Nutt's trial, temporary insanity had emerged as a popular and effective plea for defendants who killed for honor. There were two legal doctrines regarding the culpability of the mentally ill: the M'Naghten rule and the irresistible impulse test. Under the M'Naghten rule, named for an English case that lent credibility to the doctrine, a defendant was guilty if he *understood* the legal consequences of his actions. The irresistible impulse test looked beyond understanding to *self-control*—a defendant who suffered from an "irresistible impulse" to commit a crime was not legally responsible. No jurisdiction adopted the irresistible impulse test as a stand-alone doctrine, but in the late nineteenth century, several states (including Pennsylvania) used it as an ancillary to the M'Naghten rule, affording defendants the opportunity to evade conviction by either a lack of understanding or an absence of control. The irresistible impulse test resonated in a modernizing society characterized by the loss of individual autonomy. A defendant who was powerless was necessarily guiltless.[18]

James's legal team planned to follow a common strategy of attorneys who defended honor killers, predicating a temporary insanity plea on a combination of the irresistible impulse test and the concept of monomania—an obsessive preoccupation with one thing. According to this line of reasoning, the dishonor of a man's female kin drove him into a state of monomaniacal fixation on vengeance. Overcome by an irresistible impulse to kill, the man slew the seducer. Then, rather conveniently, his insanity remitted because the source of his mania was no longer alive. Framed in these terms, the illicit practice of honor killing offered a pretense to legality. Although it was hardly coherent to describe revenge as both an honor-bound duty and the product of a diseased mind, this inconsistency bespoke an American justice system laboring to reconcile traditional values with a modern society.[19]

The sole subject of discussion on the streets of Pittsburgh that Sunday was the pending Nutt trial. There was nothing yet to witness, but eager throngs nevertheless gathered near the jailhouse, pulsing with excitement about the affair that had captivated the national imagination and even made global headlines. Newspapers in countries as disparate as Mexico, Australia, England, Panama, Guyana, and Scotland covered the story. And in a hopeful sign for James, the press reported that a resident of Ohio, who was considered a "champion dreamer," envisioned an acquittal for the defendant during a recent slumber.[20]

Early the next morning, well before the day's session was to begin, the dim passageways that wound to the courtroom were packed with men. The horde futilely banged against the locked entry to the chamber. In the words of one journalist, the "mass of struggling humanity" continued to grow until it poured into the street. Fifth Avenue was filled with the sounds of vendors hawking booklets about the notorious Dukes trial from the previous March. The Pittsburgh-based publisher Stevenson & Foster preemptively acquired the rights to the transcript of James's trial, which soon sold in published form for 25¢ a piece (around $6 today).[21]

When Captain Nutt's brother Stephen arrived at the train station in Pittsburgh, an enterprising reporter immediately seized upon him. The correspondent asked whether the rumors

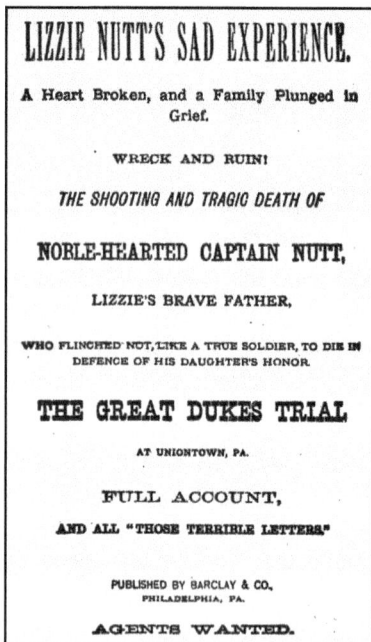

Pamphlet

A popular booklet about the Dukes trial affair sold outside the Allegheny County courthouse in Pittsburgh.

Source: Lizzie Nutt's Sad Experience: A Heart Broken, and a Family Plunged in Grief. Wreck and Ruin! (Philadelphia: Barclay, 1886), 17.

were true that James had once demonstrated a tendency toward "uncontrollable passion" by killing a pig. Stephen Nutt had no knowledge of such a slaughter and remarked that an incident of that sort would hardly amount to a grave offense anyhow. "Myself, or anybody else is liable to kill a hog if we would get angry with it for some mischief done," he insisted.[22]

At 9:00 A.M., court officers relegated the anxious throng inside the building to the floor landing, barricading the stairwells leading to the courtroom. "We do not propose to admit any but respectable people," it was announced. One of the men impaneled for jury duty cried out, "I am a juryman!" The crowd responded, "Yer a liar." But the juror, armed with his court summons, was allowed to pass through.[23]

When the courtroom finally opened, Judge Edwin Stowe took to the bench, the jurors to their box, and the lawyers to their tables. For the defense were the veterans of the Dukes trial, Boyd and Playford, alongside Swartzwelder, Major Brown, and another newcomer, General William Blakely of the Allegheny County bar. Senator Voorhees would not arrive until the following day. His absence was not unsurprising at this early stage of the trial—Voorhees's primary responsibility was not the minutia of jury selection or even the examination of witnesses but rather a stirring closing argument that would win the jurors' affections. Two of James's uncles were in attendance; his mother and sister, however, had not yet come to Pittsburgh. The Commonwealth featured the same three attorneys who had been present in the Fayette County courthouse in December: Congressman Boyle's son, John; Isaac Johnson, who continued to represent the Commonwealth in this case although his term as district attorney had ended; and the shrewd Pittsburgh local, David Patterson. Two of Dukes's brothers appeared before long. Absent was Dukes's stepfather, Asbury Struble, who was suffering from rheumatism.[24]

The court crier and county detective delivered James through the jail passageway to the prisoner's dock in the courtroom. James's pale face betokened the toll of his lengthy incarceration. When the courtroom was finally opened to the public, it took no more than five minutes for excited spectators to fill the space available. The doors were then swiftly shut and the trial commenced. After the court clerk finished reciting the indictment, James pleaded, "Not guilty." With this, the defendant was removed from the prisoner's dock and seated with his legal team.[25]

Attention turned to the selection of jurors. From a panel of sixty, the first juror called was a steelworker who was already familiar with the case but affirmed that he could render a verdict on the basis of evidence presented in court. He was admitted to the jury box. Judge Stowe had little interest in Judge Willson's inflexible rule that any juror with a preexisting opinion be dismissed, and it was evident that Stowe's court, accordingly, would meet with greater success in jury selection. Over the next several hours, the lawyers for both sides worked their way through the panel. A stoic James studied every potential juror and then looked to his attorneys as if searching for some hint of their own assessment.[26]

At one point during these proceedings, a spectator asked the court crier to pass a bouquet of flowers to James. The crier delivered the impressive collection of roses to General Blakely, who turned them over to his client. Judge Stowe was not pleased. "There must be no more of that," scolded the judge. "If I observe any persons bringing bouquets into court, I shall certainly have them committed." The crowd in the courtroom was audibly disconcerted by Judge Stowe's abrupt remarks, prompting the crier to bellow, "Order!" Although the threat of imprisonment preempted any more floral offerings to the defendant, these particular flowers were not confiscated from James. They remained on his table, petals pointed toward the bench.[27]

By 2:00 P.M., with the panel exhausted and the jury still two men short of a dozen, court adjourned for an hour. Four of the sheriff's deputies spent this time impaneling thirty bystanders from the building and surrounding streets. James repaired to his jail cell during the recess. When the selection of jurors finally resumed, James reappeared, this time without his bouquet, which he had left behind. Mrs. Nutt and Lizzie, meanwhile, arrived at the train station in Pittsburgh and were quickly taken to the courthouse.[28]

The day's most contentious moment came just after the eleventh juror was selected from the new panel of bystanders. According to one journalist, Patterson's eyes "snapped with fire," and he accused General Blakely of receiving clandestine signals—it was unclear from whom—to admit or reject a given juror. Judge Stowe decided to let the matter rest, and jury selection continued until the seventeenth bystander was agreed on to fill the final seat in the jury box.[29]

The twelve men who would hear the case claimed a diverse range of occupations. There was the druggist, the laborer, the bricklayer, the tax collector, the clerk, the sanitary inspector, the engineer, the steelworker, the plumber, the coal merchant, the farmer, and the carpet dealer. Although eclectic in their professions, these jurors were nearly uniform in their politics—eleven Republicans and a lone Democrat. It would soon surface that one of these men had fought alongside Captain Nutt in the Civil War and another had come close to murdering the seducer of his own daughter, facts that almost certainly would have disqualified them had they been known during jury selection.[30]

The court clerk swore in the jurors and read aloud the indictment against the prisoner a final time. As the clerk spoke, James's eyes remained fixed on the dozen men who could set him free or condemn him to the gallows. Judge Stowe adjourned court until the following morning. James was led back to his cell and the jury taken to the St. Clair Hotel for dinner.[31]

General Blakely expressed a confidence bordering on hubris about the defense's chances of success, boasting to the press, "A school boy could conduct the defense with that jury and obtain an acquittal." Blakely and his co-counselors spent the night strategizing with Treasurer Baily as they awaited the arrival of Senator Voorhees the following day. Meanwhile, Mrs. Nutt and Lizzie retired to the home of Major Brown, where they stayed as his guests for the duration of the trial. They were hardly the only ones who made the journey from Uniontown. Some 150 of their neighbors traveled to Pittsburgh for the trial, many opting to lodge at the Central Hotel or Monongahela House. They arrived to find Pittsburgh alive with endless chatter about James.[32]

Not long after sunrise the next morning, onlookers began to assemble in the passageway to the courtroom, hoping to gain entry to the spectacle that was making national headlines. The horde grew even larger, noisier, and rowdier than the previous day's throng. In an effort to contain the unruly masses, a court official dispensed tickets to ensure the admission of members of the bar, jurors, and witnesses. Select others received tickets as well, including several ministers and "a fair sprinkling of ladies," according to one report. Some of the witnesses—there were more than 100 summoned between the two sides—scalped their tickets for upward of $5 (equivalent to $125 today), knowing that they would be let in regardless.[33]

At 9:30 A.M., Judge Stowe instructed the court crier to clear the stairs and hallways of the residual crowd and promised imprisonment for any loiterers. Ten minutes later, the attorneys took their places. Senator Voorhees remained absent; for now, the defense was joined by Mrs. Nutt and Lizzie as well as Clark Breckenridge and his wife. James's mother and sister were both shrouded in mourning garb, their somber expressions largely hidden from view by their veils. Also in attendance was Treasurer Baily. The officers tasked with maintaining an orderly procession found themselves overrun by a swarm of witnesses who stormed into the courtroom. Eventually James appeared, surveying the crowd upon arrival. The jurors sat stiffly in their box.[34]

Ex–District Attorney Isaac Johnson delivered a terse opening argument for the Commonwealth. He began by emphasizing to the jurors that each was chosen precisely because his answers under questioning showed him to be dispassionate to the satisfaction of both the Commonwealth and the defense. Johnson reviewed the facts of the case and claimed that James's target practice on the afternoon of Dukes's death demonstrated the premeditated nature of the defendant's lethal assault. He closed his remarks with an appeal for impartiality:

All that the Commonwealth asks you to do is hear the testimony here in Court, to hear the charge of His Honor and find a verdict according to that evidence, as you have sworn to do. I know that it is not a light duty. Where the burden is easy, where the duty is light, where the responsibility is not seen, the weak, the timid, alike with the strong, the honest and the brave, can perform that duty. But where the responsibility is heavy, where the duty is great, the weak and the timid hesitate, falter, pause and turn back, and their duty remains undone, but the strong, the vigorous and the honest, as the Commonwealth believes each of you to be, go on to the end—follow the evidence whithersoever it leads, render a verdict according to that evidence, and then their duty is done. When you do that, gentlemen of the jury, the prisoner has no right to complain, and I assure you the Commonwealth will have no cause to murmur.

James, his mother, and sister alike looked downward throughout Johnson's address.[35]

The Commonwealth opened its case by calling five eyewitnesses to the shooting. This exercise was little more than perfunctory because there had never been any doubt or denial that James Nutt killed Nicholas Dukes. The Commonwealth then summoned to the stand Officer Pegg, the policeman who arrested James outside the post office. Pegg recalled how James told him on their walk to jail that if a stray bullet had hit anyone else, "I am sorry for it, but for Dukes I couldn't help it." Lucius Martin, another police officer who had heard James's comment, testified next and corroborated Officer Pegg's story. The press described the Commonwealth's eliciting of this testimony from Pegg and Martin as a "great blunder" because it tended to support the defense's claim that James acted on an irresistible impulse.[36]

The following witness, Coroner Sturgeon, had possession of the relevant physical evidence in the case. He presented to Judge Stowe the pistol that James had used to gun down Dukes as well as the second firearm that James had kept in his pocket but had not needed to accomplish his mission. The judge closed one eye and looked down the barrel of the first weapon. "Take care, they're loaded!" warned the coroner. Because James had fired five shots, there was still one bullet in the chamber; the other gun remained fully loaded. Both pistols were now emptied as a precaution. Coroner Sturgeon testified to the course of the three bullets that penetrated Dukes's chest and produced the two balls that he had pulled out of the corpse. (Sturgeon would keep those bullets for the rest of his long life.) A juror requested to see the third ball. "It is in the heart of Dukes," the coroner replied.[37]

During Coroner Sturgeon's cross-examination, Playford hoped to show that on June 13, Dukes was armed with the very revolver he had used to kill Captain Nutt.

"When you made this examination of Dukes, what did you find on him?" Playford inquired.

Patterson was quick to protest: "Stay; we object."

"I think we can show what condition Dukes was in at that time. Can't I find out what was on the person of Dukes at that time?"

"No, sir," responded Judge Stowe. "It is not part of the cross-examination, except testimony connected with the killing. If you want to get it in for the defense, this is not the time or place to do it." Before Coroner Sturgeon was dismissed, he offered one final piece of evidence: Dukes's bullet-riddled, blood-stained coat.[38]

The Commonwealth called two more residents of Uniontown who had seen James shoot Dukes; they corroborated the testimony of the other eyewitnesses. Playford did not abandon his efforts to show that Dukes was carrying a gun at the time of his death. When the latter of these witnesses described seeing Dukes on the post office floor, Playford asked,

"Did you notice any pistol or anything of that kind?"

Again, Patterson challenged this line of questioning: "Stay; I object."

"I can certainly show that, your Honor," pleaded Playford.

Judge Stowe shot back, "No. I won't let you show a thing tending to sustain your position." This kind of combative back and forth kept the crowd in rapt attention. It was 11:50 A.M., and court adjourned for lunch.

The afternoon session was marked by the long-anticipated arrival of Senator Daniel Voorhees. The Commonwealth called still more eyewitnesses to the shooting. During cross-examination, Playford pressed one in particular, a local carpenter, for details that would lend credibility to an insanity defense. He asked the witness to "state whether Nutt had not been wild with excitement at that time?"

"He looked to me just like a wild man," the witness confirmed.[39]

Having firmly established that James had killed Dukes, the Commonwealth turned to the target practice undertaken by the defendant and his uncles, Stephen Nutt and Jim Wells. The first witness to this effect was Johnny Messmore, a pasty nine-year-old boy who had been playing with one of the younger Nutt children on the afternoon of Dukes's death and had seen James and his uncles shooting at a board.

Judge Stowe questioned the child to assess his competency to give testimony.

"What is an oath?" the judge inquired.

"It's the truth," Johnny affirmed.

"And what happens to little boys who don't tell the truth?"

"They go to the bad place."

"—And sometimes to the penitentiary," Judge Stowe added. The witness was deemed competent. Johnny Messmore proceeded to describe, without pause or calculation, the target practice as well as Stephen Nutt's remark to his nephew, "Don't fail." The defense decided not to cross-examine the child. Next, the Commonwealth questioned several additional witnesses who had seen or heard the gunfire at the Nutt estate during the target practice.[40]

Ex-Sheriff Hoover offered the day's final testimony. He alleged that on James's first night in jail, the defendant discussed Dukes's death with him in a manner that suggested premeditation. According to Hoover, James said, "It had to be done, and I done it. And I was prepared to do it." With this, the Commonwealth rested its case. James maintained his composure throughout the proceedings, although the edges of his mouth twitched sporadically. For her part, Lizzie broke down and cried for much of the afternoon session.[41]

The defense was not yet prepared to open its case because Senator Voorhees had only recently arrived and the rest of James's legal team had not yet had time to confer with him. It was now 3:30 P.M. and Judge Stowe adjourned court until the following day, with William Playford set to deliver the opening argument for the defense. Ten months earlier, Playford's closing remarks in the Dukes trial failed to persuade a jury to bring justice to Captain Nutt's killer. With James facing the prospect of the hangman's noose, the next morning offered Playford his chance for redemption.[42]

· *Twelve* ·

DEFENSE

As court reconvened for the third day of the trial, temperatures dipped into the teens. More onlookers than ever before packed into the courtroom to hear Playford's opening remarks. He began by highlighting the central theme of the defense's case: James Nutt was overcome by an "irresistible impulse" when he unloaded round after round into Nicholas Dukes. Playford reminded the jurors of James's comment to Officer Pegg that he "couldn't help it." "That, gentlemen of the jury, is the truth," contended Playford.

> We will endeavor to show you, before we close this case, that he was no more responsible for what he did on the occasion than if he had not fired the pistol at all. . . . *His mind at that time was in such a diseased condition, brought about by the wrongs that he and his family had suffered, that he was unable to control his will; that the killing of Nicholas Lyman Dukes was to him an uncontrollable, irresistible impulse; that he had no longer the power to choose between peace and war.*

Playford then tried to cast the events preceding Duke's death in the most sympathetic light possible. He described James Nutt as victim to a familial disposition toward mental illness. James was also slow in intellect and impulsive in nature (traits that the medical establishment considered conducive to insanity). According to Playford, Captain Nutt's sudden death shattered James, who was deeply attached to his father. James failed to return to his commercial school in Rochester after the funeral and instead brooded about the Nutt home with a loss of purpose. And, at that point in time—noted Playford—James had not even learned of the substance of the infamous letters. He was present, however, in the Fayette County courthouse in March when Dukes's letters were read aloud. No one had been more deeply disturbed by the accusations of Lizzie's impurity than James. Playford alleged that James's despair developed into a monomaniacal fixation on vengeance. He would neither eat by day nor sleep by night, passing the small hours pacing in his bedroom. Finally, on June 13, James snapped.[1]

At times, Playford's opening argument veered away from an emphasis on James's purported insanity and toward a distinct—even contradictory—thesis that anyone similarly situated would be justified in committing homicide. "Not in a single instance, in fifty years," Playford maintained,

> has there been a conviction of a man who slew the seducer of his wife, where it was clearly established that he had done it; or where a man had been convicted for the killing of one who had seduced his sister. . . . Courts and juries may fail, as they sometimes do, but just as sure as the Lord reigns above, no man who

ever committed such crimes, as Dukes committed against the Nutt family can go unpunished. . . . Gentlemen, it was the hand of fate that did the shooting. It was the redress of society for the great wrong that this man had committed upon the household of Captain Nutt.

Referring to the prosecution, Playford proclaimed, "Now they would have you erect a gibbet for the hanging of James Nutt, the son. You won't do it. You cannot do it. No twelve Indians would do it, much less citizens of Allegheny County, and of this Commonwealth." Playford concluded by minimizing the significance of the target practice preceding Dukes's death. The very fact that James and his uncles conducted the shooting in the middle of the day, within the view and earshot of so many people, belied any notion that it was part of some surreptitious and premeditated scheme to kill Dukes.[2]

The audience was notably moved by Playford's words. James tried his best to maintain control over his emotions but tears streamed down his face. Although mourning veils covered the faces of James's mother and sister, their own expressions of sorrow became visible when, through the windows of the courtroom, the rising sun reflected for a passing moment off their tear-soaked cheeks.[3]

The defense's first witness was Dr. Smith Fuller, who had a long history with the Nutts. He had served as their family doctor for almost twenty years. During the tortured final moments of Captain Nutt's life, Dr. Fuller was among those physicians summoned to his deathbed. Dr. Fuller also had the honor of opening the indignation meeting in Uniontown in the wake of Dukes's acquittal. Now he testified as a medical expert about a patient he had treated since childhood.

"I would ask you this question, Doctor," Major Brown began. "From your intimate knowledge of James Nutt during nearly his whole lifetime, and down to the present, what is your opinion of James Nutt's mental capacity, and state whether or not he is more or less deficient in all the attributes of intellect?"

The Commonwealth objected, contending that Dr. Fuller's knowledge of mental illness had not been established. Judge Stowe overruled the objection and Dr. Fuller responded:

"I have always believed him to be mentally imbecile, and more or less deficient in all the attributes of intellect."

"Now, Doctor, does that mental condition that you have spoken of tend to destroy his self-control?"

"It would, sir."

"Would it, in your opinion, tend to the production of insanity under the influence of violent disturbance of the feelings, as of rage or grief?"

"It would, in my judgment."

"When any deep impression is established in his mind, as enmity, or for a great injury to himself or to those nearly related to him, would he be inclined to harbor this feeling for a long period of time?"

"I think he would, sir."

"That is your judgment?"

"That is my opinion; yes, sir."

"Would or would not this enmity be likely to increase and become more uncontrollable or menacing towards its object by the lapse of time?"

"It would increase, sir, in my judgment."

"Would he be likely to dwell upon the great injury inflicted upon him by the slayer of his father until he became a monomaniac upon the subject of avenging his father's death?"

"He would be very liable to become a monomaniac under those circumstances, more so than a person of sound mind would be."

"Please state further: Do you think that in this state of mind he would conceive the act of vengeance to be the discharge of duty, or not?"

"I think he would; he would probably do that."

"Are weak, feeble-minded people predisposed to monomania?"

"They are, sir."

It is incomprehensible why the Commonwealth failed to object to this line of questioning on the grounds of leading the witness.

During cross-examination, David Patterson tried to raise doubts about Dr. Fuller's competency to testify on insanity.

"Well, Doctor, have you made any special study of mental diseases?" inquired Patterson.

"Oh, no, sir," Dr. Fuller conceded. "I am only a general practitioner, that is all."[4]

Mrs. Nutt was next called to the stand. Her lengthy testimony—which lasted the rest of the morning session and continued after the midday recess—portrayed James as doltish and impetuous since childhood. She described how James developed an early fascination with firearms and from the age of ten always carried his own gun. James's lawyers hoped to establish with this testimony that their client had not armed himself in a premeditated fashion on June 13 with the intent of shooting Dukes; rather, the defendant was always in possession of a firearm and so happened to have ready access to one when the irresistible impulse to kill overtook him.[5]

According to Mrs. Nutt, her son was despondent following his father's death. James's condition only grew worse after he heard Dukes's letters read aloud in court, she said. Although he remained silent about his inner turmoil, the signs of James's anguish were conspicuous. His appetite waned, and he was prone to sulk about the house, sometimes giving way to tears. Mrs. Nutt further testified that after Dukes was set free, James received a stream of mail about the trial from every corner of the country, including letters, newspaper clippings, and copies of sermons. He saved these materials in a trunk and pored over them repeatedly. When Dukes moved back to Uniontown a few weeks after his acquittal, James sometimes crossed his path in town, returning home in a state of agitation. Mrs. Nutt had worried for her son's safety, suspecting that Dukes feared reprisal from James and might try to kill him preemptively. Accordingly, she warned James to stay away from his father's murderer.[6]

The defense called Mrs. Nutt's mother, Grandma Wells, who corroborated her daughter's testimony in full. Stephen Nutt followed; he, too, depicted his nephew as a slow-witted, impulsive boy who was crestfallen after Captain Nutt's demise. Stephen also addressed the details of the much-discussed target practice. He recalled that they had stood about sixteen feet from the board, and James fired the first shot to establish a mark. Although neither uncle came closer than six inches to that target, James displayed impressive accuracy, hitting the board less than an inch from the original bullet hole. When Stephen unloaded another round, he missed the board completely, he said, a confession that elicited laughter from the courtroom. On the question of whether he uttered the cryptic admonition, "Don't fail," Stephen swore that he had no memory of making any such statement to James. He claimed that if he told his nephew not to fail, it was in reference to protecting Mrs. Nutt's vegetables from potato bugs or perhaps cutting the grass, not an allusion to an assault on Dukes. Stephen Nutt emphatically denied that he had any prior knowledge of James's pending attack, declaring, "I desire to state that as the truth, not only to the jury, but to the world." He insisted that, in fact, he had warned his nephew on several occasions to keep his distance from Dukes.[7]

Mrs. Nutt's brother, Jim Wells, was next in the succession of relatives who took the stand for the defense. His account of James as emotionally distraught conformed to the preceding testimony. It had been a difficult day in court for the defendant. He passed the hours fidgeting uncomfortably in his seat and frequently broke into tears. Still, Playford's masterful opening and Major Brown's skillful questioning of the witnesses impressed the members of the local bar in attendance. Whether the jury, too, was swayed remained a matter for speculation.[8]

When court opened the next morning, Lizzie Nutt was notably absent. She had been relegated to bed by what one reporter referred to as "a severe attack of nervous prostration."[9]

The defense recalled Jim Wells to the stand, and the questioning turned to the subject of the target practice. Wells testified that he had not heard Stephen Nutt tell James, "Don't fail." He, too, claimed that he had cautioned James to avoid Dukes and denied any prior knowledge that James would shoot Dukes. The defense called still more relatives—Mrs. Nutt's cousin and yet another uncle of the defendant—who reinforced the image of a disconsolate James in the months following his father's death.[10]

The morning session also featured the witness who had fallen ill in September and shrugged off death threats in December, Clark Breckenridge. Finally on the stand, Breckenridge revealed how Captain Nutt's revolver came into James's possession. Breckenridge was among the executors of Nutt's estate, and James approached his cousin shortly after the Dukes trial at the bank where Breckenridge worked and inquired about the gun. "Mother said I could have it as it was my father's," James told him. Breckenridge replied that he himself might find use for the firearm but James was insistent and Breckenridge acquiesced. Coroner Sturgeon had retained custody of the weapon until Dukes's acquittal, at which point he turned the revolver over to Playford's law partner, A. D. Boyd. So Breckenridge escorted James to Boyd's office, where the lawyer who had failed to obtain a legal execution of Dukes handed James the gun that he would later use to do away with his father's killer. Under cross-examination from Patterson, Breckenridge provided an eyewitness account of Captain Nutt's death.[11]

When court reconvened in the afternoon, Major Brown sought to offer evidence that Dukes carried a revolver of his own, as well as a knife, on the day of his death. The defense hoped to show that Dukes outfitted himself with weapons because even he understood that his sins against the Nutt family must be repaid in blood. As Playford had said of Dukes in his opening argument,

> His fate was sealed just as unerringly as destiny itself. He knew it when he armed himself with [a] revolver and bowie-knife. He knew that there was a hand somewhere, invisible and unseen, waiting for him, and in his heart of hearts he knew that he must be ever ready to stand on his defense. He could no more walk this earth unharmed.

The Commonwealth protested that any evidence to those ends was irrelevant and thus inadmissible. After all, Dukes made no use of the weapons on the night of his death nor had he issued prior threats to the defendant. Judge Stowe sustained the objection.[12]

The defense proceeded to call Leonora Philipps, who had served as James's teacher for a year when he was a teenager. She characterized his intellect as "much below average" and found that he made no progress despite her providing individual lessons to him after school. Major Brown also submitted records from the 1860s documenting that two of James's relatives on his father's side were legally certified "lunatics."[13]

James's legal team turned to the physicians whose testimony concerning his mental health was vital to his case. The first to take the stand was Dr. A. M. Pollock. Marshall Swartzwelder, for the defense, opened the questioning by asking Dr. Pollock about his experience with insanity in his four decades as a medical practitioner.

"During the course of my life I have seen a great deal of mental diseases," Dr. Pollock testified, "and have kept moderately up with the literature of it; I never paid any special attention to it. As far as I have had an opportunity of observing the disease, I feel competent to give an opinion as an expert, if the question arose."

Patterson interjected: "I submit the question to your Honor as to the competency of this witness to testify as an expert in this matter."

Judge Stowe acknowledged, "It is a pretty hard question to determine who are experts. The Doctor has not made it a specialty as I understand it." The complexities of modern society demanded that members of the learned professions become increasingly specialized. Amid this transition from generalism to specialism, sorting out which physicians possessed the requisite expertise to testify was no easy task. Whatever misgivings Judge Stowe might have had were, in the end, not sufficient to dismiss Dr. Pollock. "By his long practice and familiarity with diseases, and having given it some attention, I think he is competent," the judge concluded. "At all events, he comes so near the line that I don't think I ought to exclude him."[14]

With the witness's expertise passing muster, Swartzwelder posed to Dr. Pollock a "hypothetical case" with facts identical to those set forth by the defense concerning James. At the time, American courts disallowed lawyers from simply asking experts to weigh in on the "ultimate issue" for the jury to decide; that would have usurped the jury's prerogative. Judges, therefore, permitted attorneys to pose hypothetical questions to expert witnesses based on alleged facts that had been submitted in evidence. If the jurors found the factual premises of the question to be true, then they could accept the expert's answer. In this way, courts preserved roles for expert witnesses and lay jurors alike. Swartwelder's hypothetical case emphasized in particular James's weak intellect, despair over his father's death, reaction to Dukes's letters, comment to Officer Pegg—"I couldn't help it"— and the family history of lunacy.[15]

Swartzwelder inquired, "Assuming this to be true, the facts as set forth in this hypothetical case, what is your opinion as to the condition of mind of James Nutt at the time of the firing of this pistol?" Dr. Pollock responded, "The probability is that his mind would not be in a sane condition." The physician further testified that an insane mind could curb an instinct to kill for an extended period of time before eventually submitting to the homicidal urge. The mere presence of Dukes on the street would have been to James "like waving a red flag at a mad bull."[16]

In his cross-examination of Dr. Pollock, Patterson raised a telling question: could a person be free from insanity, then, during the commission of a criminal act, experience a fleeting moment of insanity, only to revert back to a previously sane state directly after the crime? Pollock conceded that such a scenario would indeed be "exceptional."[17]

Patterson moved swiftly to exploit the weakness. He posited his own hypothetical case, in which James exhibited sane behavior just before the shooting by chatting leisurely with a friend, and again after by voicing remorse over the possibility that a stray bullet had hurt an innocent bystander. "What would be your judgment then," asked Patterson, "as to whether the act arose from an insane mind, or from the passions of a sane mind?" Dr. Pollock would not budge from his earlier position, contending that pre-existing insanity could possibly have made no outward showing until an "aggravating occurrence" unleashed a "sudden explosion" of "homicidal mania."[18]

The next physician to testify, Dr. W. H. Daly, had a similar background to the preceding witness—he had treated mental diseases in his many years of medical practice but claimed no particular specialty in the subject. Like Dr. Pollock, Dr. Daly concluded that, based on the hypothetical case, James's lethal vengeance was likely the result of an "uncontrollable impulse." For now, the Commonwealth chose not to cross-examine the witness.[19]

Dr. James Ewing approached the stand. He had been the first physician on the scene at the Jennings House to attend to Captain Nutt's mortal wound, but Dr. Ewing was not in court to rehash the events of that fateful Christmas Eve. Instead, he spoke to James's mental state. Dr. Ewing brought with him the most impressive bona fides yet to the trial, having worked at the Dixmont Insane Asylum for more than two years.[20]

In response to the defense's hypothetical case, Dr. Ewing determined that James Nutt probably suffered from insanity at the time of Dukes's death. During cross-examination, Patterson asked Dr. Ewing to infer from the Commonwealth's version of the hypothetical case—in which James appeared sane immediately before and after the shooting—the chances that the defendant had in fact labored under a diseased condition of mind. Dr. Ewing adhered to his contention that James was most likely insane at the time of the act. But whereas Dr. Pollock stated that a flash of insanity bookended by sane behavior was an unusual occurrence, Dr. Ewing testified that ephemeral instances of insanity were actually common. Patterson saw his opening.

"Is that the doctrine of the authorities?" asked Patterson.

"Yes, sir," Dr. Ewing responded.

"Upon what do you rely for that doctrine?"

"Just general reading on the subject and experience."

"Can you refer to any recognized medical authority who accepts that doctrine?"

"I think that is the accepted doctrine of all the authorities."

"Can you refer to any special one?"

Dr. Ewing could not.[21]

With the testimony of the two physicians in conflict, the Commonwealth recalled Dr. Daly in the hopes of further highlighting the lack of uniformity among the defense's medical experts. Patterson requested that Dr. Daly state whether scientific authorities believed in the rarity of quickly passing insanity, as Dr. Pollock suggested, or its regularity, as Dr. Ewing claimed. Dr. Daly suggested that even the authorities themselves failed to reach consensus on this point. He noted that there were "very high authorities" to be found who supported either position. Indeed, Dr. Daly was correct—the leading experts at the time disagreed on the existence of temporary insanity. When asked to name an American authority who subscribed to the notion of fleeting insanity, Dr. Daly fared better than Dr. Pollock, referencing William Hammond's recently published textbook, *A Treatise on Insanity in Its Medical Relations*. Hammond was the first doctor in the United States to specialize exclusively in neurology, a branch of medicine that at the time encompassed psychoses. He had also testified as an expert in two prominent trials on behalf of defendants who pled insanity after the commission of honor killings.[22]

The defense called Dr. Charles C. Wiley, who had spent six years at Dixmont, including a stint as superintendent of the asylum. He considered James's homicide, as described in the defense's hypothetical case, to be "the act of an irresistible, uncontrollable impulse." When the defense concluded its questioning of Dr. Wiley, Swartzwelder turned to the Commonwealth:

"Cross-examine, gentleman."

"We have no questions to ask the doctor," was Patterson's unexpected response, causing a stir in the courtroom.[23]

Patterson was saving his fire for the following witness, Dr. David W. Riggs, a former assistant surgeon in the army. Like many of the day's physicians under examination, Dr. Riggs had no special expertise in mental illness but had treated some cases of that variety. He, too, found James Nutt to be of "unsound mind" based on the hypothetical case posed by the defense. Under cross-examination, Dr. Riggs affirmed his belief that continuously sane behavior may be punctuated by a single moment of insanity.

"You have treated such cases?" asked Patterson.

"Yes, sir," Dr. Riggs answered.

"Doctor, what necessity would there be for the treatment of cases of that kind, if the insanity passed away immediately after the act?"

"Nothing if the insanity passed away."

Patterson sprung his trap. If an instant of transient insanity required no treatment, then surely Dr. Riggs had *not* in fact dealt with such patients, contrary to his testimony just a moment earlier.

"Well, that is the question I put to you," Patterson explained, "whether you have had under your care, cases where there have been no manifestations of insanity until a sudden outburst occurred, manifesting unsoundness of mind, and then all manifestations of unsoundness of mind passing away at once—have you treated such cases?"

Dr. Riggs succumbed. "No, sir."

"You don't know in your experience of any such cases, doctor?"

"No, sir; where—"

"That's all, doctor," interrupted Patterson.[24]

At this point, the defense recalled Dr. Fuller, the Nutt family physician. Dr. Fuller had already testified, based on his many years of experience with the defendant, that James's mental ability was impaired. But the defense had not yet posed the hypothetical case to him. Now given that opportunity on the stand, Dr. Fuller embarked on a lengthy diatribe in which, contrary to the other medical witnesses, he suggested that James's killing of Dukes had been very much premeditated. The defendant did not experience a momentary flash of insanity, Dr. Fuller claimed, but rather suffered from the sort of mania that involved careful and deliberate plotting. As Dr. Fuller explained it, "Like other maniacs, he was crafty. There is no set of men so crafty as maniacs; there is no set of men who so quietly, so noiselessly, and without a word concoct, develop and execute a plan. A sane man won't do it half so well." The Commonwealth declined to cross-examine and court adjourned for the day.[25]

On Friday, January 18, the Allegheny County courthouse opened for the fifth day of the *Commonwealth v. James Nutt*. The courthouse's system for seating observers was markedly better organized than at the start of the week, and a methodical admission of onlookers replaced the jostling that had been commonplace days earlier. Lizzie was still confined to bed. Although Mrs. Nutt continued to attend the trial, she did not fare much better than her daughter. She passed the day with her hands covering her face, her weary body rocking back and forth.[26]

The defense began the proceedings by recalling Dr. Fuller. Having testified in his capacity as James's lifelong physician and as an expert on the matter of insanity, he now spoke in a third role—as a member of the school board in Uniontown when James was a student. That experience, shared Dr. Fuller, had only served to reinforce his impression of James as a "mental imbecile."[27]

Four more general practitioners each shared his professional opinion that James had suffered from mental illness when he pulled the trigger of his father's gun. Thus concluded the medical testimony. Whatever inconsistencies Patterson exposed among the ten physicians who took the stand and whatever doubts he may have raised about their expertise, all had responded uniformly to the hypothetical case—James Nutt had been insane.[28]

Major Brown moved to admit as evidence Dukes's notorious letters to Captain Nutt as well as Nutt's reply. The Commonwealth raised no objections. The previous March, the reading of Dukes's letters in court prompted James to commit homicide; now, these same letters would be recited once more to exonerate James for that very killing. As it had in March, the task fell to Playford.

Ladies excused themselves from the courtroom before the rehearsal of Dukes's words. The eyes of the crowd followed Mrs. Nutt closely as she made her way toward the exit, with several female family members in tow. James appeared riddled with angst, and he too was removed from the courtroom.[29]

The jurors leaned forward intently as Playford began to read. His pacing was deliberate, his enunciation precise. The members of the jury box remained motionless throughout the reading, save for their faces, as looks of anticipation quickly turned to exasperation. A reporter remarked of the scene, "It was like digging the bones of dead men from their graves and flaunting their rotting cerements in the face of the living." After Playford finished all three letters, court adjourned for lunch.[30]

When the proceedings resumed, excerpts from the *Republican Standard*'s coverage of the Dukes trial were read into the record. According to Mrs. Nutt's testimony, this newspaper in particular consumed James's attention in the months between Dukes's acquittal and his death. With this, Senator Voorhees announced that the defense closed its case.[31]

The Commonwealth had the opportunity to call rebuttal witnesses, whose testimony was by rule limited to the refutation of specific evidence offered by the defense. Ex–District Attorney Isaac Johnson examined nine such witnesses during the remainder of the afternoon session in the hopes of establishing James's sanity. They included schoolmates of the defendant, men who worked at the Nutt estate, and other townsfolk who were familiar with James. Although only a medical expert could offer an opinion on the hypothetical case, a layman was permitted to state whether in his personal interactions with the defendant he had seen symptoms of insanity.[32]

Johnson asked each witness whether James displayed an unsound mind. To what was surely the frustration of the Commonwealth, much of the testimony actually strengthened the defense's case. Although four of the nine witnesses answered as expected that James had displayed no signs of insanity, another four maintained that they lacked sufficient opportunity to observe James and, accordingly, could draw no firm conclusions about his mental condition. One flatly declared that James was indeed of "unsound mind." Under cross-examination from Major Brown, one of these witnesses, a childhood companion of the defendant, confirmed that the other boys in Uniontown had considered James "crazy." Another of these rebuttal witnesses, a Uniontown journalist, provided testimony during cross-examination that supported the defense's theory that their client was a monomaniac. "Sometimes he would dwell on one subject for two or three months," the journalist told the court. Attorneys for the defense were buoyant as they watched the Commonwealth suffer misfortune at the hands of its own witnesses until court adjourned for the day. The Commonwealth would have to wait until the following morning to reverse the damage, if possible.[33]

Lizzie reappeared in court at her mother's side the next day—the trial's sixth—exhibiting signs of a full recuperation. James, too, looked revitalized; in the wake of the Commonwealth's disastrous performance the day before, the defendant had enjoyed his soundest night of sleep since coming to Pittsburgh. His eyes were notably free of the bloodshot sorrow that had plagued them for much of the week.[34]

The Commonwealth began the morning session by requesting permission from Judge Stowe to admit to the stand two rebuttal witnesses who were prepared to testify that months before Dukes's death, James made comments indicating his desire for vengeance. If allowed, this evidence would undermine the defense's theory that James had acted on a sudden and irresistible impulse. The defense objected to both witnesses on the grounds that their statements lay outside the permissible sphere of rebuttal witness testimony. Judge Stowe concurred, ruling, "While the proposed evidence would have been entirely competent for the Commonwealth in chief, I do not consider it proper now offered by way of rebuttal to [the] defendant's case."[35]

The Commonwealth enjoyed better luck with its subsequent two witnesses, whom Judge Stowe allowed to testify that they saw James encounter Dukes on a number of instances in Uniontown following Dukes's acquittal. Prosecutors hoped to show that the sight of Dukes on several occasions clearly had *not* provoked in James an irrepressible, homicidal urge.[36]

The Commonwealth then revived for a final time its failed strategy of calling James's acquaintances and asking them to infer whether his mind were diseased. To this end, Johnson examined Robert Hunt, a close friend of James since boyhood, who corroborated the well-established proposition that the defendant possessed an inferior intellect. "He never learned very fast," Hunt recalled, adding, "but still he could keep up to me." The crowd rewarded Hunt's self-deprecation with laughter. During cross-examination, Major Brown elicited testimony from Hunt in support of the defense—the witness described James as quick to temper, which dovetailed with the defense's theory that the shooting of Dukes was impulsive rather than premeditated.[37]

Patterson submitted as evidence a copy of Congressman Boyle's closing argument from the Dukes trial and official documentation of Dukes's acquittal. "May it please the court, the Commonwealth here rests its case," announced Patterson. Judge

Stowe inquired whether the defense had any evidence to offer in challenge to the rebuttal testimony. "We have nothing, your Honor," Senator Voorhees replied.[38]

After a recess for lunch, the defense attempted a stunning gambit. Swartzwelder proposed that the court forgo closing arguments altogether and proceed immediately to the judge's charge. He claimed that the verdict was inevitable and there was little point in delaying James's deliverance. The courtroom was shocked. Lawyers for the Commonwealth jumped to their feet and objected to such an extraordinary departure from trial procedure.[39]

Judge Stowe sided with the Commonwealth—closing arguments would be presented in accordance with protocol. Many in attendance thought that the defense was merely bluffing. Perhaps James's legal team knew that the Commonwealth would never accede to its request and made the suggestion purely to signal confidence in its case to the jurors. It was now a Saturday, and court adjourned until Monday morning.[40]

The intervening Sabbath was a time for prayer. James attended the religious service available to prisoners in the local jail. The jurors were permitted to worship at the Smithfield Street Methodist Episcopal Church after court officials received assurances that the resident minister would not make reference to the Nutt trial. Meanwhile, Mrs. Nutt and Lizzie discreetly joined the congregation of the North Avenue Methodist Church. At his hotel, Senator Voorhees read from the Bible. The hour was soon approaching when Voorhees would need to marshal his rare oratorical gifts and persuade twelve men to spare the life of an American hero.[41]

· *Thirteen* ·

DECISION

WHEN THE TRIAL RESUMED ON JANUARY 21, THE ORDERLY
seating of spectators that characterized the latter days of the
trial gave way to the chaos that marked its start. Around 2,000
curiosity seekers were turned away at the doors; the elbowing
among them was intense. Some men were hurt, albeit not seri-
ously, and a few women fainted. The prisoner was conveyed to
his seat at 9:00 A.M. His mother and sister assumed their usual
places behind him.[1]

Each side was allotted up to three and a half hours to address
the jury. Isaac Johnson, the ex–District Attorney from Fayette
County, spoke first for the Commonwealth. Knowing full well that
the crowd's sympathies lay with the prisoner, Johnson seemed
anxious. His hands quivered as he grasped the railing that sepa-
rated the jury from the rest of the courtroom; Johnson's voice
was no less shaky. According to Johnson, James Nutt was hardly
a monomaniac who suddenly snapped into an ephemeral state
of insanity at the sight of his father's killer on that fateful night.
Rather, the defendant deliberately waited for an opportune moment

and when given a clear line of sight to Dukes's back, he fired. Johnson highlighted evidence that suggested premeditation, including Stephen Nutt's alleged exhortation, "Don't fail," as well as Sheriff Hoover's testimony that James, just hours after the shooting, insisted, "It had to be done; I have done it, and I was prepared to do it."[2]

It was striking, Johnson noted, that those who testified to James's alleged distress in the months preceding Dukes's death were all related to the defendant, whereas disinterested townsfolk—who witnessed James encounter Dukes on the street without incident— saw in the defendant no signs of aggravation. Johnson then made the ill-advised decision to chastise Mrs. Nutt for allowing her admittedly feeble-minded son to carry a firearm since boyhood. This reproach brought hisses from the audience and the court crier in turn demanded quiet. An acquittal now, warned Johnson, would serve as an invitation to every potential vigilante and undermine social order. Johnson concluded his fifty-minute address with an appeal to the rule of law: "The time has not yet come when wrongs done—no matter what they may be—are sufficient legal excuse for taking life."[3]

Before David Patterson used the balance of the Commonwealth's time, the defense presented its closing argument, with Major Brown speaking first and Senator Voorhees following. The courtroom fell silent as Major Brown's slim frame rose, his pallid face bearing an expression of solemnity. He began by countering the Commonwealth's suggestion that setting James free would lead to an anarchic string of extralegal killings. There would be no need for that kind of bloodshed, Major Brown explained, because "there are no Dukes alive to-day, unless you would find one among the twelve men made infamous by having acquitted him." With this, the crowd broke into applause.[4]

Major Brown rehearsed the tragic succession of events that culminated in Dukes's death, beginning with the infamous letters that constituted an "attack upon the citadel of virtue and honor." After that calamitous Christmas Eve, James returned home to a father lifeless in his coffin, a mother ill with grief, and a sister reeling from accusations of impropriety. When Dukes walked free, the world cried out for justice, and James was moved "to avenge his father's death, and his sister's imputed dishonor." The unrivaled indignities to which James was subjected would have induced a man of soundest possible mind to insanity, all the more so an "imbecile" such as the defendant.[5]

The medical experts all agreed that James suffered from insanity on the evening in question, Major Brown reminded the jurors. What's more, James told Officer Pegg in the heat of the moment, "I couldn't help it," further suggesting a case of impulsive insanity. And the Commonwealth's rebuttal witnesses largely reinforced the defense's case. Major Brown compared Dukes to Judas, an analogy that drew applause from the courtroom. Judas at least had been contrite, Brown noted. Dukes, on the other hand, showed no remorse, instead parading the streets of Uniontown after his trial with brazen disregard for the Nutts. Major Brown closed his remarks by exhorting the jurors "to meet the prayer of civilization, and restore this boy to his broken-hearted mother. Your debt of honor demands it, decency claims it, immortal truth and impartial justice require it."[6]

After a midday recess, court reconvened for the address that the eager throng had long awaited. Two members of the judiciary took advantage of their status as judges to secure optimal seats for viewing the performance, joining Judge Stowe on the bench. Senator Voorhees, with his light hair and dark eyes, began his appeal.[7]

Never in American history, claimed Voorhees, had a jury returned an unfavorable verdict to a defendant who spilled blood for honor: "No man, young or old, father or son, brother or whatever relation he bore to the family—the male member of it who avenged its outraged honor as this boy has done, has ever had the hand of the law laid upon him." Senator Voorhees recognized that, technically, the letter of the law criminalized killings of the variety perpetrated by his client, and he used his closing argument to advocate reform that would bring the law into formal accord with the findings of juries:

> One of the problems to me, gentlemen of the jury, has been for some time past what the law ought to do to move up to the findings of juries . . . so as to make one in harmony with the other, for the written law of juries in every part of the civilized globe is, that the man who invades another man's home and rifles that home of its honor, takes his life in his hands. . . . Do you say that it is injurious to the peace and welfare of society to ho such a doctrine? On the contrary, it is a preserver of society.

By upholding cherished values such as female purity, honor killing undergirded rather than undermined the social order.[8]

To be sure, Senator Voorhees paid lip service to the defense's insanity plea, arguing that "the destruction of a home" creates an "uncontrollable impulse even in sound minds." But he also explicitly insisted of James's vengeance, "Such an act is right in itself." In that vein, Voorhees suggested that had *he* been the man in whom Captain Nutt confided his troubles with Dukes, "I would have told him, 'take a double-barrel shot gun, fill it four inches deep in each chamber with buckshot and kill him on the street wherever you may see him.' May God forget me in mercy if I wouldn't have told him so." The crowd broke into applause yet again, prompting Judge Stowe to threaten arrest for any further clamor.[9]

Senator Voorhees suggested, just as William Playford had, that the hand of fate was at work in Dukes's death. After all, James used his dead father's pistol, the bullets penetrated their target with uncanny precision, and Dukes perished within feet from where he had deposited his letters to Captain Nutt. "Does it not seem to you, gentlemen, that there is a power in these things that defies analysis in court?" Voorhees inquired. Dismissing Johnson's criticism that Mrs. Nutt should not have allowed her son to use a pistol at such a young age, Senator Voorhees asked, "Has he killed anybody that ought not to have been killed?" Judge Stowe was chagrined at the muffled laughter that escaped from the mass of sympathetic onlookers. Voorhees rebuked Johnson: "What right has he to complain that this boy had a pistol in his hands? I thank God that he had a pistol, and I thank God he knew how to use it." And so did the nation, as Senator Voorhees was eager to point out: "The sound of the shot rang through this country, and brought no regrets."[10]

Voorhees repudiated Dukes's allegations about Lizzie, observing that she had plainly not born a child. He acknowledged that, in theory, Lizzie could have been pregnant and undergone an abortion, but she was under intense public scrutiny after her father's death, rendering impossible such an illicit arrangement. No, Lizzie had rejected Dukes's sexual advances; his subsequent letters were undoubtedly "the revenge of baffled lust." Senator Voorhees closed by admonishing the jurors not to condemn James to the gallows, warning ominously, "Gentlemen of the jury, take this case, and let a verdict of guilty be rendered, and see what it would be like."[11]

Over the course of the nearly two hours that Voorhees spoke, many of the women in attendance were moved to tears, and two of the jurors frequently dried their eyes. After Voorhees finished, it was some time before the proceedings could continue as people crowded the senator to shake his hand. Even one of the guest members of the judiciary who was sitting with Judge Stowe descended from the bench and, with watery eyes, approached Senator Voorhees to express gratitude for his touching words.[12]

The courtroom went quiet as Patterson rose to offer his summation to the jury. He removed his brown and blue scarf, placed it on a stack of papers, and began to speak. There lay at the heart of this case a harsh and inescapable truth, said Patterson: "James Nutt shot down a human being on the public streets of a neighboring town with a deadly weapon." Patterson castigated Senator Voorhees for trying to frighten the jurors into an acquittal. Whereas "the learned Senator from Indiana comes to picture to you the terror that would follow you if you dare to render a verdict of conviction," Patterson challenged the jury to defy this kind of scaremongering. Nor should sentimentality influence the verdict; the rule of law was the only sure guide:

> Gush, mere gush, is short lived; but the law which preserves our lives, our property, and everything of value to us on this earth, is needed, and will be needed, long after you and I are gone, and James Nutt and his family are unheard of.

Patterson rejected the proposition that the American justice system had never punished the perpetrator of an honor killing, referencing an 1874 trial over which Judge Stowe himself had presided alongside another judge. In that case, a man stabbed his sister's seducer to death and the court's charge to the jury set forth that the circumstances provoking the assault were insufficient to reduce the crime from murder to manslaughter, much less justify an acquittal.[13]

Patterson dismissed the testimony of the "so-called medical experts," emphasizing that all but two were general practitioners with no particular focus on mental illness. The defendant's failure to exhibit signs of insanity at any point before or after the shooting suggested that James's condition of mind was sound. And the medical testimony was inconsistent. Patterson contended that James's lethal action was motivated by something other than insanity. Captain Nutt had warned Dukes that even if he died defending his daughter's honor, vengeance would still come. "My accidental death will not stop proceedings nor gain you immunity," Nutt wrote. James understood his father's letter as essentially posthumous instructions to finish the deed, claimed Patterson. America itself had demanded as much:

> The public press, and the citizens in their public meetings, and the general temper all over the land . . . led this young man not to insanity—nothing of the kind—but to the belief of a sane mind, that if he would commit this act he would not be punished for it, but would be applauded.

Confident that he would be exalted as a hero and absolved of wrongdoing, James decided to take another man's life.[14]

Turning to Dukes's letters, Patterson intimated that the allegations about Lizzie were perhaps partly true. James thus far had remained still during Patterson's remarks, but now he coiled his hands into fists and clenched his jaw. Patterson also dismissed the notion that fate was at play; it had been Clark Breckenridge, not fate, who furnished James with his father's gun. The accuracy of the defendant's shots, moreover, were the unsurprising result of his long-standing experience with firearms, including the target practice with his uncles hours before the fatal encounter. Patterson predicted that if society embraced extralegal vengeance as readily as Senator Voorhees did, countless women were destined to join Captain Nutt's wife and Dukes's mother in mourning. After speaking for more than two hours, Patterson closed by reminding the jurors that they had sworn an oath to God to adhere to the law and would, accordingly, answer to the "great Being" when "you come to give in your last account."[15]

In sharp contrast to Senator Voorhees's easy affability, Patterson's delivery was methodical, his approach calculated, his tone icy. "His eyes cast down," wrote one reporter, "to dig the foundation for a gallows." Patterson required no superfluous room for pacing as he spoke, only enough space to press his right index finger into his left palm to emphasize a given point. At his side for ready reference were seven books of law, from which he read aloud intermittently. Patterson seemed oblivious to the packed crush of spectators and instead fixed his gaze on the twelve men in the jury box. Although the jurors were weary from a long week of testimony and argument, Patterson commanded their attention throughout his address. One of the jurors who had cried during Senator Voorhees's argument now fidgeted in his chair. The others patiently absorbed Patterson's words, periodically eyeing the defendant's reaction. Few in the crowd could claim to have anticipated such a strong close for the Commonwealth.[16]

After a recess, court reconvened in the early evening for Judge Stowe's charge to the jury. He thanked both sets of lawyers for maintaining a high sense of professionalism amid this public spectacle. Turning to the jurors, the judge impressed upon them that they acted not on their own behalves but as agents of the law who were bound by its dictates:

> You have nothing to do with the result of your verdict. If it should bring disastrous results, it is the law that produces them. If it should bring joy and rejoicing to sorrowing hearts, it is the law that brings them about.

He explained the various grades of homicide and elaborated on the legal doctrines concerning insanity, concluding that the case before the jury rested on one fundamental matter: "In order to relieve the prisoner from legal responsibility for the killing of Dukes, the jury must be satisfied from the evidence that, at the time of the killing, his will was so far overmastered and controlled that he was powerless to resist the commission of the act."[17]

Judge Stowe expressed incredulity that a flash of insanity could take hold of a person at the moment a crime was committed, without a hint of insanity beforehand or afterward. Still, the judge acknowledged that every physician under examination testified that James Nutt had indeed been insane when he pulled the trigger. The jurors were in no way beholden to the medical testimony, Stowe informed them, and were free to afford it whatever weight they saw fit.[18]

Because of the unique circumstances of this case, the burden of proof differed from that of a typical criminal trial, and Judge Stowe clarified the standard under which the defense here labored. Usually, the burden fell to the Commonwealth to prove a defendant's guilt beyond a reasonable doubt. However, James's lawyers conceded that their client killed Nicholas Dukes. The question was merely whether the defendant suffered from an insanity that provoked in him an irresistible impulse to avenge his father's death. It was insufficient for the defense merely to raise a reasonable doubt about James's sanity; the prisoner's lawyers needed to establish that, more likely than not, he acted at the behest of a diseased mind.[19]

Judge Stowe reminded the jury that there was no legal protection for honor killing. "You must not forget, from first to last," he counseled,

> that the law does not under any circumstances justify a private citizen in taking it into his own hands by way of punishment or revenge. No wrongs, however great or aggravating, of a character

such as those alleged to have been heaped upon the prisoner, his father, or the members of his family, can operate as any legal excuse for the killing of Dukes.

The judge concluded his charge with a plea for dispassion, calling on the jurors to render their verdict "regardless of fear, favor or affection." Throughout the charge, James stared intently at Judge Stowe. At one point, Lizzie lifted her veil and took in her surroundings before covering her face once more.[20]

It was now 7:50 P.M., and the dozen men in the jury box retired from the courtroom to determine whether James would return to Uniontown in a coffin. The prisoner appeared unsettled as he watched them depart. But when Mrs. Nutt and Lizzie came over to comfort James, his distress melted into a smile.[21]

Judge Stowe expected that the jury might render its verdict quickly and kept the court open for the time being. After forty minutes passed with no indication that the jury would return imminently, court adjourned. The failure of the jury to summarily acquit the defendant was a source of concern for James's supporters. Still, the pool halls of Pittsburgh were offering three-to-one odds that James would walk free.[22]

The jury reached its verdict the next day at 7:00 A.M. As court prepared to reconvene in a few hours' time, spectators gathered in droves and tensely waited for the opening of the courtroom. The entrance to the chamber was finally unlocked at 9:00 A.M., and the crowd surged forward. Forty-five minutes passed before the defendant arrived. The jury box remained empty. James's relatives stared expectantly at the door through which the jurors were to emerge, although Mrs. Nutt and Lizzie were absent. Theirs had been a restless night, and they elected to wait for the news in Major Brown's office nearby.[23]

Amid the throng that packed the courtroom, rumors spread that the verdict was acquittal. Others expressed anxiety that the length of time required by the jury to reach consensus was an indication that it found the defendant guilty as charged. At 10:00 A.M., the twelve members of the jury appeared.[24]

For seven months, the American people awaited the trial of James Nutt. For seven days, they read in the papers the testimony, the evidence, and the arguments. Now, finally, the jury was prepared to announce whether James's defense of his family's honor would cost him his life.

James was not seated with his counsel but rather locked in the prisoner's box. As he faced the prospect of dying a martyr, the full gravity of the circumstances appeared to overcome him. Never before had he seemed so alone.[25]

"Let there be no demonstration of approval or disapproval," Judge Stowe mandated.

"Prisoner, stand up," the court clerk instructed James. The clerk turned to the jurors and asked, "Gentlemen, have you agreed upon a verdict?"

"We have," they responded.

"What say you, guilty or not guilty?"

"Not guilty," replied the foreman.[26]

A thousand voices cried out in celebration. Men who had been waiting in the hallway heard the cheering and raced downstairs, proclaiming to the crowds in the street, "Acquitted! Acquitted!" The news was instantly carried by word of mouth throughout the city. Amid subfreezing temperatures, the streets of Pittsburgh exploded with jubilee. Some danced, others sobbed for joy. Major Brown's son caught wind of the excitement and ran to deliver the news to James's mother and sister. "They're cheering, they're cheering," he relayed. "It's all right. He's acquitted." Lizzie began to weep uncontrollably and touched her lips to her mother's weary face. Mrs. Nutt, moist with tears of her own, kept repeating the words, "Thank God, thank God." Only a day before, she feared she would have to bury her eldest son alongside his father. With the law's assent, James Nutt would live, and with him, the cause of honor.[27]

· *Fourteen* ·

Vindication

🌿

When the foreman announced the verdict, James collapsed into his chair as if in shock. It was then clarified that the jury had not found the defendant simply not guilty; rather, James was not guilty by reason of insanity. Unless and until the court declared that the insanity was temporary and the defendant of sound mind once again, he would remain in the custody of the state. "The prisoner is remanded to jail," Judge Stowe announced. James made his way through a cheering crowd to the passageway that led from the courtroom back to his cell. As the members of the jury exited the chamber, enthusiastic spectators reached out their hands in congratulations. An acquittal on the grounds of insanity had hardly been a foregone conclusion for these jurors—on the first ballot, only six favored that verdict. Three proposed finding James not guilty without any mention of insanity, and another three found him guilty as charged. It appeared that not guilty by reason of insanity was a compromise verdict to bring these various contingencies into accord.[1]

Major Brown made a motion for the court to inquire into his client's current mental state, insisting, "I have no doubt in my own mind of his sanity at the present time." Judge Stowe agreed to hold a hearing the following day to determine whether the insanity that had absolved James from guilt was now replaced by a sane condition of mind that would justify his release.[2]

Although the judge had been a paragon of impartiality throughout the proceedings, his true sentiments became evident after court adjourned for the day. He descended from the bench bearing a smile and began to shake hands with those who had labored for acquittal. Judge Stowe's public duty had required a fastidious adherence to the law, but now he felt free to advocate honor killing. "For my own private self I have no hesitancy in saying a proper retribution followed the acts of a villain," he confessed to the press. "I could scarcely have done less as a private individual myself." Had James been found guilty, Stowe would have gladly added his name to a petition for a pardon. The judge also quoted with pride his son, who vowed, "If that man had shot down my father in the way he killed Captain Nutt, I would not have shot him—I'd have cut him up so that there would not have been a piece as big as an inch left of him." A wide grin spread across Judge Stowe's face as he recalled his son's willingness to resort to bodily mutilation.[3]

Harrisburg had teemed with anticipation all morning. The offices of American Rapid and Western Union in the capital were inundated with requests for any word of the verdict. Finally, at 10:30 A.M., the *Harrisburg Telegraph* posted the news on its office windows and passersby voiced their exuberance. A. D. Boyd, for the defense, personally telegraphed Treasurer Baily to inform him of the jury's decision. And, as expected, reports of the acquittal were met with celebration in Uniontown.[4]

Mrs. Nutt and Lizzie were flooded with friends who came to Major Brown's office to share in this moment of joy punctuating a long year of sorrow. The dozen men who acquitted James soon arrived and provided Mrs. Nutt with a handwritten duplicate of their verdict.[5]

Her son may not have been guilty but neither was he free. As he had for the past seven months, James spent the night in jail.

Several physicians appointed by Judge Stowe met with James in his cell the next morning to assess his mental state. In an indication of Stowe's sympathy for the defendant, most of the doctors whom the judge tapped for this duty had appeared as expert witnesses for the defense. Court reconvened later that morning. In came James, light-hearted and smiling. His uncles Stephen Nutt and Jim Wells were in attendance. Again, Mrs. Nutt and Lizzie chose to wait in Major Brown's office.[6]

Although not a physician, the warden of the jail in Pittsburgh was the first on the stand, swearing under oath that James was the sanest prisoner who had ever come into his custody. Four medical witnesses then testified that James was now of sound mind and posed no threat to the public. Major Brown prepared to call a fifth expert but Judge Stowe interrupted: "I do not think more testimony necessary." In truth, before the day's testimony began, the judge had already drafted a decision authorizing James's release. After referring to the relevant law concerning the discharge of the formerly insane, Judge Stowe turned to the acquitted and, with a warm countenance, said, "James, you can go."[7]

As soon as Stowe uttered his final declaration setting James at liberty, spectators swarmed "Young Nutt" to offer their congratulations. He eventually emerged on the street and, surrounded by an applauding crowd of hundreds, walked to Major Brown's office. When James arrived, his mother and sister sobbed as they enveloped him in their arms.[8]

Strangers came forward to request James's autograph, and he willingly obliged. Some of the jurors reappeared; one even offered to assist James if he encountered any trouble from Dukes's friends. "Jimmy, if they do anything to you in Fayette, send them down and we will see to them," the juror assured him. The crush of onlookers grew so immense that the police had to disperse the crowd to keep the street clear. In speaking to the press, James denied that his attack on Dukes was premeditated; indeed, he claimed to have no recollection of killing Dukes at all. "The time from I began to shoot till I quit is now, and always has been, a blank to me," James maintained. He also confirmed that no one in his family had directed him to seek vengeance. The country may have lionized James, but he rejected any pretenses to courage. "I am no hero," James insisted, "nor do I want to be."[9]

The press was eager to know what James planned to do with his life but he admitted that he was unsure. General Blakely suggested that James should work on his Uncle Jim's farm. A more unusual opportunity had already surfaced—an entrepreneurial museum manager offered James a substantial sum to put himself on display. James showed no indication that he would accept.[10]

A carriage soon arrived to carry James and his family to Major Brown's home for lunch. Afterward, the Nutts set off for the Grant Street train station to commence the southward journey home. Hordes of people lined the railway at every stop along the way to voice their support for James. At the station in Union-town, an admiring throng awaited the village's most celebrated citizen. Mrs. Nutt requested that no formal ceremonies be conducted upon their arrival. Still, many in the crowd reached out their hands to James before he boarded his carriage for the short ride to his father's mansion.[11]

James's acquittal was front-page news nationwide. The press coverage focused on the widespread support for this vindication of honor. In West Virginia, the *Wheeling Register* anticipated, "Thousands, nay millions, will learn with joy this morning that James Nutt has been restored a free man to the home into which so much sorrow has come and whose honor he so well defended." The *Trenton Evening Times* reported that "even without evidence of insanity the public would have felt that only justice had been done by the son." The jury in James's trial was hardly singular in a nation committed to honor killing. As the *New York Herald* asked rhetorically, "How many men are there who would not hesitate to act as James Nutt did under the same provocation, and how many jurors are there who would not do as the Pittsburg jury has done?" Among those countrymen delighted by the acquittal was the president, Chester Arthur. "I am glad the young man has got off," affirmed the president. "Anything else would have been an outrage on the reputation of the Keystone State." James G. Blaine—a former secretary of state and future Republican nominee for the presidency—was even more emphatic in his advocacy of honor killing: "I should say that Nutt was justified in shooting Dukes if ever man were justified in taking the life of another, and that the jury was justified in acquitting him."[12]

Newspapers across the country not only described popular approval of the trial's outcome but also joined the public in endorsing the verdict. In Indiana, the *Fort Wayne Daily News* declared, "No one who loves justice can regret the action of the jury." Louisville's *Courier-Journal* lauded the jurors for recognizing that James had fulfilled his obligation to "vindicate the majesty of that higher law which is supreme, and which must continue to be relied on until our courts do their duty." In the same vein, the *New Haven Evening Register* reasoned, "If deliberate murder was ever justifiable, that of the murder of the coward Dukes by James Nutt was." Although the jury was overwhelmingly Republican, there were no accusations of political scheming. Honor was a value spanning partisan divides, and papers of every persuasion championed James's freedom.[13]

According to the *Morning Oregonian*, James's shooting of Dukes was not an indication of the defendant's insanity but rather the best evidence of a sound mind. "The killing of the foul monster Dukes was an act of the highest and most approved sanity," the *Oregonian* insisted. The press largely lamented that James's attorneys had to resort to an obviously fictional insanity plea when their client was, of course, sane and the killing warranted. As Washington, DC's *Evening Critic* asserted,

The jury did right in acquitting young Nutt. But it did wrong in rendering a verdict of "not guilty *because of insanity.*" There is no doubt but that jury believed young Nutt did right in killing the seducer of his sister and the murderer of his father. Why not have said so without qualification.

The *Cincinnati Commercial Gazette* suggested that a straight not-guilty verdict would have had greater chilling effect on would-be seducers by serving as "public notification that, if the law fails to convict for murder, and worse than murder, he who is most deeply wounded by its inefficiency is justified in inflicting punishment."[14]

Several newspapers contended that the best means to reconcile society's support for honor killing with laws that prohibited the practice was for states to legalize honor-bound bloodshed. Echoing Senator Voorhees's closing argument, the *Decatur Daily Republican* in Illinois advised,

> There ought to be a statute more clearly defining what constitutes justifiable homicide, so that the man who, like James Nutt, avenged the death of his father and vindicated the honor of his sister, would not have to claim that he was insane in order to escape punishment that he in no way deserved.[15]

Although the support for James's release was broad, a minority of papers voiced discontent with his acquittal. The *New York Times* denounced the verdict as reflecting a lack of "regard for the sanctity of human life and for the laws of the land." Still, the *Times* had to concede that its perspective ran counter to that of the general public: "It must be admitted that popular sympathy was so clearly on the side of the prisoner at the bar that his conviction would have been greeted with a burst of wrath."[16]

Whether one stood with the majority in celebrating James's liberty or spoke out against the conventional wisdom by decrying lawlessness, few, if any, believed that James Nutt had been insane for even a moment. The perverse irony of the Dukes–Nutt affair was that James's insanity would prove, in the end, neither fictional nor temporary.

Epilogue

By the 1890s, James Nutt had returned to obscurity, managing a farm that his mother owned near Horton, Kansas. The editor of the *Horton Headlight*, Lucien Smyth, thought that his readers might appreciate how a local resident once played a central role in an episode of national renown. On January 17, 1895, Smyth published a brief article recounting the great Dukes–Nutt saga. The story was a harmless human-interest piece, but it stirred something deep within James. He confronted Smyth in the editor's office armed with a fully loaded revolver, intending to repay the editor's ink with blood. Known for his sunny temperament and cordial manner, Smyth desperately searched for words of appeasement. He eventually prevailed upon James that the article intended no offense, and James wandered out as night approached.[1]

The demons that haunted James had retreated only briefly. On his way home, James stopped at the Payton family residence. James knew the Paytons well—they had worked on his farm at one point and considered James akin to a brother. It was close to

9:00 P.M. and the evening was unusually cold, even for February. Mr. Payton was away in Missouri working as an ice-cutter, but his wife Jesse, a twenty-eight-year-old mother of five, invited James in and offered to prepare supper. After finishing his meal and praising Jesse for her kindness, James inexplicably drew his revolver and began to fire at his hostess. The Payton's hired hand, Leonard Colnan, heard shooting and burst into the house to find Jesse reeling from gunshot wounds. James turned his weapon on Colnan and struck him with his final two bullets. Despite his pain, Colnan mustered the strength to seize an ax and battered James into submission. He bound James's limbs and set off for help from the nearest neighbor, a half-mile away.[2]

Jesse Payton's condition was deemed critical and her prospect of survival limited. Colnan, it appeared, would recover. A constable escorted a blood-spattered James into the custody of the sheriff. At first, James was taken to the nearby community of Muscotah, but the presence of a lynch mob there demanding James's life prompted the authorities to move him to a jail in Atchinson, some twenty-five miles to the east. Asked whether he had any statement to make, James said only, "No, I have not. Please keep it quiet so that mother will not hear of it. She has had enough trouble already."[3]

Indeed, Mrs. Nutt had bore sorrows even greater than her husband's untimely death. In 1884, several months after James was acquitted for killing Dukes, she buried two of her daughters— Annie, age sixteen, and Nellie, not yet a teenager—who both died from contaminated water. Lizzie, at least, offered a ray of light amid the dark clouds of Mrs. Nutt's life, marrying a traveling salesman from a nearby town. But this latest tragedy in Kansas could not possibly escape Mrs. Nutt's attention. James's previous celebrity ensured that his assault at the Payton home became a national story. His mother received word of the attack shortly after James's arrest.[4]

Miraculously, Jesse Payton recovered. James would stand trial for attempted double murder. As he waited in the county jail for his court date, James could at least look forward every Sunday to two visitors—his wife, whom he married almost two years earlier, and their baby. James's lawyer sought a change of venue to a neighboring county given the strong local antipathy toward his client but the court refused.[5]

In a trial that made headlines nationwide, a haggard-looking James sat beside his spouse, and together they listened to Jesse Payton on the witness stand recite the details of the attack that nearly claimed her life. Once more, James pled insanity. His counsel submitted evidence of his hereditary disposition for mental illness; James's mother and one of his brothers provided depositions testifying to the defendant's weak mind. But these efforts proved futile. The public that once championed James as an American icon turned against him in the wake of his senseless violence. There were no adoring crowds to greet him, no subscription funds to pay for his defense, no sympathetic editorials demanding his freedom. When the Kansas jury found him guilty, James remained stoic. He was sentenced to fifteen years in the state penitentiary.[6]

In 1884, James had insisted on the day of his release that he was no hero. Perhaps he knew then that when he lodged a fatal bullet in the heart of his father's assassin, it was not honor alone that compelled him.

Afterword

T HE DUKES–NUTT AFFAIR REVEALS THAT A CULTURE OF honor—including its sanction of extralegal killing—was not unique to the American South but in fact a national phenomenon during the Gilded Age. Endorsements of the vigilante execution attempted by Captain Nutt and carried out by his son could be found in newspapers from states as varied as Massachusetts, Nevada, Ohio, Georgia, Oregon, and New York. The minority who spoke out against honor killing conceded that public opinion was squarely behind the Nutt family. Public subscription funds nationwide paid for James's legal counsel. Perhaps most striking was the array of government officials—legislators, judges, even the president (a New Yorker no less)—who advocated the violent defense of honor outside the boundaries of the law. The killings in Uniontown and the ensuing trials compelled Americans in every region to express an abiding commitment to the so-called "unwritten law" that one man could kill another who violated the honor of his female relative.[1]

Violence lay at the core of honor—if a patriarch were unwilling to resort to physical, even lethal, aggression in defense of honor, then the ideal was nothing more than an illusion. But if honor were prized above life itself, then its power was great indeed to reinforce social norms and punish deviants. Honor-bound violence assumed three primary forms: the duel, the lynch mob, and the lone vigilante. All three were present in the Dukes–Nutt saga.[2]

Formal dueling, a European import, was a highly ritualistic affair for gentlemen, complete with an elaborate set of rules. When a given party was offended, he did not demand satisfaction directly from his adversary but rather issued a letter to the offending party that was handled by a friend, known as a "second." The adversary, in turn, offered a reply through a second of his own. This reply may have put forward reparation for the offense or not, but in either case all correspondence was written in a gentlemanly manner. Seconds shouldered the responsibility of calming their principals and encouraging amends. Any communication between the principals occurred strictly between their seconds.[3]

If peaceful reconciliation were not forthcoming, the offended principal issued a challenge to a duel, which his opponent was obliged to accept. The seconds agreed on the time and location of the duel, as well as the distance at which the principals could fire at each other. A duel typically ended after either principal hit his opponent, irrespective of the degree of injury. In the event that each principal missed the other, the seconds were empowered to negotiate an end to the matter, although a duel based on an egregious offense may well have continued.[4]

The lethal encounter between Nicholas Dukes and Captain Nutt did not subscribe strictly to these conventions, but, as was often the case with Northern dueling, it appropriated many elements of the dueling ritual. For one, Dukes and Nutt exchanged written communications in advance indicating that a deadly affray was at hand and agreeing to meet within a predetermined time frame and location. The language of their letters—"Dear sir," "Very respectfully, A. C. Nutt"—conformed to the standards of gentlemanly correspondence. Most significantly, each was prepared to take the life of another and risk his own in defense of his honor. Contemporaries understood the bout between Dukes and Nutt to have been a duel. Indeed, the front-page headline in the next day's *New York Times* used the word "duel" to describe the altercation.[5]

The lynch mob offered a second variety of honor killing. Because lynch mobs involved the participation of townsfolk, they embodied the conviction that upholding honor was a communal obligation. Residents of Uniontown in particular and Fayette County in general did not view the Dukes–Nutt affair as a personal matter confined to the parties directly involved. Rather, the defense of honor implicated the entire village. After Dukes's acquittal, his mock lynching on the streets of Uniontown displayed local residents' desire to collectively reappropriate from the legal system the responsibility of justice. Dukes, of course, did not ultimately meet his demise at the hands of a mob, but several of the indignation meetings across Fayette County can rightly be considered lynch mobs insofar as they featured congregations of people who explicitly threatened Dukes's life. The rhetoric that infused these gatherings bespoke a self-conscious anxiety about the loss of local honor in the eyes of the nation. Notably, the indignation meetings were led by professional elites, including doctors, lawyers, editors, merchants, educators, and military officers. These were the very people who could have used their authority to help render honor killing obsolete. Instead, they exalted it. "Lynch law" may be best remembered as a tool of white supremacy in the South during the Gilded Age, but the Dukes–Nutt story illustrates that lynching was limited to neither that purpose nor region.[6]

Alongside the duel and the lynch mob, the lone vigilante committed honor-bound homicide. He acted as an individual albeit with the endorsement of the community. Whereas the traditional duelist placed a premium on affording his opponent a fair fight, the lone vigilante's paramount concern was vengeance at all costs. James Nutt was one of many contemporary avengers of honor who fit this description. Their murder trials often inspired popular sympathy and extensive news coverage. It is worth noting that several of these high-profile trials took place north of the Mason–Dixon Line. In 1867, an army general murdered a well-known politician in Albany for the seduction of his wife. Two years later, a Tammany Hall crony defended his honor by shooting a venerated journalist in the *New York Tribune* offices for luring away his spouse, an accomplished actress. Harry Thaw, heir to a great railroad future, murdered his wife's lover, the acclaimed architect Stanford White, on the roof of Madison Square Garden in 1906. Each of these defendants was ultimately set free.[7]

In a modernizing world characterized by the erosion of autonomy, honor killing reinvested individuals and communities with a sense of agency. Uniontown of the nineteenth century was typical of American villages that were jolted from their quiet, insular existence into vast networks of transportation, communication, and industry. The opportunities afforded by the spread of train tracks, telegraph lines, and factories came at a cost—townsfolk increasingly found their daily lives shaped by forces beyond their grasp.

This forfeiture of local independence was acutely felt in the realm of criminal justice. Over the course of the nineteenth century, a bureaucratizing and professionalizing legal system diminished the role of the general public in criminal law. The growth of plea bargaining meant that fewer cases ever reached trial, with outcomes shaped by state prosecutors rather than juries composed of everyday citizens. Even when juries did hear cases and returned guilty verdicts, pardons were common across the country. Pennsylvania instituted a Board of Pardons in 1873, betokening an age in which remote government officials rather than local communities served as the final arbiters of justice. Felons of an earlier generation were subjected to corporal punishment in the town square where villagers witnessed justice in action, but the development of the modern prison complex relegated convicts to isolated cells away from the public eye. In the same vein, the executions of death row inmates—formerly spectacles for all to see—were now carried out in the privacy of prison yards. Honor killing, therefore, repudiated not only the target who violated the code of honor but also a modern justice system that disempowered laymen. The graves of men like Dukes were testaments to the violent struggle waged by ordinary people to regain some measure of control over their lives and their communities.[8]

Modernization also spawned a crisis of manhood that the honor code promised to remedy. Constrained by the regimentation of the modern workplace and alarmed by women demanding equal rights, men feared that the traditional ideal of rugged masculinity had become hopelessly elusive. That men were eager to reassert their manhood was evident in nearly every aspect of the Dukes–Nutt story. William Playford lauded Captain Nutt's threatening letter to Dukes as "noble and manly." The press also used the term "manly" to describe James Feather's testimony against Dukes. The vaunted manhood of Nutt and Feather threw into high relief Dukes's supposed lack of manliness. Following the Dukes verdict, Lizzie openly questioned the manhood of her former fiancé. The members of the Pennsylvania House of Representatives considered the prospect of seating Dukes an affront to their masculinity. One legislator's resolution to expel Dukes condemned his behavior as "disgraceful to him as a man." The jurors who acquitted Dukes were no better on that count, derided in the press as having "dishonored their own manhood."[9]

Notions of manliness were bound up with the Victorian premium on female chastity. Indeed, the greatest indication of one's manhood was his tenacity in guarding the sexual purity of his female relatives. (Unmarried men were supposed to be celibate as well but male purity had nowhere near the cultural importance of womanly virtue.) As the economy shifted from agriculture to industry, thereby relocating work outside the home, fathers and brothers struggled to keep watch over their daughters and sisters. Gilded-Age courtship was largely unchaperoned because of the changing nature not only of work but also of architecture. During the colonial era, houses often consisted of one large room and thus offered little expectation of privacy. Captain Nutt's mansion was a consummate example of the kind of seclusion that a modern home, complete with many rooms, could afford a daughter hosting a suitor. The lack of parental oversight in parlors of residences such as Nutt's was a source of alarm for contemporary moralists anxious to police the boundaries of premarital romance.[10]

Given the dire consequences for an otherwise chaste woman who fell prey to a suave man, the latter half of the nineteenth century saw a wave of laws against "seduction"—that is, a man taking a woman's virginity under the false pretense that he would later wed her. American courts had recognized since colonial times a common law tort for seduction, allowing the fathers (and in some instances mothers) of seduced women to recover monetary damages. But increasing angst about female purity stoked by modernization led numerous states to criminalize seduction. Pennsylvania's adoption of a seduction statute in 1843 prefigured a national trend that accelerated in the Gilded Age. As Pennsylvania's judiciary interpreted that law, a "vile and corrupt" woman who indulged "in her own lustful propensities" would naturally find no protection under the act, but the statute did extend to a reformed woman who, after a solitary lapse, was now "walking in the fear of God, and in the path of virtue."[11]

The Victorian milieu was, counterintuitively, a highly sexualized one. Only in a world where people failed to practice abstinence outside of marriage did the need arise to exalt purity so vocally. Moreover, a fixation on suppressing sexual activity still amounted to a fixation on sex. The keen interest with which

Americans read about the lascivious details of the Dukes–Nutt affair was one index of the centrality of sex to the Victorian imagination.[12]

The Victorian attitude toward sex was not the only one expressed in the late nineteenth century. There was no single, monolithic sexual culture. For instance, working-class norms surrounding sex were relatively permissive. But one of the central lessons of the Dukes–Nutt saga is that an ideal of sexual purity was real enough that people were willing to kill and die for it—at least among middle-class professionals and their families. Nicholas Dukes was, after all, a Princeton alumnus and representative-elect to the General Assembly; Lizzie Nutt was the daughter of a prominent official at the Pennsylvania Treasury. For men and women of their station, pretenses to sexual abnegation were vital to their self-definition, especially as they sought to distinguish themselves from the lower classes. So cherished was womanly purity within the middle class that its denigration constituted a graver offense than murder—a theme echoed in the Fayette County courthouse, the press, and the House of Representatives.[13]

Although the historical record is frustratingly sparse when it comes to Lizzie Nutt, the documents that do survive suggest that she both subscribed to and subverted conventional gender roles. On the one hand, she wholly endorsed the Victorian premium on female chastity. On the other, Lizzie suggested that she planned to avenge her own honor rather than cede that responsibility to a man. As she told the press in the wake of Dukes's death, "The only thing I regret about the shooting, is that I did not do it myself. I had made up my mind if he remained here to kill him, and would have done so had the opportunity been presented." In her own way, Lizzie poignantly embodied the tension between the traditional and the modern.[14]

Although the honor code resonated with a majority in the Gilded Age, it was not an ideal left wholly uncontested. Some papers, for instance, condemned the calls for lynching Dukes, declined to applaud James's vengeance, and criticized the latter's acquittal. These editorialists readily conceded that they stood opposite the prevailing sentiment in the country. Still, they offer an indication that at least some Americans valued the rule of law over the demands of honor—a position that would ultimately win out in history.[15]

The efficacy of the rule of law is a central, if not determinative, indicator of modernity. A modern state and a modern economy require the stability that law provides. On a foundational level, a society cannot be considered fully modern when its members undermine the state's monopoly on violence, reject its established legal system, and distribute justice according to their own whims. The Dukes–Nutt affair reveals that most Americans in the Gilded Age were willing to subjugate law to honor, at least in circumstances like those concerning Nicholas Dukes and the Nutt family.[16]

The ideal of honor did not necessarily undermine the formal legal system—those who subscribed to the honor code sought to reconcile, however precariously, the vigilantism it often demanded with the proceedings that law required. As Captain Nutt's letter intimated, he expected a jury to acquit him for killing Dukes in a "legal farce"; honor killing and the legal system could work in tandem, not tension. Adherents to honor's dictates hardly considered the code an invitation to anarchy. After all, law and honor alike were intended to safeguard rather than undermine widely cherished social values. A delicate balance could endure so long as the law bent, in any way necessary, to legitimate honor-bound bloodshed. But if the justice system rendered a verdict that conflicted with honor's imperatives, then the community would be forced to choose between law and honor. For the people of Uniontown, the decision was not difficult. Editorialists who encouraged the mob lynching of Dukes and lauded James's homicide expressly looked to honor killing to provide the social stability that the law did not. Senator Voorhees likewise described the code of honor as a "preserver of society."[17]

Eventually, Americans came to privilege law over honor. In this light, Dukes was a prophet of modernity. He initially extolled honor as stridently as anyone. Balking at the prospect of marriage to the supposedly promiscuous Lizzie Nutt, Dukes informed her father, "My honor is as dear to me as yours is to you, and I prefer to die rather than to live a life of such shame." Yet Dukes's open letter, written after his acquittal and released following his death, explicitly rejected the code of honor for which he had once been willing to lay down his life: "Honor is a delusion and a mockery." Dukes instead touted the rule of law; he contrasted the behavior of Captain Nutt, incendiary newspapers, and Uniontown mobs with his own newfound commitment to legalism. Nicholas Dukes's conversion from a disciple of honor to an adherent of law prefigured the later national transition from an acceptance of honor killing to a state monopoly on violence characteristic of a modern society. That said, it is unclear when the culture of honor killing lost mainstream acceptance in the United States. As late as 1934, a publication no less esteemed than the *Yale Law Journal* advocated the legalization of honor killing.[18]

The Dukes trial was, in one sense, a proxy battle between the code of honor and the rule of law, between tradition and modernity. On one side stood the Commonwealth, which valorized honor killing. On the other was the defense, pleading with the jurors to abide by the law. Considering that Captain Nutt indicated in writing a determination to kill Dukes, that Nutt had stormed into Dukes's room, and that inconsistencies surfaced between the self-professed eyewitnesses to the shooting, surely the verdict of the Dukes jury was not preposterous. The defense, after all, needed only to establish a reasonable doubt about the guilt of its client. But if the Dukes jurors' willingness to follow the evidence was a triumph of law over honor, it was a hollow victory when viewed in light of the trial's violent aftermath.[19]

The *Commonwealth v. James Nutt* reprised the contest between the code of honor and rule of law, only now it was the prosecution demanding adherence to the law and the defense upholding the right of a man to spill blood for the honor of his family. In the opening statement for the defense, Playford insisted that Dukes's death was "the redress of society for the great wrong that this man had committed upon the household of Captain Nutt." Indeed, it was. Dukes violated the sacrosanct value of female purity and American society demanded his corpse as reparation. Conversely, David Patterson for the Commonwealth called on the jurors to resist Senator Voorhees's vague threat about the comeuppance awaiting them should they fail to acquit and likewise to curb their sympathies for a grieving Nutt family. The rule of law could be their only directive.[20]

It is tempting, then, to interpret James's acquittal as the defeat of law at the hands of honor. For the most part, it was. But the truth is more complex. Honor killing lay outside the letter of the law. And so James's attorneys coupled their invocation of honor with a temporary insanity plea that, however unsupported by evidence, at least had a legal basis. This strategy constituted an acknowledgment that honor had to be packaged with the trappings of the law. If the celebration of honor by James's lawyers reflected the staying power of tradition in the Gilded Age, then their coincident reliance on an insanity plea—with its nod to the rule of law—indicated that the birth of modern America was at hand.[21]

The Dukes–Nutt affair vividly illustrates the necessity of the rule of law and the perils of its absence. Any legal system will, at times, produce results that the public abhors. But rejecting the law for its perceived shortcomings invites only greater injustice still. The verdict of the Dukes jury struck Americans as an outrageous miscarriage of justice that required murder as a remedy. And so the nation cheered when James Nutt drew blood from his father's assassin, only to react with horror when he struck again years later. "If men were angels," James Madison famously wrote, "no government would be necessary." Yet no angels walk among us, and so we strive to live by the rule of law. It is an ideal born of man's eternal struggle against the devil within himself.

NOTES

Prologue

1. Grady McWhiney, *Cracker Culture: Celtic Ways in the Old South* (Tuscaloosa: University of Alabama Press, 1988), 149–69; Michael J. Pfeifer, *Rough Justice: Lynching and American Society, 1874–1947* (Urbana: University of Illinois Press), 122–24; Bertram Wyatt-Brown, *Southern Honor: Ethics and Behavior in the Old South* (1982; Oxford University Press, 2007), 19; Edward L. Ayers, *Vengeance and Justice: Crime and Punishment in the Nineteenth Century American South* (New York: Oxford University Press, 1984), 19.

2. Thomas L. Haskell, *The Emergence of Professional Social Science: The American Social Science Association and the Nineteenth-Century Crisis of Authority*, (Urbana: University of Illinois Press, 1977), 27–42; James W. Carey, *Communication as Culture: Essays on Media and Society*, revised ed. (New York: Routledge, 2009), 156–72; Martin J. Sklar, *The United States as a Developing Country: Studies in U.S. History in the Progressive Era and the 1920s* (New York: Cambridge University Press, 1992), 39; Cary Boucock, *In the Grip of Freedom: Law and Modernity in Max Weber* (Toronto: University of Toronto Press, 2000), 69. The phrase "island communities" appears in Robert H. Wiebe, *The Search for Order, 1877–1920* (London: Macmillan, 1967), xiii.

3. Pfeifer, *Rough Justice*, 3; Wyatt-Brown, *Southern Honor*, 458–60.

4. Michael Kimmel, *Manhood in America: A Cultural History*, 3rd ed. (New York: Oxford University Press, 2012), 61–67, 77.

5. Jayme A. Sokolow, *Eros and Modernization: Sylvester Graham, Health Reform, and the Origins of Victorian Sexuality in America* (Rutherford, NJ:

Fairleigh Dickinson University Press, 1983), 12–15, 33–4, 84. Quotation appears in Karen Lystra, *Searching the Heart: Women, Men, and Romantic Love in Nineteenth-Century America* (New York: Oxford University Press, 1989), 58.

Chapter 1

1. Franklin Ellis, *A History of Fayette County, Pennsylvania: With Biographical Sketches of Many of Its Pioneers and Prominent Men* (Philadelphia: Everts, 1882), 333; *Lizzie Nutt's Sad Experience: A Heart Broken, and a Family Plunged in Grief. Wreck and Ruin!* (Philadelphia: Barclay, 1886), 34, 38; "What Lizzie Nutt Says," *The Times* (Philadelphia), March 16, 1883, 1; "Lizzie Nutt's Sorrow," *Atlanta Constitution*, June 20, 1883, 1; Dukes suggested that he viewed Lizzie as an adult woman rather than an impressionable girl in a letter reprinted in Edward J. Donnelly, *Trial of James Nutt for the Killing of N. L. Dukes at Uniontown, Fayette County, Pennsylvania, PA., June 13th, 1883: Containing a Complete History of the Dual Tragedy, Letters and Expert Testimony. Also, the Medical Expert Testimony, Verbatim; Speeches, Rulings, Charge of the Court, Points of Counsel, Portraits, etc.* (Pittsburgh: Stevenson & Foster, 1884), 29. Note that more than one edition of both *Lizzie Nutt's Sad Experience* and *Trial of James Nutt* exist and not all are identical—see Thomas M. McDade, *The Annals of Murder: A Bibliography of Books and Pamphlets on American Murders from Colonial Times to 1900* (Norman: University of Oklahoma Press, 1961), 215–16.

2. *Sad Experience*, 34.

3. Ibid., 34–35.

4. Ibid., 35–36.

5. Ibid., 36.

6. Ibid., 36–37.

7. Ibid., 37–38; James S. Witherspoon, "Reexamining *Roe*: Nineteenth-Century Abortion Statutes and the Fourteenth Amendment," *St. Mary's Law Journal* 17 (1985): 33n15; Estelle B. Freedman and John D'Emilio, *Intimate Matters: A History of Sexuality in America* (New York: Harper & Row, 1988), 66. Quotations appear in ibid.

8. *Sad Experience*, 38.

9. Ibid.; Freedman and D'Emilio, *Intimate Matters*, 77. Quotation appears in ibid.

10. *Sad Experience*, 51, 30; "A Woman in the Case," *New Haven Evening Register*, January 23, 1884, 3; "Not Guilty," *Genius of Liberty* (Uniontown, PA), March 15, 1883, 1. Quotation appears in *Sad Experience*.

11. Freedman and D'Emilio, *Intimate Matters*, 68, 77; Karen Lystra, *Searching the Heart: Women, Men, and Romantic Love in Nineteenth-Century America* (New York: Oxford University Press, 1989), 76.

12. Freedman and Emilio, *Intimate Matters*, 68, 77; James Dunlop, *The General Laws of Pennsylvania, from the Year 1700, to April 1849*, 2nd ed. (Philadelphia: Johnson, 1849), 1012. The language of the Pennsylvania statute was modified slightly in 1860—see *Penal Laws of Pennsylvania: Passed March 31, 1860* (Harrisburg, PA: Hamilton, 1860), 15.

13. *Sad Experience*, 38, 41.

14. Ibid., 41.

15. Ibid., 41–42.

16. Ibid., 42.

17. "Not Guilty," *Genius of Liberty* (Uniontown, PA), March 15, 1883, 1; *Sad Experience*, 42. Quotation appears in *Sad Experience*. Dukes wrote his reply on December 19, he mailed it on December 20, and Nutt received it on December 21.

18. *Sad Experience*, 43; *Penal Laws of Pennsylvania*, 15. Quotations appear in *Sad Experience*.

19. *Sad Experience*, 43.

20. Ibid., 43–44.

21. Ibid., 44.

22. Ibid., 30; Donnelly, *James Nutt*, 17. Quotation appears in *James Nutt*. Note that there is a discrepancy between these two sources, both of which describe Pickard's testimony concerning the date of Dukes's purchase—the former suggests December 22, the latter December 21. Regarding the origins of Dukes's gun model, see Robert J. Neal and Roy G. Jinks, *Smith and Wesson, 1857–1945* (South Brunswick, NJ: Barnes, 1966), 63–65; Roy G. Jinks, *History of Smith & Wesson: No Thing of Importance Will Come without Effort* (North Hollywood, CA: Beinfeld, 1977), 128–30.

23. Donnelly, *James Nutt*, 67.

Chapter 2

1. Franklin Ellis, *A History of Fayette County, Pennsylvania: With Biographical Sketches of Many of Its Pioneers and Prominent Men* (Philadelphia: Everts, 1882), 358; H. W. Brands, *Andrew Jackson: His Life and Times* (New York: Anchor Books, 2006), 279–86, 297–99, 303–4, 400.

2. Ellis, *Fayette County*, 358–59; Jonathan E. Helmreich, *Through All the Years: A History of Allegheny College* (Meadville, PA: Allegheny College, 2005), 52–57; Lawrence L. Pelletier, *From a Reliance on the Smiles of Heaven: The Story of Allegheny College* (New York: Newcomen Society in North America, 1966), 18; Julie Reuben, *The Making of the Modern University: Intellectual Transformation and the Marginalization of Morality* (Chicago: University of Chicago Press, 1996), 22; Caroline Winterer, "The Humanist Revolution in America, 1820–1860: Classical Antiquity in the Colleges," *History of Higher Education Annual* 18 (1998): 112.

3. Ellis, *Fayette County*, 358–59; "Fearful Tragedy," *Genius of Liberty* (Uniontown, PA), December 28, 1882, 1; Helmreich, *Through All the Years*, 53.

4. Adam Clarke Nutt, "The Western Continent as a Field of Laudable Ambition," 45, 50, 51, 54, Philo-Franklin Literary Society Prize Essays, 1857–1873, 45–57, RG3 Dean of Students, Allegheny College Archives, Wayne and Sally Merrick Historical Archival Center, Pelletier Library, Allegheny College, Meadville, PA; "Catalogue of the Philo-Franklin Literary Society of Allegheny College: Embracing the Names of Honorary Members, Alumni, Undergraduates and Present Members; Together with the Constitution and By-Laws and the origin, articles and restrictions of the Woodruff and Kalamathean prize medals. 1860. Buffalo Commercial Advertiser Steam Press," 46, RG3 Dean of Students, Allegheny College Archives; Ellis, *Fayette County*, 359. Quotations appear in "Western Continent."

5. Nutt, "Western Continent," 56.

6. Edward J. Donnelly, *Trial of James Nutt for the Killing of N. L. Dukes at Uniontown, Fayette County, Pennsylvania, PA., June 13th, 1883: Containing a Complete History of the Dual Tragedy, Letters and Expert Testimony. Also, the Medical Expert Testimony, Verbatim; Speeches, Rulings, Charge of the Court, Points of Counsel, Portraits, etc.* (Pittsburgh: Stevenson & Foster, 1884), 6; John M. Sacher, "'A Soldier's Life Is a Hard One at Best': Soldiers in the American Civil War," in Lisa Tendrich Frank and Peter C. Mancall, eds., *Civil War: People and Perspectives* (Santa Barbara, CA: ABC-CLIO, 2009), 4–10;

7. Lorien Foote, *The Gentlemen and the Roughs: Violence, Honor, and Manhood in the Union Army* (New York: New York University Press, 2010), 86, 80, 117; "Proclamation by the President," *New-York Times*, April 15, 1861, 1. Quotation appears in *New-York Times*.

8. Donnelly, *James Nutt*, 6; William A. Dobak, *Freedom by the Sword: The U.S. Colored Troops, 1862–1867* (New York: Skyhorse, 2013), 2–10, 13;

Emancipation Proclamation, January 1, 1863, Presidential Proclamations, 1791–1991, Record Group 11, General Records of the U.S. Government, National Archives; Dudley Taylor Cornish, *The Sable Arm: Negro Troops in the Union Army, 1861–1865* (New York: Longmans, Green, 1956), 29–30. Quotation appears in Emancipation Proclamation.

9. Samuel P. Bates, *History of Pennsylvania Volunteers, 1861–5* (Harrisburg, PA: Singerly, 1871) 5: 941–42, 925; Dobak, *Freedom by the Sword*, 47–54.

10. Dobak, *Freedom by the Sword*, 65–68; Bates, *History of Pennsylvania Volunteers*, 925–26.

11. Betty J. Ownsbey, *Alias "Paine": Lewis Thornton Powell, the Mystery Man of the Lincoln Conspiracy* (Jefferson, NC: McFarland, 1993), 76–100.

12. Quotations appears in ibid., 149.

13. Donnelly, *James Nutt*, 6; Ellis, *Fayette County*, 359; Sean Dennis Cashman, *America in the Gilded Age: From the Death of Lincoln to the Rise of Theodore Roosevelt* (New York: New York University Press, 1984), 215–16.

14. Ellis, *Fayette County*, 359; Donnelly, *James Nutt*, 6; "An Unpopular Verdict," *The Sun* (Baltimore), March 15, 1883, 1; Philadelphia *Press* excerpted in "Shocking Tragedy," *Republican Standard* (Uniontown, PA), December 28, 1882, 1.

15. Donnelly, *James Nutt*, 6; "Shocking Tragedy," *Republican Standard* (Uniontown, PA), December 28, 1882, 1; "Fearful Tragedy," *Genius of Liberty* (Uniontown, PA), December 28, 1882, 1; Ellis, *Fayette County*, 359.

16. Ellis, *Fayette County*, 314, 341; James Hadden, *A History of Uniontown: The County Seat of Fayette County, Pennsylvania* (Akron, OH: New Werner, 1913), 707. Quotation appears in *Uniontown*.

17. Fearful Tragedy," *Genius of Liberty* (Uniontown, PA), December 28, 1882, 1; Lynn Dumenil, *Freemasonry and American Culture, 1880–1930* (Princeton, NJ: Princeton University Press, 1984), 9, 23–24; Ellis, *Fayette County*, 342–44.

18. Donnelly, *James Nutt*, 6; "Fearful Tragedy," *Genius of Liberty* (Uniontown, PA), December 28, 1882, 1; "Shocking Tragedy," *Republican Standard* (Uniontown, PA), December 28, 1882, 1; Ellis, *Fayette County*, 359.

19. "Paper Book of Appellants, Supreme Court of Pennsylvania, Eastern District, January Term, 1889 . . . F. C. Breckenridge, James Wells, and Stephen R. Nutt," 4, 34, Dukes–Nutt Tragedy Vertical File, Pennsylvania Room, Uniontown Public Library; Cashman, *America in the Gilded Age*, 228.

20. Donnelly, *James Nutt*, 7; "An Interview with Dukes," *The Times* (Philadelphia), March 16, 1883, 1. On "white swelling," see Charles L.

Scudder, "White Swelling of the Knee," *Boston Medical and Surgical Journal* 131 (August 2, 1894): 101.

21. Don Oberdorfer, *Princeton University: The First 250 Years* (Princeton, NJ: Trustees of Princeton University), 72–83. Quotation appears on page 72.

22. Donnelly, *James Nutt*, 7; "The Nutt Trial," *The Times* (Philadelphia), December 1, 1883, 1; "Fearful Tragedy," *Genius of Liberty* (Uniontown, PA), December 28, 1882, 1.

23. James A. Kehl, *Boss Rule in the Gilded Age: Matt Quay of Pennsylvania* (Pittsburgh: University of Pittsburgh Press, 1981), 52; Gregory J. Dehler, *Chester Alan Arthur: The Life of a Gilded Age Politician and President* (New York: Nova History, 2007), 65–66.

24. Kehl, *Boss Rule*, 52–55; "Fearful Tragedy," *Genius of Liberty*, December 28, 1882, 1.

25. Edward C. Allison, *The Dukes–Nutt Tragedies* (Uniontown, PA: The "Democrat" Print, 1883), 12.

26. Hadden, *Uniontown*, 12.

27. Ibid., 432.

28. Ibid., 432–39; Ellis, *Fayette County*, 340. Quotations appear in ibid., 435, 436.

29. Hadden, *Uniontown*, 428–29.

30. Ibid., 441; Robert V. Bruce, *Bell: Alexander Graham Bell and the Conquest of Solitude* (1973; Ithaca, NY: Cornell University Press, 1990), 181. Quotation appears in *Bell*. Note that Broadway was later changed to Beeson Avenue.

31. Thomas J. Schlereth, *Victorian America: Transformations of Everyday Life, 1876–1915* (New York: HarperCollins, 1991), 54–55; Ellis, *Fayette County*, 345.

32. Carmen DiCiccio, *Coal and Coke in Pennsylvania* (Harrisburg: Commonwealth of Pennsylvania, Pennsylvania Historical and Museum Commission, 1996), 23, 61, 39–41.

33. Advertisements, *Republican Standard* (Uniontown, PA), December 21, 1882, 2.

34. Hadden, *Uniontown*, 811–12; Schelerth, *Victorian America*, 286; Ellis, *Fayette County*, 279–364; "Neighborhood News," *Republican Standard* (Uniontown, PA), January 4, 1883, 1.

35. Donnelly, *James Nutt*, 36; Hadden, *Uniontown*, 418–19. Quotation appears in *Uniontown*.

36. Ellis, *Fayette County*, 289–90; Hadden, *Uniontown*, 149, 705.

Chapter 3

1. Edward J. Donnelly, *Trial of James Nutt for the Killing of N. L. Dukes at Uniontown, Fayette County, Pennsylvania, PA., June 13th, 1883: Containing a Complete History of the Dual Tragedy, Letters and Expert Testimony. Also, the Medical Expert Testimony, Verbatim; Speeches, Rulings, Charge of the Court, Points of Counsel, Portraits, etc.* (Pittsburgh: Stevenson & Foster, 1884), 70; "The Uniontown Murder," *Harrisburg Telegraph*, December 28, 1882, 1; "Fearful Tragedy," *Genius of Liberty* (Uniontown, PA), December 28, 1882, 1. Quotation appears in *Genius of Liberty*.

2. "Fearful Tragedy," *Genius of Liberty* (Uniontown, PA), December 28, 1882, 1; Edward C. Allison, *The Dukes–Nutt Tragedies* (Uniontown, PA: The "Democrat" Print, 1883), 7; "The Hearing," *Republican Standard* (Uniontown, PA), January 4, 1883, 1; "Speech of Charles E. Boyle," *Genius of Liberty* (Uniontown, PA), April 5, 1883, 2.

3. "Fearful Tragedy," *Genius of Liberty* (Uniontown, PA), December 28, 1882, 1

4. "Fearful Tragedy," *Genius of Liberty* (Uniontown, PA), December 28, 1882, 1; "The Hearing," *Republican Standard* (Uniontown, PA), January 4, 1883, 1; Donnelly, *James Nutt*, 8; "The Hearing," *Republican Standard* (Uniontown, PA), January 4, 1883, 1. Quotation appears in *James Nutt*.

5. Donnelly, *James Nutt*, 8, 27; "Not Guilty," *Genius of Liberty* (Uniontown, PA), March 15, 1883, 1. Quotations appear in both sources.

6. "Not Guilty," *Genius of Liberty* (Uniontown, PA), March 15, 1883, 1; "Speech of Charles E. Boyle," *Genius of Liberty* (Uniontown, PA), April 5, 1883, 3; "The Hearing," *Republican Standard* (Uniontown, PA), January 4, 1883, 1; "Shocking Tragedy," *Republican Standard* (Uniontown, PA), December 28, 1882, 1. Quotations appear in both articles in *Genius of Liberty*.

7. Donnelly, *James Nutt*, 27. For a physical description of Dukes's frame, see "The Nutt Tragedy," *Atlanta Constitution*, June 17, 1883, 3.

8. Donnelly, *James Nutt*, 27–28.

9. "Not Guilty," *Genius of Liberty* (Uniontown, PA), March 15, 1883, 1; "The Hearing," *Republican Standard* (Uniontown, PA), January 4, 1883, 1. Quotation appears in *Republican Standard*.

10. "The Hearing," *Republican Standard* (Uniontown, PA), January 4, 1883, 1; "Not Guilty," *Genius of Liberty* (Uniontown, PA), March 15, 1883, 1. Quotation appears in *Republican Standard*.

11. "Not Guilty," *Genius of Liberty* (Uniontown, PA), March 15, 1883, 1.

12. Ibid.; "Shocking Tragedy," *Republican Standard* (Uniontown, PA), December 28, 1882, 1.

13. Donnelly, *James Nutt*, 28; "Shocking Tragedy," *Republican Standard* (Uniontown, PA), December 28, 1882, 1; "Fearful Tragedy," *Genius of Liberty* (Uniontown, PA), December 28, 1882, 1; "Not Guilty," *Genius of Liberty* (Uniontown, PA), March 15, 1883, 1. Quotations appear in "Not Guilty," *Genius of Liberty*.

14. "Shocking Tragedy," *Republican Standard* (Uniontown, PA), December 28, 1882, 1; "Not Guilty," *Genius of Liberty* (Uniontown, PA), March 15, 1883, 1.

15. "Shocking Tragedy," *Republican Standard* (Uniontown, PA), December 28, 1882, 1; "Fearful Tragedy," *Genius of Liberty* (Uniontown, PA), December 28, 1882, 1. Quotation appears in *Genius of Liberty*.

16. "Shocking Tragedy," *Republican Standard* (Uniontown, PA), December 28, 1882, 1; "Fearful Tragedy," *Genius of Liberty* (Uniontown, PA), December 28, 1882, 1.

17. "Shocking Tragedy," *Republican Standard* (Uniontown, PA), December 28, 1882, 1; "Fearful Tragedy," *Genius of Liberty* (Uniontown, PA), December 28, 1882, 1; *Corpus Juris Secundum: A Contemporary Restatement of American Law as Derived from Reported Cases and Legislation* (St. Paul, MN: Thomas/West, 2007), 18: 280. Quotation appears in *Republican Standard*.

18. "Shocking Tragedy," *Republican Standard* (Uniontown, PA), December 28, 1882, 1; "A Dastardly Murder," *Harrisburg Telegraph*, December 26, 1882, 1. Quotations appear in *Republican Standard*.

19. "Shocking Tragedy," *Republican Standard* (Uniontown, PA), December 28, 1882, 1; "A Distressing Affair," *The Patriot* (Harrisburg, PA), December 25, 1882, 1; "Fearful Tragedy," *Genius of Liberty* (Uniontown, PA), December 28, 1882, 1. Quotation appears in *Genius of Liberty*.

20. "Fatal Impromptu Duel," *New-York Times*, December 25, 1882, 1; "The Father of a Ruined Girl Shot Dead by Her Deceiver," *Albuquerque Journal*, December 27, 1882, 3; "A Daughter's Honor," *Chicago Daily Tribune*, December 27, 1882, 10; "A Prominent Pennsylvanian Shot Dead by a Lawyer," *San Francisco Chronicle*, December 25, 1882, 3; "A Tragedy in High Life," *Worcester Daily Spy* (MA), December 25, 1882, 1. For additional coverage, see "A Pennsylvania Tragedy," *Galveston Weekly News*, December 28, 1882, 6; "Terrible Shooting Affair," *Bangor Daily Whig and Courier*, December 25, 1882, 3; "The Nutt Tragedy," *Omaha Daily Bee*, December 28, 1882, 5; "A Heart Broken Father Murdered by the Seducer

of His Daughter," *Newark Advocate* (OH), December 26, 1882, 1; "The Uniontown Mystery," *New Haven Evening Register*, December 26, 1882, 3; "A Seducer's Shot," *Kansas City Star*, December 26, 1882, 4; "The Uniontown Tragedy," *National Republican* (Washington, DC), December 26, 1882, 1; "The Cause of the Shooting of Captain Nutt," *Arkansas Daily Gazette* (Little Rock), December 27, 1882, 1; "A Tragedy at Uniontown," *The Sun* (Baltimore), December 25, 1882, 4; "A Nut Cracked," *Daily Herald* (Grand Forks, Dakota Territory), December 27, 1882, 1; "A State Cashier Killed," *New York Tribune*, December 25, 1882, 5; "A Sensational Killing," *Cincinnati Daily Gazette*, December 25, 1882, 1; "Sunday Horrors," *Wheeling Register*, December 25, 1882, 1; "Shocking Tragedy," *New York Herald*, December 25, 1882, 8; "An Exciting Tragedy," *Springfield Daily Republican* (MA), December 25, 1882, 5; "Shot through the Brain," *Plain Dealer* (Cleveland), December 26, 1882, 5; "Strong Feeling against Dukes," *Omaha Daily News*, December 27, 1882, 4; "The Pennsylvania Tragedy," *Duluth Daily Tribune*, December 28, 1882, 1; "The Nutt Tragedy," *Daily State Gazette* (Trenton), December 30, 1882, 2; "The Dukes–Nutt Tragedy," *Inter Ocean* (Chicago), December 27, 1882, 3; "The Uniontown Sensation," *Bismark Tribune*, December 29, 1882, 5; "He Admits She Was an Angel, But Wouldn't Marry Her," *Dunkirk Evening Observer* (NY), December 26, 1882, 1; "Uniontown, PA," *Courier Journal* (Louisville), December 25, 1882, 2; "Through the Brain," *Cincinnati Enquirer*, December 25, 1882, 2; "Bloody Business," *Fort Wayne Sentinel* (IN), December 26, 1882, 1; "The Uniontown Tragedy," *Saint Paul Globe*, December 26, 1882, 4; "A Pennsylvania Tragedy," *Independent Record* (Helena, MT), December 28, 1882, 1; "The Pennsylvania Tragedy," *Evening Star* (Washington, DC), December 26, 1882, 2; "The Nutt Murder," *Wheeling Intelligencer*, December 26, 1882, 1; "The Dukes–Nutt Murder," *Stark Democrat* (Canton, OH), December 30, 1; "The Wrong Man Killed," *Jamestown Weekly Alert* (Dakota Territory), December 29, 1882, 1.

21. Gerald J. Baldasty, *The Commercialization of News in the Nineteenth Century* (Madison: University of Wisconsin Press, 1992), 50; Richard L. Kaplan, *Politics and the American Press: The Rise of Objectivity, 1865–1920* (New York: Cambridge University Press, 2002), 175; Hazel Dicken-Garcia, *Journalistic Standards in Nineteenth-Century America*, (Madison: University of Wisconsin Press, 1989), 172–73.

22. "The Uniontown Murder," *Harrisburg Telegraph*, December 27, 1882, 1; "Capt. Nutt's Death," *The Patriot* (Harrisburg, PA), December 28, 1882, 1; "Shocking Tragedy," *Republican Standard* (Uniontown, PA),

December 28, 1882, 1; "Capt. Nutt's Burial," *The Patriot* (Harrisburg, PA), December 27, 1882, 1.

23. "Fearful Tragedy," *Genius of Liberty* (Uniontown, PA), December 28, 1882, 1.

24. Ibid., "Shocking Tragedy," *Republican Standard* (Uniontown, PA), December 28, 1882, 1.

25. James Hadden, *A History of Uniontown: The County Seat of Fayette County, Pennsylvania* (Akron, OH: New Werner, 1913), 695–96; "Shocking Tragedy," *Republican Standard* (Uniontown, PA), December 28, 1882, 1; "Fearful Tragedy," *Genius of Liberty* (Uniontown, PA), December 28, 1882, 1.

26. "Fearful Tragedy," *Genius of Liberty* (Uniontown, PA), December 28, 1882, 1; "Shocking Tragedy," *Republican Standard* (Uniontown, PA), December 28, 1882, 1.

27. "Dukes's Deed," *The Patriot* (Harrisburg, PA), December 26, 1883, 1; "The Uniontown Murder," *Harrisburg Telegraph*, December 27, 1882, 1; "Shocking Tragedy," *Republican Standard* (Uniontown, PA), December 28, 1882, 1; "Fearful Tragedy," *Genius of Liberty* (Uniontown, PA), December 28, 1882, 1; "The Defense of James Nutt," *Harrisburg Telegraph*, June 20, 1883, 1; "Paper Book of Appellants in the Supreme Court of Pennsylvania, Eastern District, January Term, 1889 . . . J. K. Ewing and A. D. Boyd," 4, Dukes–Nutt Vertical Folder, Pennsylvania Room, Uniontown Public Library; "Nutt's Oil Speculation," *Harrisburg Telegraph*, March 29, 1886, 1.

28. "Uniontown," *Philadelphia Inquirer*, December 27, 1882, 1; "Fearful Tragedy," *Genius of Liberty* (Uniontown, PA), December 28, 1882, 1. Quotation appears in *Philadelphia Inquirer*.

29. "Not Guilty," *Genius of Liberty* (Uniontown, PA), March 15, 1883, 1.

30. "Shocking Tragedy," *Republican Standard* (Uniontown, PA), December 28, 1882, 1; "Fearful Tragedy," *Genius of Liberty* (Uniontown, PA), December 28, 1882, 1. Quotation appears in *Genius of Liberty*.

31. "Fearful Tragedy," *Genius of Liberty* (Uniontown, PA), December 28, 1882, 1; "The Uniontown Murder," *Harrisburg Telegraph*, December 27, 1882, 1. Quotation appears in *Genius of Liberty*.

32. "Uniontown," *Philadelphia Inquirer*, December 27, 1882, 1; "Capt. Nutt's Death," *The Patriot* (Harrisburg, PA), December 28, 1882, 1; Allison, *Dukes–Nutt*, 20; "The Uniontown Murder," *Harrisburg Telegraph*, December 27, 1882, 1; *Penal Laws of Pennsylvania: Passed March 31, 1860* (Harrisburg, PA: Hamilton, 1860), 23. Quotation appears in *Philadelphia Inquirer*.

Chapter 4

1. "Fearful Tragedy," *Genius of Liberty* (Uniontown, PA), December 28, 1882, 1; Franklin Ellis, *A History of Fayette County, Pennsylvania: With Biographical Sketches of Many of Its Pioneers and Prominent Men* (Philadelphia: Everts, 1882), 353–54; Edward C. Allison, *The Dukes–Nutt Tragedies* (Uniontown, PA: The "Democrat" Print, 1883), 21. Quotation appears in *Dukes–Nutt.*

2. Fearful Tragedy," *Genius of Liberty* (Uniontown, PA), December 28, 1882, 1; "Shocking Tragedy," *Republican Standard* (Uniontown, PA), December 28, 1882, 1; Robert M. Ireland, "Privately Funded Prosecution of Crime in the Nineteenth-Century United States," *American Journal of Legal History* 39 (January 1995): 43–58; Ellis, *Fayette County*, 353.

3. "Over Capitol Hill," *The Patriot* (Harrisburg, PA), June 30, 1883, 1; John Woolf Jordan and James Hadden, eds., *Genealogical and Personal History of Fayette County, Pennsylvania* (New York: Lewis, 1912), 2: 353; "The Nutt Trial," *The Times* (Philadelphia), December 1, 1883, 1.

4. Allison, *Dukes–Nutt*, 21.

5. James Hadden, *A History of Uniontown: The County Seat of Fayette County, Pennsylvania* (Akron, OH: New Werner, 1913), 464.

6. Ellis, *Fayette County*, 352–53; "Official Footings," *Republican Standard* (Uniontown, PA), November 16, 1882, 1; "Shocking Tragedy," *Republican Standard* (Uniontown, PA), December 28, 1882, 1; "Fearful Tragedy," *Genius of Liberty* (Uniontown, PA), December 28, 1882, 1. Quotation appears in *Genius of Liberty.*

7. Edward J. Donnelly, *Trial of James Nutt for the Killing of N. L. Dukes at Uniontown, Fayette County, Pennsylvania, PA., June 13th, 1883: Containing a Complete History of the Dual Tragedy, Letters and Expert Testimony. Also, the Medical Expert Testimony, Verbatim; Speeches, Rulings, Charge of the Court, Points of Counsel, Portraits, etc.* (Pittsburgh: Stevenson & Foster, 1884), 7; Jordan and Hadden, *Genealogical and Personal History*, 1:125, 1:129; "E. C. Higbee," *Daily News Standard* (Uniontown, PA), February 14, 1938, 4.

8. "Fearful Tragedy," *Genius of Liberty* (Uniontown, PA), December 28, 1882, 1.

9. "Nutt–Dukes," *Genius of Liberty* (Uniontown, PA), June 21, 1883, 1; "Dukes' Last Will," *The Times* (Philadelphia), June 26, 1883, 2; "Dukes's Crime," *Genius of Liberty* (Uniontown, PA), January 4, 1883, 1. Quotations appear in "Nutt–Dukes," *Genius of Liberty.*

10. Pennsylvania Constitution of 1874, Article I, Section 14; "The Hearing," *Republican Standard* (Uniontown, PA), January 4, 1883, 1; "Nutt's Trial Postponed," *The Times* (Philadelphia), December 6, 1883, 1; "Dukes's Crime," *Genius of Liberty* (Uniontown, PA), January 4, 1883, 1. Quotations appear in Pennsylvania Constitution and *Genius of Liberty*.

11. "Dukes's Crime," *Genius of Liberty* (Uniontown, PA), January 4, 1883, 1; "Captain Nutt's Murderer," *Harrisburg Telegraph*, December 30, 1882, 1.

12. "The Hearing," *Republican Standard* (Uniontown, PA), January 4, 1883, 1; "Dukes's Crime," *Genius of Liberty* (Uniontown, PA), January 4, 1883, 1; "The State—House of Representatives," *Philadelphia Inquirer*, January 3, 1883, 1.

13. Willard Glazier, *Peculiarities of American Cities* (Philadelphia: Hubbard Brothers, 1886), 200–5.

14. Ibid., 201–3.

15. "On the Hill," *The Patriot* (Harrisburg, PA), December 29, 1882, 1.

16. "The State—House of Representatives," *Philadelphia Inquirer*, January, 3, 1883, 1.

17. "Will Dukes Go to Harrisburg?" *Republican Standard* (Uniontown, PA), January 11, 1883, 1; "A House Curiosity," *The Patriot* (Harrisburg, PA), January 10, 1883, 4; "Will Dukes Go to Harrisburg?" *Republican Standard* (Uniontown, PA), January 11, 1883, 1. Quotation appears in *The Patriot*.

18. "Dukes, the Murderer," *Harrisburg Telegraph*, January 11, 1883, 4; "Dukes and His Seat," *Republican Standard* (Uniontown, PA), January 18, 1883, 3; "State Capital," *Philadelphia Inquirer*, January 12, 1883, 1. Quotation appears in *Philadelphia Inquirer*.

19. "Dukes in the City," *The Patriot* (Harrisburg, PA), January 12, 1883, 1; "Dukes and His Seat," *Republican Standard* (Uniontown, PA), January 18, 1883, 3; "Dukes, the Murderer," *Harrisburg Telegraph*, January 11, 1883, 4. Quotation appears in *Harrisburg Telegraph*.

20. "State Capital," *Philadelphia Inquirer*, January 12, 1883, 1; "Doings of Dukes," *Harrisburg Telegraph*, January 12, 1883, 4; "Dukes and His Seat," *Republican Standard* (Uniontown, PA), January 18, 1883, 3; "Doings of Dukes," *Harrisburg Telegraph*, January 12, 1883, 4; "The Slayer of Captain Nutt," *The Times* (Philadelphia), January 14, 1883, 2.

21. "Capt. Nutt's Murderer at Home," *Harrisburg Telegraph*, January 20, 1883, 1.

22. "What Lizzie Nutt Says," *The Times* (Philadelphia), March 16, 1883, 1; "Memorial Services," *Republican Standard* (Uniontown, PA),

March 1, 1883, 1; "Resolution Adopted," *Republican Standard* (Uniontown, PA), January 4, 1883, 1.

23. "Memorial Services," *Republican Standard* (Uniontown, PA), March 1, 1883, 1.

Chapter 5

1. "The Dukes' Murder Trial," *Galveston Daily News* (Galveston, TX), March 15, 1883, 2; "Notes on the Trial," *Republican Standard* (Uniontown, PA), March 22, 1883, 1.

2. Altina L. Waller, *Reverend Beecher and Mrs. Tilton: Sex and Class in Victorian America* (Amherst: University of Massachusetts Press, 1982), 7–12.

3. James Hadden, *A History of Uniontown: The County Seat of Fayette County, Pennsylvania* (Akron, OH: New Werner, 1913), 404.

4. "Shame! Oh, Shame!!" *Republican Standard* (Uniontown, PA), March 15, 1883, 1; Franklin Ellis, *A History of Fayette County, Pennsylvania:With Biographical Sketches of Many of Its Pioneers and Prominent Men* (Philadelphia: Everts, 1882), 359; "The Nutt Trial," *The Times* (Philadelphia), December 1, 1883, 1; "Not Guilty," *Genius of Liberty* (Uniontown, PA), March 15, 1883, 1. Quotations appear in *Republican Standard*.

5. "Not Guilty," *Genius of Liberty* (Uniontown, PA), March 15, 1883, 1.

6. "The Dukes Homicide," *Philadelphia Inquirer*, March 12, 1883, 1; "The Dukes–Nutt Jury," *The Patriot* (Harrisburg, PA), March 12, 1883, 1; "Not Guilty," *Genius of Liberty* (Uniontown, PA), March 15, 1883, 1; "Shame! Oh, Shame!!" *Republican Standard* (Uniontown, PA), March 31, 1883, 1. Pennsylvania did not allow women onto juries until 1920—see Burnita Shelton Matthews, "The Woman Juror," *Women Lawyer's Journal* (April 1927): 15. In 1898, Utah became the first state to allow female jurors. The U.S. Supreme Court did not find the exclusion of women on juries unconstitutional until the 1975 case *Taylor v. Louisiana*, 419 U.S. 552.

7. "Not Guilty," *Genius of Liberty* (Uniontown, PA), March 15, 1883, 1; "Speech of Charles E. Boyle," *Genius of Liberty* (Uniontown, PA), April 5, 1883, 2; "Shame! Oh, Shame!!" *Republican Standard* (Uniontown, PA), March 15, 1883, 1; Ellis, *Fayette County*, 290.

8. Edward J. Donnelly, *Trial of James Nutt for the Killing of N. L. Dukes at Uniontown, Fayette County, Pennsylvania, PA., June 13th, 1883: Containing a Complete History of the Dual Tragedy, Letters and Expert Testimony. Also, the Medical Expert Testimony, Verbatim; Speeches, Rulings, Charge of the Court,*

Points of Counsel, Portraits, etc. (Pittsburgh: Stevenson & Foster, 1884), 10; "How It Was Done," *Republican Standard* (Uniontown, PA), March 22, 1883, 1.

9. "The Dukes Murder Case," *Reading Times* (Pennsylvania), March 12, 1883, 1; "On Trial," *Philadelphia Inquirer*, March 13, 1883, 1; "Shame! Oh, Shame!!" *Republican Standard* (Uniontown, PA), March 31, 1883, 1.

10. "Shame! Oh, Shame!!" *Republican Standard* (Uniontown, PA), March 15, 1883, 1; "A Careless Murder," *Harrisburg Telegraph*, March 13, 1883, 1. Quotation appears in *Harrisburg Telegraph*.

11. "On Trial," *Philadelphia Inquirer*, March 13, 1883, 1.

12. Ibid.

13. "Not Guilty," *Genius of Liberty* (Uniontown, PA), March 15, 1883, 1.

14. Ibid.

15. Ibid.

16. Ibid.; "Shame! Oh, Shame!!" *Republican Standard* (Uniontown, PA), March 15, 1883, 1.

17. "Not Guilty," *Genius of Liberty* (Uniontown, PA), March 15, 1883, 1.

18. Ibid.

19. Ibid.; "Shame! Oh, Shame!!" *Republican Standard* (Uniontown, PA), March 15, 1883, 1; Thomas J. Schlereth, *Victorian America: Transformations of Everyday Life, 1876–1915* (New York: HarperCollins, 1991), 292; "Dukes Set Free," *Somerset Herald* (Pennsylvania), March 21, 1883, 2. Quotations appear in Ibid.

20. "N. L. Dukes on Trial," *The Patriot* (Harrisburg, PA), March 13, 1883, 1; "Shame! Oh, Shame!!" *Republican Standard* (Uniontown, PA), March 15, 1883, 1; "Not Guilty," *Genius of Liberty* (Uniontown, PA), March 15, 1883, 1.

21. "N. L. Dukes on Trial," *The Patriot* (Harrisburg, PA), March 13, 1883, 1; "The Temperature," *Pittsburgh Commercial-Gazette*, March 13, 1883, 4; "A Careless Murder," *Harrisburg Telegraph*, March 13, 1883, 1; "Not Guilty," *Genius of Liberty* (Uniontown, PA), March 15, 1883, 1. Quotation appears in *Harrisburg Telegraph*.

22. "Dukes Set Free," *Somerset Herald*, March 21, 1883, 2; Untitled, *Somerset Herald*, March 21, 1883, 2; "Dukes' Letters to Nutt," *The Patriot* (Harrisburg, PA), March 13, 1883, 2.

23. "N. L. Dukes on Trial," *The Patriot* (Harrisburg, PA), March 13, 1883, 1; "On Trial For His Life," *New-York Times*, March 13, 1883, 1; "The Dukes Murder Trial," *Record Union* (Sacramento) March 13, 1883, 1; "The Dukes Murder Trial," *Daily Globe* (St. Paul, MN), March 13, 1883, 1; "Dukes–Nutt Case," *Las Vegas Daily Gazette*, March 13, 1883, 1. For other examples of press coverage of the Dukes trial, see "The Dukes–Nutt

Trial," *The Sun* (Baltimore), March 13, 1883, 1; "The Dukes–Nutt Murder Trial," *New-York Tribune*, March 13, 1883, 1; "Dukes' Infamous Deed," *Plain Dealer* (Cleveland), March 13, 1883, 1; "Sensational Testimony in the Dukes–Nutt Trial," *Jackson Daily Citizen* (MI), March 13, 1883, 1; "Dukes' Trial," *Wheeling Register*, March 13, 1883, 1; "Dukes–Nutt Murder Trial," *Evening Critic* (Washington, DC), March 13, 1883, 1; "The Dukes Trial," *Cincinnati Commercial*, March 13, 1883, 1; "The Dukes's Trial for Murder," *The Sun* (New York), March 13, 1883, 1; "The Slayer of Nutt," *National Republican* (Washington, DC), March 13, 1883, 1; "Sensational Murder Trial," *New York Herald*, March 13, 1883, 3; "The Dukes Trial," *New Haven Evening Register*, March 13, 1883, 2; "The Dukes–Nutt Murder Trial," *Evening Bulletin* (San Francisco), March 13, 1883, 3; "A Cause Celebre," *Dallas Daily Herald*, March 13, 1883, 5; "The Dukes–Nutt Murder Case," *Independent Record* (Helena, MT), March 13, 1883, 2; "Sensational Trial," *Fort Wayne Daily News* (IN), March 13, 1883, 3; "The Dukes–Nutt Murder Trial," *Courier-Journal* (Louisville), March 13, 1883, 2; "The Duke [*sic*] Murder Trial," *Morning Oregonian* (Portland), March 13, 1883, 2; "The Trap," *Cincinnati Enquirer*, March 13, 1883, 4; "Cause Celebre," *Fort Worth Daily Gazette*, March 13, 1883, 4; "The Dukes–Nutt Murder Trial," *Evening Star* (Washington, DC), March 13, 1883, 3; "The Nutt Murder," *Salt Lake Herald*, March 13, 1883, 5.

24. "Not Guilty," *Genius of Liberty* (Uniontown, PA), March 15, 1883, 1; "Shame! Oh, Shame!!" *Republican Standard* (Uniontown, PA), March 15, 1883, 1. Quotations appear in both sources.

25. "Not Guilty," *Genius of Liberty* (Uniontown, PA), March 15, 1883, 1; "Shame! Oh, Shame!!" *Republican Standard* (Uniontown, PA), March 15, 1883, 1. Quotations appear in *Genius of Liberty*.

26. "Not Guilty," *Genius of Liberty* (Uniontown, PA), March 15, 1883, 1; "Shame! Oh, Shame!!" *Republican Standard* (Uniontown, PA), March 15, 1883, 1; "The Dukes Letters Read," *The Times* (Philadelphia), March 14, 1883, 1. Quotations appear in *Genius of Liberty*.

27. "Dukes Set Free," *Somerset Herald* (PA), March 21, 1883, 2; "Dukes' Defense," *The Patriot* (Harrisburg, PA), March 14, 1883, 1; "Speech of Charles Boyle," *Genius of Liberty* (Uniontown, PA), April 5, 1883, 2; "Not Guilty," *Genius of Liberty* (Uniontown, PA), March 15, 1883, 1; "Shame! Oh, Shame!!" *Republican Standard* (Uniontown, PA), March 15, 1883, 1. Quotations appear in *Somerset Herald*; *The Patriot*; and "Speech of Charles Boyle," *Genius of Liberty*.

28. "Not Guilty," *Genius of Liberty* (Uniontown, PA), March 15, 1883, 1.

29. *Lizzie Nutt's Sad Experience: A Heart Broken, and a Family Plunged in Grief. Wreck and Ruin!* (Philadelphia: Barclay, 1886), 43.

30. "Not Guilty," *Genius of Liberty* (Uniontown, PA), March 15, 1883, 1.

31. Ibid.

32. Ibid. On the English and classical origins of castle doctrine, see Jeannie Suk, *At Home in the Law: How the Domestic Violence Revolution Is Transforming Privacy* (New Haven, CT: Yale University Press, 2009), 55–59; Numa Denis Fustel de Coulanges, *The Ancient City: A Study on the Religion, Laws, and Institutions of Greece and Rome* (1864; Kitchener, Ontario: Batoche Books, 2001), 50.

33. "Not Guilty," *Genius of Liberty* (Uniontown, PA), March 15, 1883, 1.

34. Ibid.

35. Ibid.

36. Ibid.

37. Robert M. Ireland, "Popular Justice in Pennsylvania: The Nutt–Dukes Tragedy," *Pennsylvania Magazine of History and Biography* 113 (July 1989): 402; "The Dukes Trial," *Wheeling Intelligencer*, March 14, 1883, 1; "Shame! Oh, Shame!!" *Republican Standard* (Uniontown, PA), March 15, 1883, 1. Note that Ireland's article, "Popular Justice," is the only prior scholarship on the Dukes–Nutt affair; he acknowledges the episode as an instance of Northern honor.

38. Quotations appear in "Dukes' Characteristics," *Republican Standard* (Uniontown, PA), March 22, 1883, 2; "Dukes the Infamous" *Evening Critic* (Washington, DC), March 13, 1883, 3. *Inter Ocean* reprinted in "Dirty Dukes," *Republican Standard* (Uniontown, PA), March 22, 1883, 2. See also Untitled, *Plain Dealer* (Cleveland), March 12, 1883, 2.

39. "Nearing the End," *Harrisburg Telegraph*, March 14, 1883, 1; "Shame! Oh, Shame!!" *Republican Standard* (Uniontown, PA), March 15, 1883, 4. Quotation appears in *Republican Standard*.

Chapter 6

1. "An Infamous Verdict," *Harrisburg Telegraph*, March 15, 1883, 1.

2. "Not Guilty," *Genius of Liberty* (Uniontown, PA), March 15, 1883, 1; "Law Points," *Genius of Liberty* (Uniontown, PA), April 5, 1883, 1. Quotation appears in "Law Points," *Genius of Liberty*.

3. "An Infamous Verdict," *Harrisburg Telegraph*, March 15, 1883, 1; "Speech of Charles E. Boyle," *Genius of Liberty* (Uniontown, PA), April 5, 1883, 2. Quotations appear in *Genius of Liberty*.

4. "Speech of Charles E. Boyle," *Genius of Liberty* (Uniontown, PA), April 5, 1883, 2.

5. Ibid.

6. Ibid.

7. Ibid., 2–3.

8. Ibid., 3.

9. Ibid. In fact, modern medical knowledge tells us that that scenario is entirely possible.

10. Ibid.; "N. L. Dukes Acquitted," *The Patriot* (Harrisburg, PA), March 15, 1883, 1; "Not Guilty," *Genius of Liberty* (Uniontown, PA), March 15, 1883, 1. Quotations appear in ibid. For legal doctrine concerning good character, see "Law Points," *Genius of Liberty* (Uniontown, PA), April 5, 1883, 1.

11. "Not Guilty," *Genius of Liberty* (Uniontown, PA), March 15, 1883, 1; "An Infamous Verdict," *Harrisburg Telegraph*, March 15, 1883, 1; "Shame! Oh, Shame!!" *Republican Standard* (Uniontown, PA), March 15, 1883, 4. Quotations appear in *Republican Standard*.

12. "Shame! Oh, Shame!!" *Republican Standard* (Uniontown, PA), March 15, 1883, 4.

13. Ibid.

14. Ibid.

15. Ibid.

16. Ibid.

17. "An Infamous Verdict," *Harrisburg Telegraph*, March 15, 1883, 1; Edward C. Allison, *The Dukes–Nutt Tragedies* (Uniontown, PA: The "Democrat" Print, 1883), 23; "N. L. Dukes Acquitted," *The Patriot* (Harrisburg, PA), March 15, 1. Quotations appear in *Harrisburg Telegraph* and *The Patriot*.

18. "An Infamous Verdict," *Harrisburg Telegraph*, March 15, 1883, 1; "Shame! Oh, Shame!!" *Republican Standard* (Uniontown, PA), March 15, 1883, 4.

19. "An Infamous Verdict," *Harrisburg Telegraph*, March 15, 1883, 1; "Shame! Oh, Shame!!" *Republican Standard* (Uniontown, PA), March 15, 1883, 4. Quotations appear in *Harrisburg Telegraph*.

20. "An Infamous Verdict," *Harrisburg Telegraph*, March 15, 1883, 1; "How It Was Done," *Republican Standard* (Uniontown, PA), March 22, 1883, 1.

21. "Speech of Charles E. Boyle," *Genius of Liberty* (Uniontown, PA), April 5, 1883, 2; "An Interview with Dukes," *The Times* (Philadelphia), March 16, 1883, 1. Quotations appear in *Genius of Liberty*.

22. "An Infamous Verdict," *Harrisburg Telegraph*, March 15, 1883, 1; "N. L. Dukes Acquitted," *The Patriot* (Harrisburg, PA), March 15, 1;

"The Acquittal of Dukes," *Daily Dispatch* (Richmond, VA), March 16, 1883, 3; "An Unpopular Verdict," *The Sun* (Baltimore), March 15, 1883, 1.

23. "An Infamous Verdict," *Harrisburg Telegraph*, March 15, 1883, 1; "An Unpopular Verdict," *The Sun* (Baltimore), March 15, 1883, 1; "Freeing a Fiend," *National Republican* (Washington, DC), March 15, 1883, 1. Quotations appear in *Harrisburg Telegraph*.

24. *Lizzie Nutt's Sad Experience: A Heart Broken, and a Family Plunged in Grief. Wreck and Ruin!* (Philadelphia: Barclay, 1886), 45; "The Nutt Trial," *The Times* (Philadelphia), December 1, 1883, 1; "An Infamous Verdict," *Harrisburg Telegraph*, March 15, 1883, 1. Quotation appears in *Sad Experience*.

25. "How It Was Done," *Republican Standard* (Uniontown, PA), March 22, 1883, 1.

26. "Juror Cagey's Experience," *Republican Standard* (Uniontown, PA), March 31, 1883, 4.

27. "N. L. Dukes Acquitted," *The Patriot* (Harrisburg, PA), March 15, 1; "Shame! Oh, Shame!!" *Republican Standard* (Uniontown, PA), March 15, 1883, 4. "An Infamous Verdict," *Harrisburg Telegraph*, March 15, 1883, 1.

Chapter 7

1. *Lizzie Nutt's Sad Experience: A Heart Broken, and a Family Plunged in Grief. Wreck and Ruin!* (Philadelphia: Barclay, 1886), 46.

2. Tony Horwitz, *Midnight Rising: John Brown and the Raid That Sparked the Civil War* (New York: Holt, 2011), 68–71, 177–80, 199–213, 251–53, 277.

3. "N. L. Dukes Acquitted," *The Patriot* (Harrisburg, PA), March 15, 1; "An Infamous Verdict," *Harrisburg Telegraph*, March 15, 1883, 1; *Sad Experience*, 45-6; "Shame! Oh, Shame!!" *Republican Standard* (Uniontown, PA), March 15, 1883, 4.

4. "N. L. Dukes Acquitted," *The Patriot* (Harrisburg, PA), March 15, 1; "An Infamous Verdict," *Harrisburg Telegraph*, March 15, 1883, 1. Quotation appears in *Harrisburg Telegraph*.

5. *Sad Experience*, 46; "N. L. Dukes Acquitted," *The Patriot* (Harrisburg, PA), March 15, 1; "Shame! Oh, Shame!!" *Republican Standard* (Uniontown, PA), March 31, 1883, 4; "An Interview with Dukes," *The Times* (Philadelphia), March 16, 1883, 1. Quotation appears in *Sad Experience*.

6. Quotations appear in "Dukes Acquitted—A Verdict That Amazed the Judge and Infuriated the Community," *Telegraph and Messenger* (Macon, GA), March 15, 1883, 1; "'Not Guilty'—Indignation over the Verdict in the Dukes Murder Case," *San Francisco Chronicle*, March 15, 1883, 3; "Righteous Indignation," *Kansas City Star* (MO), March 15, 1883, 4; Untitled, *Evening Star* (Washington, DC), March 15, 1883, 2.

7. Four newspapers that offered some word of support for the verdict were the *Patriot* (Harrisburg, PA), *Evening Chronicle* (Pottsville, PA), *Monitor* (Fayette County, PA), and *Lancaster Intelligencer* (PA). Among these four, the *Intelligencer*'s editorial board was split on the verdict (see "The Nutts and Dukes," *Lancaster Intelligencer*, March 15, 1883, 2), and the *Patriot* initially supported the verdict and then quickly announced its opposition (see "Acquittal of Dukes," *Patriot*, March 15, 1883, 2; "The Dukes Case," *Patriot*, March 19, 1883, 2).

8. "Shame! Oh, Shame!!" *Republican Standard* (Uniontown, PA), March 15, 1883, 4; "Dukes' Acquittal," *Philadelphia Inquirer*, March 16, 1883, 1. Quotation appears in *Philadelphia Inquirer*. For an example of riding on a rail from contemporary literature, see Mark Twain, *The Adventures of Tom Sawyer* (Hartford, CT: American, 1876), 106.

9. *Sad Experience*, 26–27.

10. *Sad Experience*, 61; "Juror Cagey's Experience" *Republican Standard* (Uniontown, PA), March 31, 1883, 4; "Here Again," *Republican Standard* (Uniontown, PA), March 22, 1883, 4.

11. "Dukes' Acquittal, *Philadelphia Inquirer*, March 16, 1883, 1; "Shame! Oh, Shame!!" *Republican Standard* (Uniontown, PA), March 15, 1883, 4; Edward J. Donnelly, *Trial of James Nutt for the Killing of N. L. Dukes at Uniontown, Fayette County, Pennsylvania, PA., June 13th, 1883: Containing a Complete History of the Dual Tragedy, Letters and Expert Testimony. Also, the Medical Expert Testimony, Verbatim; Speeches, Rulings, Charge of the Court, Points of Counsel, Portraits, etc.* (Pittsburgh: Stevenson & Foster, 1884), 26; *Sad Experience*, 27; "The Assassin Dukes," *Harrisburg Telegraph*, March 16, 1883, 1. Quotation appears in *Sad Experience*.

12. "What Lizzie Nutt Says," *The Times* (Philadelphia), March 16, 1883, 1.

13. "An Interview with Dukes," *The Times* (Philadelphia), March 16, 1883, 1.

14. Ibid.

15. "Shame! Oh, Shame!!" *Republican Standard* (Uniontown, PA), March 15, 1883, 4; "Denouncing the Verdict," *The Patriot* (Harrisburg, PA), March 16,

1883, 1; Franklin Ellis, *A History of Fayette County, Pennsylvania:With Biographical Sketches of Many of Its Pioneers and Prominent Men* (Philadelphia: Everts, 1882), 314; *Sad Experience*, 20; Donnelly, *James Nutt*, 65, 67; "The Temperature," *Pittsburgh Commercial-Gazette*, March 16, 1883, 4.

16. *Sad Experience*, 21.

17. Ibid.; "Denouncing the Verdict," *The Patriot* (Harrisburg, PA), March 16, 1883, 1. Quotation appears in ibid.

18. "Denouncing the Verdict," *The Patriot* (Harrisburg, PA), March 16, 1883, 1; *Sad Experience*, 22, 25. Quotations appear in *Sad Experience*.

19. "Denouncing the Verdict," *The Patriot* (Harrisburg, PA), March 16, 1883, 1; *Sad Experience*, 26. Quotations appear in *The Patriot*.

20. Quotations appear in untitled, *Somerset Herald* (PA), March 21, 1883, 2 and "Shame! Oh, Shame!!" *Republican Standard* (Uniontown, PA), March 15, 1883, 1. See also Philadelphia *Times* reprinted in "The Press of Verdict," *Harrisburg Telegraph*, March 15, 1883, 2; *Pittsburgh Chronicle* reprinted in "Dirty Dukes," *Republican Standard* (Uniontown, PA), March 22, 1883, 2.

21. Quotations appear in "The News in Harrisburg," *Harrisburg Telegraph*, March 15, 1883, 1; "Dukes, the Murderer," *Harrisburg Telegraph*, March 15, 1883, 4; "Dukes Did Not Come," *Harrisburg Telegraph*, March 16, 1883, 4. See also "Dukes Will Not Get His Seat," *The Times* (Philadelphia), March 16, 1883, 1; "Shame! Oh, Shame!!" *Republican Standard* (Uniontown, PA), March 31, 1883, 4.

22. *Sad Experience*, 43.

23. Karen Lystra, *Searching the Heart: Women, Men, and Romantic Love in Nineteenth-Century America* (New York: Oxford University Press, 1989), 20; "Dukes' Unblushing Baseness," *The Times* (Philadelphia), March 16, 1883, 1; "Dukes' Love Letters," *Republican Standard* (Uniontown, PA), March 22, 1883, 3. Quotations appear in *The Times* and *Republican Standard*.

24. "The Assassin Dukes," *Harrisburg Telegraph*, March 16, 1883, 1; *Sad Experience*, 28. Quotations appear in "The Assassin Dukes."

25. "A Statement from Dukes," *The Patriot* (Harrisburg, PA), March 17, 1883, 1.

26. "The Feeling at Other Points," *The Patriot* (Harrisburg, PA), March 16, 1883, 1; "Springfield," *Republican Standard* (Uniontown, PA), March 22, 1883, 1. Quotation appears in *The Patriot*.

27. "The Press and the Trial," *Republican Standard* (Uniontown, PA), March 22, 1883, 1. See the March 15, 1883 edition (actually published on March 17, 1883) for the headline.

28. "And Still Another," *Harrisburg Telegraph*, March 17, 1883, 1.

29. "Dukes Will Claim His Seat," *The Patriot* (Harrisburg, PA), March 17, 1883, 1; Untitled, *Harrisburg Telegraph*, March 17, 1883, 4; "Dukes Found Not Guilty," *The Times* (Philadelphia), March 15, 1883, 1. Quotations appear in *Harrisburg Telegraph* and "Dukes Found Not Guilty," *The Times*.

30. "Indignation Meetings," *Republican Standard* (Uniontown, PA), March 31, 1883, 3; "Connellsville Blast," *Republican Standard* (Uniontown, PA), March 22, 1883, 3. For a description of the Newmyer Opera House, see Charles Musser, *Before the Nickelodeon: Edwin S. Porter and the Edison Manufacturing Company* (Berkeley: University of California Press, 1991), 22.

31. "Indignation Meetings," *Republican Standard* (Uniontown, PA), March 31, 1883, 3; "Brownsville Indignation," *Republican Standard* (Uniontown, PA), March 22, 1883, 2; Quotation appears in "Indignation Meetings," *Republican Standard*.

32. For hanging Dukes in effigy, see "State News," *Harrisburg Telegraph*, March 19, 1883, 2. For quotations, see "A Crime without a Name," *Worcester Daily Spy* (MA), March 17, 1883, 2; Untitled, *Jackson Weekly Citizen*, April 17, 1883, 7; *Baltimore Day* reprinted in "Dirty Dukes," *Republican Standard*, March 22, 1883, 2; *Poughkeepsie Eagle* reprinted in "Dirty Dukes," *Republican Standard*, March 22, 1883, 2. For other examples of newspapers advocating lynching, see "A Mockery upon Justice," *Duluth Tribune*, March 16, 1883, 1; Untitled, *Daily Globe* (St. Paul, MN), March 15, 1883, 4. For papers suggesting that mob action was inevitable or that Dukes ought to face banishment, see "Personal and Political," *Philadelphia Inquirer*, March 16, 1883, 4; Untitled, *Evening Star* (Washington, DC), March 15, 1883, 2; *Atchison Champion* reprinted in "Dirty Dukes," *Republican Standard* (Uniontown, PA), March 22, 1883, 2; "Dukes, the Assassin, Acquitted," *Harrisburg Telegraph*, March 15, 1883, 2.

33. "Dukes Acquitted," *New York Herald*, March 15, 1883, 6. For other newspapers expressing disapproval of extralegal vengeance, see the Philadelphia *Times* reprinted in "The Press on the Verdict," *Harrisburg Telegraph*, March 15, 1883, 2; "The Dukes Acquittal," *The Patriot* (Harrisburg, PA), March 17, 1883, 2.

34. For Democratic papers advocating vigilantism, see untitled, *Plain Dealer* (Cleveland), March 12, 1883, 2; Untitled, *Daily Globe* (St. Paul, MN), March 15, 1883, 4.

35. "How It Was Done," *Republican Standard* (Uniontown, PA), March 22, 1883, 1.

36. Ibid.

Chapter 8

1. Untitled, *Philadelphia Inquirer*, March 19, 1883, 4; "The Dukes Question," *The Patriot* (Harrisburg, PA), March 20, 1883, 1; "Dukes Will Not Sit," *Republican Standard* (Uniontown, PA), March 22, 1883, 1. Quotations appear in all sources.

2. "Dukes Passes Through," *The Patriot* (Harrisburg, PA), March 21, 1883, 4; *Lizzie Nutt's Sad Experience: A Heart Broken, and a Family Plunged in Grief. Wreck and Ruin!* (Philadelphia: Barclay, 1886), 55.

3. "Dukes Passes Through," *The Patriot* (Harrisburg, PA), March 21, 1883, 4; *Sad Experience*, 57; "The Summons Served," *The Patriot* (Harrisburg, PA), March 26, 1883, 1.

4. "A Possible Sequel to the Dukes Murder Case," *Boston Evening Journal*, March 17, 1883, 1. In 1873, Congress passed the "Comstock laws" that prohibited the use of the postal service for disseminating obscenity. For double jeopardy, see the 1874 Constitution of the Commonwealth of Pennsylvania, Article I, Section 10. The Fifth Amendment to the US Constitution also prohibited double jeopardy, but in 1883, the Fifth Amendment—indeed the entire Bill of Rights—only limited the powers of the federal government, not the states. Not until *Benton v. Maryland* (1969) did the U.S. Supreme Court rule that double jeopardy applied to the states, regardless of whether or not a given state forbade it.

5. "Obscene Mailable Matter," The Patriot (Harrisburg, PA), March 21, 1883.

6. "Dukes' Case in the House," *Republican Standard* (Uniontown, PA), March 22, 1883, 1.

7. "State Legislature—House of Representatives," *Philadelphia Inquirer*, March 22, 1883, 8; *Sad Experience*, 58, 61–62. Quotations appear in *Sad Experience*.

8. *Sad Experience*, 62–63.

9. "Is Dukes in the City?" *The Patriot* (Harrisburg, PA), March 22, 1883, 1; Untitled, *The Patriot* (Harrisburg, PA), March 20, 1883, 2. Quotation appears in untitled, *The Patriot*.

10. "Dukes' Claim to a Seat," *The Patriot* (Harrisburg, PA), March 22, 1883, 1; *Sad Experience*, 61. Quotation appears in *Sad Experience*.

11. "Dukes' Claim to a Seat," *The Patriot* (Harrisburg, PA), March 22, 1883, 1. For an overview of the Buckshot War, see William Henry Egle and Joseph Ritner, "The Buckshot War," *Pennsylvania Magazine of History and Biography* 23 (1899): 137–56. During the 1860s, Stevens left his

indelible mark on American history as a leader of the abolitionist wing in the U.S. Congress.

12. "Dukes' Claim to a Seat," *The Patriot* (Harrisburg, PA), March 22, 1883, 1.

13. "Some Touching Letters," *Republican Standard* (Uniontown, PA), March 22, 1883, 1; "A Murderer's Horoscope," *Republican Standard* (Uniontown, PA), March 22, 1883, 3. Quotations appear in both sources.

14. "Vox Populi," *Republican Standard* (Uniontown, PA), March 22, 1883, 1.

15. "Harrisburg," *Philadelphia Inquirer*, March 23, 1883, 1; "The Dukes Inquiry," *The Patriot* (Harrisburg, PA), March 23, 1883, 1.

16. "Invited to Leave Town," *Republican Standard* (Uniontown, PA), March 31, 1883, 4; "Dukes in Danger," *The Patriot* (Harrisburg, PA), March 27, 1883, 1; *Philadelphia Record* reprinted in "Invited to Leave Town," *Republican Standard* (Uniontown, PA), March 31, 1883, 4. Quotations appear in *The Patriot* and *Philadelphia Record*.

17. "Invited to Leave Town," *Republican Standard* (Uniontown, PA), March 31, 1883, 4; Untitled, *Genius of Liberty* (Uniontown, PA), March 29, 1883, 4.

18. "Dukes Fails to Appear," *The Patriot* (Harrisburg, PA), March 28, 1883, 1; "In the House of Representatives Declared Vacant [*sic*]," *Republican Standard* (Uniontown, PA), March 31, 1883, 4. Quotation appears in *The Patriot*.

19. "Dukes Declines," *Harrisburg Telegraph*, March 28, 1883, 4; "In the House of Representatives Declared Vacant [*sic*]," *Republican Standard* (Uniontown, PA), March 31, 1883, 4. Quotations appear in both sources.

20. "State Legislature—House of Representatives," *Philadelphia Inquirer*, March 29, 1883, 8; Untitled, *Philadelphia Inquirer*, March 29, 1883, 1; "In the House of Representatives Declared Vacant [*sic*]," *Republican Standard*, March 31, 1883, 4. Quotations appear in both *Philadelphia Inquirer* articles.

21. "Tampering with a Witness," *Republican Standard*, March 31, 1883, 4.

22. The *Times* reprinted in "Dukes Acquitted," *Daily Republican* (Monongahela, PA), March 15, 1883, 4; "Jury Justice," *Daily Courier* (Connellsville, PA), March 16, 1883, 1; "The Matter with the Dukes Jury," *Wheeling Register*, March 17, 1883, 2; "An Unfortunate Speculation," *The Patriot* (Harrisburg, PA), March 14, 1883, 2; the Pittsburgh *Post* excerpt in "The Matter with the Dukes Jury," *Wheeling Register*, March 17, 1883, 2;

"Notes and Comments," *Republican Standard* (Uniontown, PA), March 22, 1883, 1. Quotations appear in the *Times* and "The Matter with the Dukes Jury," *Wheeling Register*.

23. "A Social Murder," *Springfield Daily Republican* (MA), March 14, 1883, 4; "A Serious Domestic Warning," *The Sun* (Baltimore), March 15, 1883, 2; "The Acquittal of Dukes," *The Times* (Philadelphia), March 15, 1883, 2; *Washington Post* reprinted in "Dirty Dukes," *Republican Standard* (Uniontown, PA), March 22, 1883, 2; Untitled, *Harrisburg Telegraph*, March 29, 1883, 2; *Lancaster Examiner*, reprinted in "Why the Blood-stained Villain Is Ostracized," *Harrisburg Telegraph*, March 19, 1883, 2. Quotations appear in *Springfield Daily Republican* and *The Times*.

24. Elizabeth Cady Stanton, *A History of Woman Suffrage* (Rochester, NY: Fowler and Wells, 1889), 1: 70–71; Sally G. McMillen, *Seneca Falls and the Origins of the Women's Rights Movement* (New York: Oxford University Press, 2008), 185–228; Michael Kimmel, *Manhood in America: A Cultural History*, 3rd ed. (New York: Oxford University Press, 2012), 62–65; Barbara J. Harris, *Beyond Her Sphere: Women and the Professions in American History* (Westport, CT: Greenwood Press, 1978), 110–13; Christopher J. Lucas, *American Higher Education: A History*, 2nd ed. (New York: Palgrave Macmillan, 2006), 160–64; Thomas D. Snyder, ed. *120 Years of American Education: A Statistical Portrait* (Washington, DC: U.S. Department of Education, Office of Educational Research and Improvement, National Center for Education Statistics, 1993), 82; Untitled, *Saint Paul Daily Globe*, July 22, 1892, 4. Quotation appears in *Saint Paul Daily Globe*.

Chapter 9

1. "Dukes, the Murderer, in Uniontown," *Harrisburg Telegraph*, April 11, 1883, 1.

2. *Chicago Times* reprinted in "Avengers after Dukes," *Plain Dealer* (Cleveland), April 5, 1883, 2; "The Nutt Tragedy," *Atlanta Constitution*, June 17, 1883, 3; Edward J. Donnelly, *Trial of James Nutt for the Killing of N. L. Dukes at Uniontown, Fayette County, Pennsylvania, PA., June 13th, 1883: Containing a Complete History of the Dual Tragedy, Letters and Expert Testimony. Also, the Medical Expert Testimony, Verbatim; Speeches, Rulings, Charge of the Court, Points of Counsel, Portraits, etc.* (Pittsburgh: Stevenson & Foster, 1884), 32. Quotation appears in *James Nutt*.

3. "Sickening Tragedy," *Genius of Liberty* (Uniontown, PA), June 14, 1883, 1; "Dukes Stoned," *Plain Dealer* (Cleveland), April 19, 1883, 1; "Dukes Shot to the Heart," *New-York Times*, June 14, 1883, 1. Quotations appear in *Plain Dealer* and *New-York Times*. Not all of Dukes's friends encouraged him to leave Uniontown—see "Uniontown's Sentiment," *The Patriot* (Harrisburg, PA), June 15, 1883, 1.

4. "Dukes Stoned," *Plain Dealer* (Cleveland), April 19, 1883, 1; Untitled, *Trenton Times*, April 29, 1883, 2; "The Temperature," *Pittsburgh Commercial-Gazette*, April 18, 1883, 4. Quotation appears in *Trenton Times*. Note that a San Francisco paper identified Annie as sixteen years old, not fifteen: "Dukes Cobblestoned," *Daily Evening Bulletin*, April 29, 1883, 1.

5. "Another Dukes Juror," *Wheeling Register*, May 5, 1883, 1; *James Nutt*, 10; "The Vig. Com." *Wheeling Register*, May 4, 1883, 1; "Will Dukes Be Disbarred," *Plain Dealer* (Cleveland), May 4, 1883, 2; *Lizzie Nutt's Sad Experience: A Heart Broken, and a Family Plunged in Grief. Wreck and Ruin!* (Philadelphia: Barclay, 1886), 57. Quotations appear in both *Wheeling Register* articles. For a relatively contemporary source associating the Mollies with criminality, see Robert A. Pinkerton, "Detective Surveillance of Anarchists," *North American Review* 173 (November 1901): 611.

6. "Dukes in Retirement," *Wheeling Register*, April 10, 1883, 1; "Dukes' Successor Named," *The Patriot* (Harrisburg, PA), April 16, 1883, 1; "Republican Nomination for the Fayette County Vacancy," *Harrisburg Telegraph*, April 18, 1883, 1; "Dukes' Successor," *The Patriot* (Harrisburg, PA), April 25, 1883, 1; "Election of Dukes' Successor," *New York Herald*, April 28, 1883, 7. Quotation appears in *Harrisburg Telegraph*.

7. "The Rule to Disbar Dukes," *Wheeling Register* (WV), May 9, 1883, 1; *Sad Experience*, 2728. Quotations appear in the *Wheeling Register*.

8. "The Charges against Dukes," *The Times* (Philadelphia), May 15, 1883, 1; Untitled, *Summit County Beacon* (Akron, OH), May 23, 1883, 3. Quotation appears in *Summit County Beacon*.

9. "The Charges against Dukes," *The Times* (Philadelphia), May 15, 1883, 1; "He Will Fight It Out," *Wheeling Register*, May 16, 1883, 1. Quotation appears in *Wheeling Register*.

10. "The Unpopularity of Dukes," *The Sun* (Baltimore), May 22, 1883, 1.

11. Donnelly, *James Nutt*, 52–53, 84–91.

12. Ibid., 78–79. Quotation appears on page 79.

13. Ibid., 36; "Sickening Tragedy," *Genius of Liberty* (Uniontown, PA), June 14, 1883, 1; "A Son Takes Vengeance," *New-York Tribune*, June 14, 1883, 1; "Life for Life," *The Patriot* (Harrisburg, PA), June 14, 1883, 1;

"Uniontown's Sentiment," *The Patriot* (Harrisburg, PA), June 15, 1883, 1; "Dukes's Violent Death," *The Sun* (Baltimore), June 14, 1883, 1; "The Temperature," *Pittsburgh Commercial-Gazette*, June 14, 1883, 4.

14. "Uniontown's Tragedy," *Harrisburg Telegraph*, June 16, 1883, 1; "Retribution," *Commercial Gazette* (Cincinnati), June 14, 1883, 1; "A Son Takes Vengeance," *New-York Tribune*, June 14, 1883, 1.

15. "Dukes Shot to the Heart," *New-York Times*, June 14, 1883, 1; "Dukes's Violent Death," *The Sun* (Baltimore), June 14, 1883, 1; "Nutt–Dukes," *Genius of Liberty* (Uniontown, PA), June 21, 1883, 1; "Uniontown's Sentiment," *The Patriot* (Harrisburg, PA), June 15, 1883, 1. "Uniontown's Tragedy," *Harrisburg Telegraph*, June 16, 1883, 1; Donnelly, *James Nutt*, 39, 40, 49; "Another Dukes–Nutt Tragedy," *Record-Union* (Sacramento), June 14, 1883, 2.

16. "Sickening Tragedy," *Genius of Liberty* (Uniontown, PA), June 14, 1883, 1; Donnelly, *James Nutt*, 40; "Avenged," *Cincinnati Enquirer*, June 14, 1883, 1. Quotations appear in *James Nutt* and *Cincinnati Enquirer*.

17. "Uniontown's Sentiment," *The Patriot* (Harrisburg, PA), June 15, 1883, 1; Donnelly, *James Nutt*, 44. Quotations appear in *The Patriot*.

18. "Uniontown's Sentiment," *The Patriot* (Harrisburg, PA), June 15, 1883, 1; "Avenged," *Cincinnati Enquirer*, June 14, 1883, 1; "Retribution," *Commercial Gazette* (Cincinnati), June 14, 1883, 1; Donnelly, *James Nutt*, 38.

19. Donnelly, *James Nutt*, 40; "Nutt–Dukes," *Genius of Liberty*, June 21, 1883, 1; "The Uniontown Tragedy," *The Times* (Philadelphia), June 15, 1883, 1; "The Avenger's Deed," *Harrisburg Telegraph*, June 15, 1883, 1. Quotations appear in *James Nutt*.

20. Donnelly, *James Nutt*, 40; "Nutt–Dukes," *Genius of Liberty* (Uniontown, Pennsylvania), June 21, 1883, 1. Quotations appear in *James Nutt*.

21. "Sickening Tragedy," *Genius of Liberty* (Uniontown, PA), June 14, 1883, 1; "Nutt–Dukes," *Genius of Liberty* (Uniontown, PA), June 21, 1883, 1; "Retribution," *Commercial Gazette* (Cincinnati), June 14, 1883, 1.

22. "Retribution," *Commercial Gazette* (Cincinnati), June 14, 1883, 1; Donnelly, *James Nutt*, 42; "A Son Takes Vengeance," *New-York Tribune*, June 14, 1883, 1. For a list of jurors, see, "Nutt–Dukes," *Republican Standard*, June 21, 1883, 1, Historic Newspaper Collection, Pennsylvania Room, Uniontown Public Library.

23. "The Uniontown Tragedy," *The Times* (Philadelphia), June 15, 1883, 1.

24. "Nutt-Dukes," *Republican Standard*, June 21, 1883, 1, Historic Newspaper Collection, Pennsylvania Room, Uniontown Public Library;

"Triumph of Justice," *Harrisburg Telegraph*, June 14, 1883, 1; "Life for Life," *The Patriot* (Harrisburg, PA), June 14, 1883, 1. Quotations appear in *The Patriot*.

25. "Life for Life," *The Patriot* (Harrisburg, PA), June 14, 1883, 1.

26. "The Nutt Tragedy," *Atlanta Constitution*, June 17, 1883, 3; "Dukes's Violent Death," *The Sun* (Baltimore), June 14, 1883, 1.

27. "Avenged," *Cincinnati Enquirer*, June 14, 1883, 1; Donnelly, *James Nutt*, 57.

28. "Uniontown's Sentiment," *The Patriot* (Harrisburg, PA), June 15, 1883, 1; Karen Rae Mehaffey, *Rachel Weeping: Mourning in Nineteenth Century America* (Northville, MI: Moss Rose Books, 2006), 7. It was not unusual for barbers to perform the work of undertakers.

29. "The Uniontown Tragedy," *The Times* (Philadelphia), June 15, 1883, 1; "Nutt–Dukes," *Genius of Liberty* (Uniontown, PA), June 21, 1883, 1. Quotation appears in *Genius of Liberty*. For an example of a sympathetic comment concerning Mrs. Struble from someone who demonized her son, see Senator Voorhees's remarks in Donnelly, *James Nutt*, 167.

30. "Nutt–Dukes," *Genius of Liberty* (Uniontown, PA), June 21, 1883, 1; "The Uniontown Tragedy," *The Times* (Philadelphia), June 15, 1883, 1. Quotation appears in *Genius of Liberty*.

31. "The Uniontown Tragedy," *The Times* (Philadelphia), June 15, 1883, 1; "The Uniontown Tragedy," *Evening Critic* (Washington, DC), June 14, 1883, 1; "The Killing of Dukes," *The Patriot* (Harrisburg, PA), June 15, 1883, 1.

32. Quotations appear in untitled, *New Haven Evening Register*, June 15, 1883, 2; Untitled, *Saint Paul Daily Globe* (MN), June 14, 1883, 4; Untitled, *Atlanta Constitution*, June 15, 1883, 4; "The Unwritten Law of Homicide," *Plain Dealer* (Cleveland), June 14, 1883, 2; *Pittsburgh Commercial-Gazette* reprinted in "Dukes Shot Dead!" *Daily Republican* (Monongahela, PA), June 14, 1883, 1. For examples of Democratic papers that supported James, see the citations for the *Plain Dealer, Daily Globe*, and *Atlanta Constitution* above as well as "The Pennsylvania Tragedy," *Daily Picayune* (New Orleans), June 16, 1883, 4; "A Noble Act," *Wheeling Register*, June 15, 1883, 2. For instances of Republican endorsements of James, see untitled, *Morning Oregonian* (Portland), June 15, 1883, 2; "Justice at Last," *Harrisburg Telegraph*, June 14, 1883, 2; Untitled, *Daily Republican* (Monongahela, PA), June 16, 1883, 4. For examples of front-page headlines across the country, see "A Murderer's Fate," *Boston Daily Advertiser*, June 14, 1883, 1; "Avenged," *Daily Evening Bulletin* (San

Francisco), June 14, 1883, 1; "A Son's Vengeance," *Waco Daily Examiner* (TX), June 14, 1883, 1; "Dukes Shot to the Heart," *New-York Times*, June 14, 1883, 1; "Retributive Justice," *Independent Record* (Helena, MT), June 14, 1883, 1; "Retaliation—Dukes Murdered," *St. Albans Daily* Messenger (VT), June 14, 1883, 1; "Revenged at Last," *Columbus Daily Enquirer-Sun* (GA), June 14, 1883, 1; "Murder Repaid," *Oshkosh Daily Northwestern* (WI), June 14, 1883, 1; "Blood for Blood," *National Republican* (Washington, DC), June 14, 1883, 1; "A Son Takes Vengeance," *New-York Tribune*, June 14, 1883, 1; "Dukes Killed by Nutt's Son," *Trenton Times*, June 14, 1883, 1; "Dukes's Violent Death," *The Sun* (Baltimore), June 14, 1883, 1; "Death for Dukes," *Plain Dealer* (Cleveland), June 14, 1883, 1; "Avenger of Blood," *Philadelphia Inquirer*, June 14, 1883, 1; "Retribution," *Commercial Gazette* (Cincinnati), June 14, 1883, 1; "Dukes, the Uniontown, Pa., Scoundrel, Killed by Capt. Nutt's Son," *Duluth Daily Tribune*, June 14, 1883, 1; "Life for Life," *The Patriot* (Harrisburg, PA), June 14, 1883, 1; "Avenged His Father's Murder," *Jackson Daily Citizen* (MI), June 14, 1883, 1; "The Uniontown Tragedy," *Evening Critic* (Washington, DC), June 14, 1883, 1; "Vengeance," *New York Herald*, June 14, 1883, 3; "A Serpent Slain," *Wheeling Register* (WV), June 14, 1883, 1; "Dukes Done For," *Dallas Daily Herald*, June 14, 1883, 1; "Avenged," *Cincinnati Enquirer*, June 14, 1883, 1; "Dukes Dead," *Reading Times* (PA), June 14, 1883, 1; "Captain Nutt's Murder Avenged!" *Lebanon Daily News* (PA), June 14, 1883, 1; "A Life for a Life," *Delaware County Daily Times* (Chester, PA), June 14, 1883, 1; "Dukes, the Murderer, Slain by His Victim's Son," *Alton Evening Telegraph* (IL), June 14, 1883, 1; "Dukes Shot Dead!" *Daily Republican* (Monongahela, PA), June 14, 1883, 1; "Revenged His Father's Death," *Fort Wayne Daily Sentinel* (IN), June 14, 1883, 1; "Revenged at Last," *Evening Observer* (Dunkirk, NY), June 14, 1883, 1; "Blood for Blood," *Daily Gazette and Bulletin* (Williamsport, PA), June 14, 1883, 1; "Triumph of Justice," *Harrisburg Telegraph*, June 14, 1883, 1; "Dukes Killed," *Lancaster Intelligencer* (PA), June 14, 1883, 1; "Dukes Shot," *Salt Lake Daily Herald*, June 14, 1883, 1; "Dukes Done For," *Daily Globe* (St. Paul, MN), June 14, 1883, 1; "Dukes Shot and Killed," *The Sun* (NY), June 14, 1883, 1; "Dukes' Fate," *Wheeling Intelligencer* (WV), June 14, 1883, 1.

33. "The Youthful Avenger," *Trenton Times*, June 14, 1883, 2. See also "The Nutt–Dukes Tragedies," *The Times* (Philadelphia), June 16, 1883, 4; "The Death of Dukes," *Springfield Daily Republican* (MA), June 15, 1883, 4; *Philadelphia North American* reprinted in "The Press on the Shooting," *Harrisburg Telegraph*, June 15, 1883, 2.

34. "The Dukes Tragedy," *The Patriot* (Harrisburg, PA), June 14, 1883, 2; "Dukes Shot to the Heart," *New-York Times*, June 14, 1883, 1; "Gath's Letter," *The Times* (Philadelphia), June 17, 1883, 5. Quotation appears in "Gath's Letter."

35. Untitled, *Record-Union* (Sacramento), June 16, 1883, 4. For other examples of newspapers blaming Dukes's death on the jury that acquitted him, see Untitled, *New Haven Evening Register*, June 14, 1883, 2; "A Terrible Retribution," *The Sun* (Baltimore), June 14, 1883, 2; *Pittsburgh Times* reprinted in "Dukes Shot Dead!" *Daily Republican* (Monongahela, PA), June 14, 1883, 1; "The Vendetta in Pennsylvania," *The Times* (Philadelphia), June 14, 1883, 2; *Philadelphia Press* reprinted in "The Press on the Shooting," *Harrisburg Telegraph*, June 15, 1883, 2; Untitled, *Commercial Gazette* (Cincinnati) June 15, 1883, 4; *New York World* and *Cincinnati Enquirer* reprinted in "Various Opinions," *Wheeling Register*, June 16, 1883, 1; "The Pennsylvania Tragedy," *Daily Picayune* (New Orleans), June 16, 1883, 4; "He Will Not Be Punished," *Daily Gazette* (Kalamazoo, MI), June 15, 1883, 2. For the potential of James's trial to redeem the honor of Pennsylvania, see untitled, *Dallas Daily Herald*, June 16, 1883, 4.

36. Quotations appear in untitled, *Wheeling Register*, June 14, 1883, 2; "The Killing of Dukes," *New-York Times*, June 14, 1883, 4. For locals' concern about James's trial, see "The Dukes Affray," *Plain Dealer* (Cleveland), June 14, 1883, 1. For additional examples of press coverage that predicted popular support for James Nutt, see "The Death of Dukes," *Springfield Daily Republican* (MA), June 15, 1883, 4; "The Dukes Tragedy," *The Patriot* (Harrisburg, PA), June 14, 1883, 2; "The Killing of Dukes," *New-York Times*, June 14, 1883, 4; *Pittsburg Dispatch* reprinted in "Dukes Shot Dead!" *Daily Republican* (Monongahela, PA), June 14, 1883, 1; Untitled, *Wilmington Morning Star* (NC), June 15, 1883, 2; Untitled, *Trenton Evening Times*, June 17, 1883, 2. For the inevitability of James's acquittal, see untitled, *New Haven Evening Register*, June 14, 1883, 2; *Pittsburg Dispatch* reprinted in "Dukes Shot Dead!" *Daily Republican* (Monongahela, PA), June 14, 1883, 1; "The Unwritten Law of Homicide," *Plain Dealer* (Cleveland), June 14, 1883, 2; "The Nutt–Dukes Tragedies," *The Times* (Philadelphia), June 16, 1883, 4.

37. Untitled, *Evening Star* (Washington, DC), June 14, 1883, 2. For other examples of editorial criticism of James, see *Pittsburg Dispatch* reprinted in "Nutt–Dukes," *Genius of Liberty* (Uniontown, PA), June 21, 1883, 1; Pittsburgh *Times* reprinted in "Dukes Shot Dead!" *Daily*

Republican (Monongahela, PA), June 14, 1883, 1. For commentary on how few papers condemned James, see untitled, *Wheeling Register*, June 15, 1883, 2. James Nutt's detractors, like his supporters, came from both political parties. For a Republican paper that did not support James, see Untitled, *Worcester Daily Spy* (MA), June 15, 1883, 2; for Democratic opposition to James, see "Sickening Tragedy," *Genius of Liberty* (Uniontown, PA), June 14, 1883, 1.

38. "The Avenger's Deed," *Harrisburg Telegraph*, June 15, 1883, 1; "Nutt–Dukes," *Genius of Liberty* (Uniontown, PA), June 21, 1883, 1; "Dukes's Violent Death," Baltimore *Sun*, June 14, 1883, 1. Quotations appear in the *Harrisburg Telegraph*.

39. "The Avenger's Deed," *Harrisburg Telegraph*, June 15, 1883, 1.

40. "Uniontown's Tragedy," *Harrisburg Telegraph*, June 16, 1883, 1; "The Nutt Tragedy," *Atlanta Constitution*, June 17, 1883, 3; "Dukes–Nutt," *Chicago Tribune*, June 15, 1883, 5; Robert M. Ireland, "Popular Justice in Pennsylvania: The Nutt–Dukes Tragedy," *Pennsylvania Magazine of History and Biography* 113 (July 1989): 408n20. Quotations appear in *Harrisburg Telegraph*.

41. "Nutt–Dukes," *Genius of Liberty* (Uniontown, PA), June 21, 1883, 1; "Dukes Bemains [sic] Buried," *Harrisburg Telegraph*, June 18, 1883, 1.

42. "Nutt-Dukes," *Genius of Liberty* (Uniontown, PA), June 21, 1883, 1; "Dukes Bemains [sic] Buried," *Harrisburg Telegraph*, June 18, 1883, 1; "The Funeral of N. L. Dukes," *The Times* (Philadelphia), June 18, 1883, 3. Depending on the publication, reporters spelled the name of Dukes's brother either "Lewis" or "Louis."

43. "Nutt–Dukes," *Genius of Liberty* (Uniontown, PA), June 21, 1883, 1; "In Remembrance of Dukes," *The Patriot* (Harrisburg, PA), June 18, 1883, 1. Quotation appears in *Genius of Liberty*. Robert Ireland puts the number of Dukes's funeral attendees at close to 500 in "Popular Justice," 407, compared to 2,000 mourners at Adam Nutt's funeral, as described in *Genius of Liberty* (Uniontown, PA), "Fearful Tragedy," December 28, 1882, 1.

44. Ireland, "Popular Justice," 407; "In Remembrance of Dukes," *The Patriot* (Harrisburg, PA), June 18, 1883, 1. Quotation appears in *The Patriot*.

45. Untitled, *Harrisburg Telegraph*, June 19, 1883, 2; "The Death of Dukes," *The Times* (Philadelphia), June 18, 1883, 3; "Lizzie Nutt's Sorrow," *Atlanta Constitution*, June 20, 1883, 1. Quotations appear in *The Times* and *Atlanta Constitution*.

Chapter 10

1. "The Defense of James Nutt," *Harrisburg Telegraph*, June 20, 1883, 1; "The Uniontown Tragedy," *The Times* (Philadelphia), June 15, 1883, 1; "Raising a Fund for Young Jim Nutt," *The Times* (Philadelphia), June 27, 1883, 2; "Dukes Bemains [*sic*] Buried," *Harrisburg Telegraph*, June 18, 1883, 1.

2. "The Uniontown Tragedy," *The Times* (Philadelphia), June 15, 1883, 1; "Nutt's Trial Postponed," *The Times* (Philadelphia), December 6, 1883, 1; "In Court," *Genius of Liberty* (Uniontown, PA), December 6, 1883, 1; "Not Guilty," *Genius of Liberty* (Uniontown, PA), January 24, 1884, 1; "The Nutt Trial," *The Times* (Philadelphia), January 14, 1884, 1.

3. "The Dukes Tragedy," *The Patriot* (Harrisburg, PA), June 23, 1883, 1; "The Uniontown Tragedy," *The Times* (Philadelphia), June 15, 1883, 1.

4. "Lizzie Nutt's Sorrow," *Atlanta Constitution*, June 20, 1883, 1; "Uniontown's Tragedy," *Harrisburg Telegraph*, June 16, 1883, 1.

5. "The Avenger's Deed," *Harrisburg Telegraph*, June 15, 1883, 1.

6. "The Defense of James Nutt," *Harrisburg Telegraph*, June 20, 1883, 1; "Nutt–Dukes," *Genius of Liberty* (Uniontown, PA), June 21, 1883, 1; "Dukes' Last Will," *The Times* (Philadelphia), June 26, 1883, 2; Edward J. Donnelly, *Trial of James Nutt for the Killing of N. L. Dukes at Uniontown, Fayette County, Pennsylvania, PA., June 13th, 1883: Containing a Complete History of the Dual Tragedy, Letters and Expert Testimony. Also, the Medical Expert Testimony, Verbatim; Speeches, Rulings, Charge of the Court, Points of Counsel, Portraits, etc.* (Pittsburgh: Stevenson & Foster, 1884), 26; "The Will of Dukes," *Harrisburg Telegraph*, June 26, 1883, 1. Quotations appear in *James Nutt* and "The Will of Dukes," *Harrisburg Telegraph.*

7. "State Notes," *Harrisburg Telegraph*, July 20, 1883, 2; "How Jim Nutt Plays Seven-up," *The Patriot* (Harrisburg, PA), July 20, 1883, 2; "A Statement from Dukes," *Harrisburg Patriot*, March 17, 1883, 1; "A Dead Murderer's Plea," *New-York Times*, August 10, 1883, 1–2. For other examples of press coverage of Dukes's letter, see "Dukes in His Own Defense," *The Times* (Philadelphia), August 10, 1883, 1; "Dukes, the Assassin," *Chicago Daily Tribune*, August 10, 1883, 6; "Dukes in His Own Defense," *Courier-Journal* (Louisville, KY), August 12, 1883, 12; "From the Grave," *Atlanta Constitution*, August 12, 1883, 3; "Dukes in Justification," *New Haven Evening Register*, August 10, 1883, 3; "A Voice from the Tomb," *The Sun* (Baltimore), August 10, 1883, 1; "Dukes' Defense," *Daily Gazette* (Kalamazoo,

MI), August 11, 1883, 1. Some of the papers reprinted the letter in full, whereas others published excerpts.

8. Donnelly, *James Nutt*, 27–28.

9. Ibid., 28–29.

10. Ibid., 29.

11. Ibid., 29–30; Melissa Murray, "Marriage as Punishment," *Columbia Law Review* 112 (January 2012): 12. Quotations appear in ibid. For the Pennsylvania seduction statute, see James Dunlop, *The General Laws of Pennsylvania, From the Year 1700, To April 1849*, 2nd ed. (Philadelphia: Johnson, 1849), 1012. The language of the statute was modified slightly in 1860—see *Penal Laws of Pennsylvania: Passed March 31, 1860* (Harrisburg: Hamilton, 1860), 15.

12. Donnelly, *James Nutt*, 29–30.

13. "Dukes' Claim to a Seat," *The Patriot* (Harrisburg, PA), March 22, 1883, 1; "Dukes in His Own Defense," *The Times* (Philadelphia), August 10, 1883, 1. Quotation appears in *The Patriot*.

14. Untitled, *Cincinnati Enquirer*, August 11, 1883, 4; Untitled, *New York Tribune*, August 11, 1883, 4; "A Voice from the Grave," *Wheeling Register*, August 11, 1883, 2. Quotation appears in *New York Tribune*. For other examples of editorial comment that was critical of Dukes's statement, see "Much Better," *Harrisburg Telegraph*, August 13, 1883, 2; Untitled, *Inter Ocean*, August 11, 1883, 12; "Dukes' Self-Condemnation," *The Times* (Philadelphia), August 10, 1883, 2.

15. "Senator A. J. Herr," *Harrisburg Telegraph*, August 20, 1883, 4; "The Nutt Trial," *The Times* (Philadelphia), December 1, 1883, 1. Quotation appears in *The Times*.

16. Thomas Cushing, *The History of Allegheny County, Pennsylvania* (Chicago: Warner, 1889), 276; "Nutt's Trial Postponed," *The Times* (Philadelphia), December 6, 1883, 1; "The Nutt Trial," *The Times* (Philadelphia), December 1, 1883, 1. Quotation appears in *History of Allegheny County*.

17. Leonard S. Kenworthy, *The Tall Sycamore of the Wabash: Daniel Wolsey Voorhees* (Boston: Humphries, 1936), 43; "The Nutt Trial," *The Times* (Philadelphia), December 1, 1883, 1.

18. Henry D. Jordan, "Daniel Wolsey Voorhees," *Mississippi Valley Historical Review* 6 (March 1920): 533–34; Thomas B. Long, "Daniel W. Voorhees," in Daniel Wolsey Voorhees, *Forty Years of Oratory* (Indianapolis and Kansas City: Bowen–Merrill, 1898), 1:5; Steven Lubet, *John Brown's Spy: The Adventurous Life and Tragic Confession of John E. Cook* (New Haven, CT: Yale University Press, 2012), 244–45.

19. Jordan, "Voorhees," 533, 543; Lee Chambers-Schiller, "Seduced, Betrayed, and Revenged: The Murder Trial of Marry Harris," in Michael A. Bellesiles, ed., *Lethal Imagination: Violence and Brutality in American History* (New York: New York University Press, 1999), 185; John D. Lawson, ed., *American State Trials* (St. Louis: Thomas Law Book, 1936), 17: 234, 17: 299–300. Quotations appear in *American State Trials*, 17: 299–300.

20. J. Thomas Schard, *History of Western Maryland* (Philadelphia: Everts, 1882), 1:423; *Trial of Harry Crawford Black for the Killing of Col. W. W. McKaig, Jr.: In the Circuit Court of the Sixth Judicial Circuit of Maryland, Sitting at Frederick City, April 11, 1871, before Hon. W. P. Maulsby, Chief Justice, Hon. John A. Lunch, Associate Justice, Hon. J. Veirs Bowic, Associate Justice* (Washington, DC, 1871), 31, 140. Quotation appears in *Trial of Harry Crawford Black*, 140.

21. L. F. Johnson, *Famous Kentucky Tragedies and Trials* (Louisville, KY: Baldwin Law Book, 1916), 233–34; "The Sanctity of Home," *Courier-Journal* (Louisville, KY), May 16, 1883, 5. Quotations appear in both sources.

22. "A Postponement of the Nutt Trial Probable," *The Times* (Philadelphia), September 5, 1883, 1; "The Nutt Trial Postponed," *The Times* (Philadelphia), September 6, 1883, 4.

23. "The Nutt Trial," *The Times* (Philadelphia), December 1, 1883, 1.

24. Ibid.; "In Court," *Genius of Liberty* (Uniontown, PA), December 6, 1883, 1.

25. "Young Nutt's Trial," *The Times* (Philadelphia), December 5, 1883, 1.

26. Untitled, *The Times* (Philadelphia), December 5, 1883, 2; "The Nutt Trial," *The Times* (Philadelphia), December 1, 1883, 1. Quotations appear in both sources.

27. "Young Nutt's Defense," *The Times* (Philadelphia), November 16, 1883, 1; "The Trial of James Nutt," *Harrisburg Telegraph*, November 19, 1883, 1; "News in the State," *The Patriot* (Harrisburg, PA), October 16, 1883, 2.

Chapter 11

1. "Jim Nutt Gets No Jury," *The Courier* (Connellsville, PA), December 7, 1883, 1.

2. Ibid., "Nutt's Trial Postponed," *The Times* (Philadelphia), December 6, 1883, 1; "In Court," *Genius of Liberty* (Uniontown, PA), December 6, 1883, 1.

3. "The Nutt Trial," *The Times* (Philadelphia), December 1, 1883, 1; "Nutt's Trial Postponed," *The Times* (Philadelphia), December 6, 1883, 1; "The Avenger's Deed," *Harrisburg Telegraph*, June 15, 1883, 1; "In Court," *Genius of Liberty* (Uniontown, PA), December 6, 1883, 1. Quotations appear in *Genius of Liberty*.

4. "In Court," *Genius of Liberty* (Uniontown, PA), December 6, 1883, 1.

5. "Nutt's Trial Postponed," *The Times* (Philadelphia), December 6, 1883, 1; "In Court," *Genius of Liberty* (Uniontown, PA), December 6, 1883, 1.

6. "Nutt's Trial Postponed," *The Times* (Philadelphia), December 6, 1883, 1; "In Court," *Genius of Liberty* (Uniontown, PA), December 6, 1883, 1.

7. "Nutt's Trial Postponed," *The Times* (Philadelphia), December 6, 1883, 1.

8. "In Court," *Genius of Liberty* (Uniontown, PA), December 6, 1883, 1.

9. Ibid.; "Jim Nutt Gets No Jury," *The Courier* (Connellsville, PA), December 7, 1883, 1. Quotation appears in *The Courier*.

10. "Sudden Change of Venue," *Harrisburg Telegraph*, December 6, 1883, 1; "Nutt's Trial Postponed," *The Times* (Philadelphia), December 6, 1883, 1; "Jim Nutt Gets No Jury," *The Courier* (Connellsville, PA), December 7, 1883, 1; "Paragraphic Items," *The Patriot* (Harrisburg, PA), December 10, 1883, 1. Quotation appears in *Harrisburg Telegraph*. The press echoed Patterson's contention that Pittsburgh embraced James's honor killing even more than did Fayette County—see "The Trial of Nutt," *The Patriot* (Harrisburg, PA), December 6, 1883, 1. The trial was originally scheduled for January 7, 1884, but was later changed to January 14—see "The Date of Young Nutt's Trial," *The Patriot* (Harrisburg, PA), December 10, 1883, 1; "The County Capital," *Daily Courier* (Connellsville, PA), December 21, 1883, 4.

11. "Friends of Nutt Threatened," *The Times* (Philadelphia), December 26, 1883, 1; "James Nutt's Secret Foes," *The Times* (Philadelphia), December 27, 1883, 1; "A Fiend's Cowardice," *Harrisburg Telegraph*, December 26, 1883, 1. Quotation appears in "Friends of Nutt Threatened," *The Times*.

12. "The Nutt Trial," *Genius of Liberty* (Uniontown, PA), January 17, 1884, 1.

13. Willard Glazier, *Peculiarities of American Cities* (Philadelphia: Hubbard Brothers, 1886), 335–38.

14. Ibid.; S. J. Kleinberg, *The Shadow of the Mills: Working-Class Families in Pittsburgh, 1870–1907* (Pittsburgh: University of Pittsburgh Press,

1989), 86–87, 224–26; James Parton, "Pittsburg," *Atlantic Monthly* 21 (January 1868): 21; Joseph Frazier Wall, *Andrew Carnegie* (New York: Oxford University Press, 1970), 386. Quotations appear in ibid.; *Atlantic Monthly*; *Andrew Carnegie*.

15. Kleinberg, *Shadow of the Mills*, 12, 84–85; Glazier, *American Cities*, 337; Joel A. Tarr, *Transportation Innovation and Changing Spatial Patterns in Pittsburgh, 1850–1934* (Chicago: Public Works Historical Society, 1978), 6–14.

16. "James Nutt at Pittsburg," *The Times* (Philadelphia), January 13, 1884, 2; "Sunday's News Budget," *The Patriot* (Harrisburg, PA), January 15, 1884, 1; "The Nutt Trial," *The Times* (Philadelphia), January 14, 1884, 1; "The Case of James Nutt," *Harrisburg Telegraph*, January 14, 1884, 1; "The Nutt Trial," *Genius of Liberty* (Uniontown, PA), January 17, 1884, 1. Quotation appears in the *Genius of Liberty*.

17. Thomas Keneally, *American Scoundrel* (London: Chatto & Windus, 2002), 107–98. Quotations appear on 127, 174, and 175. The Sickles trial offered the first widely known plea of temporary insanity but not its seminal use—see Robert M. Ireland, "Insanity and the Unwritten Law," *American Journal of Legal History* 32 (April 1988): 162.

18. Charles E. Rosenberg, *The Trial of Assassin Guiteau: Psychiatry and Law in the Gilded Age* (Chicago: University of Chicago Press, 1968), 53, 63–65; Ireland, "Insanity and the Unwritten Law," 164–67; Irving B. Weiner, *Handbook of Psychology* (Hoboken, NJ: Wiley, 2003), 11: 391.

19. Ireland, "Insanity and the Unwritten Law," 168–69.

20. "Sunday's News Budget," *The Patriot* (Harrisburg, PA), January 15, 1884, 1; "The Nutt Trial," *The Times* (Philadelphia), January 14, 1884, 1; "James Nutt at Pittsburg," *The Times* (Philadelphia), January 13, 1884, 2. For examples of international news coverage see "El Vengador de su Familia," *El Siglo Diez y Nueve* (Mexico City, Mexico), January 7, 1884, 2; "Our American Letter—An Expected Retribution," *Evening News* (Sydney, Australia), July 25, 1883, 3; "The United States," *The Times* (London, England), June 15, 1883, 5; "Young Nutt's Provocation," *Star and Herald* (Panama, Panama), July 9, 1883, 2; "Tragedy in Pennsylvania," *Demerara Daily Chronicle* (Georgetown, Guyana), August 15, 1883, 4; "Man-Slaying in the United States," *Aberdeen Weekly Journal* (Scotland), July 4, 1883, 6.

21. "James Nutt on Trial," *The Times* (Philadelphia), January 15, 1884, 1; "The Nutt Trial," *Genius of Liberty* (Uniontown, PA), January 17, 1884, 1; "The Dukes–Nutt Tragedies," *The Times* (Philadelphia), January 22, 1884, 2. Note that this latter source is an advertisement rather than an article.

Stevenson & Foster initially planned to sell copies for 50¢ but the actual price was 25¢. Quotation appears in *Genius of Liberty*.

22. "The Nutt Trial," *Genius of Liberty* (Uniontown, PA), January 17, 1884, 1.

23. Ibid.

24. Ibid., "James Nutt on Trial," *The Times* (Philadelphia), January 15, 1884, 1; "James Nutt on Trial," *The Patriot* (Harrisburg, PA), January 15, 1884, 1.

25. "James Nutt on Trial," *The Times* (Philadelphia), January 15, 1884, 1; "The Nutt Trial," *Genius of Liberty* (Uniontown, PA), January 17, 1884, 1; "James Nutt on Trial," *The Patriot* (Harrisburg, PA), January 15, 1884, 1. Quotations appear in *Genius of Liberty*.

26. "James Nutt on Trial," *The Times* (Philadelphia), January 15, 1884, 1; "The Nutt Trial," *Genius of Liberty* (Uniontown, PA), January 17, 1884, 1.

27. "James Nutt on Trial," *The Times* (Philadelphia), January 15, 1884, 1; "James Nutt on Trial," *The Patriot* (Harrisburg, PA), January 15, 1884, 1; "The Nutt Trial," *Genius of Liberty* (Uniontown, PA), January 17, 1884, 1. Quotations appear in *The Times*.

28. "James Nutt on Trial," *The Times* (Philadelphia), January 15, 1884, 1; "The Nutt Trial," *Genius of Liberty* (Uniontown, PA), January 17, 1884, 1.

29. "The Nutt Trial," *Genius of Liberty*, January 17, 1884, 1; "James Nutt on Trial," *The Times* (Philadelphia), January 15, 1884, 1. Quotation appears in *Genius of Liberty*.

30. "James Nutt on Trial," *The Times* (Philadelphia), January 15, 1884, 1; "The Nutt Trial," *Genius of Liberty* (Uniontown, PA), January 17, 1884, 1; Edward J. Donnelly, *Trial of James Nutt for the Killing of N. L. Dukes at Uniontown, Fayette County, Pennsylvania, PA., June 13th, 1883: Containing a Complete History of the Dual Tragedy, Letters and Expert Testimony. Also, the Medical Expert Testimony, Verbatim; Speeches, Rulings, Charge of the Court, Points of Counsel, Portraits, etc.* (Pittsburgh: Stevenson & Foster, 1884), 32; Robert M. Ireland, "Popular Justice in Pennsylvania: The Nutt–Dukes Tragedy," *Pennsylvania Magazine of History and Biography* 113 (July 1989): 409.

31. "The Nutt Trial," *Genius of Liberty* (Uniontown, PA), January 17, 1884, 1; "James Nutt on Trial," *The Times* (Philadelphia), January 15, 1884, 1.

32. "James Nutt on Trial," *The Patriot* (Harrisburg, PA), January 15, 1884, 1; "The Case of James Nutt," *Harrisburg Telegraph*, January 14, 1884, 1;

"The Nutt Trial," *Genius of Liberty* (Uniontown, PA), January 17, 1884, 1. Quotation appears in *The Patriot*.

33. "The Nutt Murder Trial," *The Times* (Philadelphia), January 16, 1884, 1; "The Nutt Trial," *Genius of Liberty* (Uniontown, PA), January 17, 1884, 1; *Johnstown Tribune* reprinted in "Another Kind of Witnesses" [*sic*], *Harrisburg Telegraph*, January 18, 1884, 2. Quotation appears in *The Times*.

34. "The Nutt Murder Trial," *The Times* (Philadelphia), January 16, 1884, 1; "James Nutt on Trial," *Harrisburg Telegraph*, January 15, 1884, 1.

35. Donnelly, *James Nutt*, 33–34; "The Nutt Murder Trial," *The Times* (Philadelphia), January 16, 1884, 1. Quotation appears on *James Nutt*, 34.

36. Donnelly, *James Nutt*, 35–41; "James Nutt's Trial," *Harrisburg Telegraph*, January 16, 1884, 1; "Second Day in Court," *The Patriot* (Harrisburg, PA), January 16, 1884, 1. The first quotation appears in *James Nutt*, 40; the phrase "great blunder" appears in both the *Harrisburg Telegraph* and *The Patriot*.

37. "The Nutt Trial," *Genius of Liberty* (Uniontown, PA), January 17, 1884, 1; Donnelly, *James Nutt*, 41-2; "Dr. John Sturgeon Has Had a Notable Medical Career," *Daily News Standard* (Uniontown, PA), March 31, 1934, 2. Quotations appear in *Genius of Liberty*.

38. Donnelly, *James Nutt*, 42; "The Nutt Trial," *Genius of Liberty* (Uniontown, PA), January 17, 1884, 1; Quotations appear in *James Nutt*.

39. "The Nutt Murder Trial," *The Times* (Philadelphia), January 16, 1884, 1; Donnelly, *James Nutt*, 43–51. Quotations appear in *James Nutt*, 45, 47.

40. "Second Day in Court," *The Patriot* (Harrisburg, PA), January 16, 1884, 1; "The Nutt Murder Trial," *The Times* (Philadelphia), January 16, 1884, 1; Donnelly, *James Nutt*, 52–56. Quotation appears in *James Nutt*, 53.

41. Donnelly, *James Nutt*, 56–57; "James Nutt on Trial," *Harrisburg Telegraph*, January 15, 1884, 1; "Second Day in Court," *The Patriot* (Harrisburg, PA), January 16, 1884, 1. Quotation appears in *James Nutt*, 57.

42. Donnelly, *James Nutt*, 57.

Chapter 12

1. "The Temperature," *Pittsburgh Commercial-Gazette*, January 17, 1884, 4; "Nutt's Defense in Court," *The Patriot* (Harrisburg, PA), January 17, 1884, 1; Edward J. Donnelly, *Trial of James Nutt for the Killing of N. L. Dukes at Uniontown, Fayette County, Pennsylvania, PA., June 13th, 1883: Containing a Complete History of the Dual Tragedy, Letters and Expert Testimony. Also, the Medical Expert Testimony, Verbatim; Speeches, Rulings, Charge*

of the Court, Points of Counsel, Portraits, etc. (Pittsburgh: Stevenson & Foster, 1884), 59–63. Quotation appears *James Nutt*, 59.

2. Donnelly, *James Nutt*, 61–66. Quotations appear on pages 61, 63, 64.

3. "James Nutt's Defense," *The Times* (Philadelphia), January 17, 1884, 1.

4. Donnelly, *James Nutt*, 67–69. For leading questions being objectionable, see Simon Greenleaf, *A Treatise on the Law of Evidence*, 14th ed., rev. Simon Greenleaf Croswell (Boston: Little, Brown, 1883), 1: 521–22.

5. Donnelly, *James Nutt*, 70–71, 76.

6. Ibid., 72–74, 77.

7. Ibid., 78–89. Quotation appears on page 88.

8. Ibid., 89–90; "The Nutt Trial," *Genius of Liberty* (Uniontown, PA), January 17, 1884, 1; "James Nutt's Defense," *The Times* (Philadelphia), January 17, 1884, 1. The Philadelphia *Times* suggested that Dr. Fuller's testimony in particular had an impact on the jury.

9. "Was Young Nutt Insane?," *The Times* (Philadelphia), January 18, 1884, 1.

10. Donnelly, *James Nutt*, 91–95, 102.

11. Ibid., 98–100. Quotation appears on page 98.

12. Ibid., 63, 106. Quotation appears on page 63.

13. Ibid., 107–8.

14. Ibid., 108–9.

15. Donnelly, *James Nutt*, 109–10; Tal Golan, "Revisiting the History of Scientific Expert Testimony," *Brooklyn Law Review* 73 (Spring 2008): 921–22.

16. Donnelly, *James Nutt*, 110–11.

17. Ibid., 112–13. Quotation appears on page 113.

18. Ibid., 113–14. Quotations appear on page 114.

19. Ibid., 115–16. Quotation appears on page 115.

20. Ibid., 116.

21. Ibid., 117–18.

22. Ibid., 119–20; Robert M. Ireland, "Insanity and the Unwritten Law," *American Journal of Legal History* 32 (April 1988): 160, 164; Frank R. Freemon, "William Alexander Hamilton: The Centenary of His Death," *Journal of the History of the Neurosciences* 10 (December 2001): 293–99; William Alexander Hammond, *A Treatise on Insanity in Its Medical Relations* (New York: Appleton, 1883); Charles E. Rosenberg, *The Trial of Assassin Guiteau: Psychiatry and Law in the Gilded Age* (Chicago: University of Chicago Press, 1968), 60. Quotation appears in *James Nutt*, 119.

23. Donnelly, *James Nutt*, 122.

24. Ibid., 122–24.

25. Ibid., 125–26. Quotation appears on page 125.

26. "The Nutt Defense All In," *The Times* (Philadelphia), January 19, 1884, 1.

27. Donnelly, *James Nutt*, 126.

28. Ibid., 127–29.

29. "The Trial of James Nutt," *Harrisburg Telegraph*, January 19, 1884, 1; "James Nutt's Weak Mind," *The Patriot* (Harrisburg, PA), January 19, 1884, 1.

30. "The Nutt Defense All In," *The Times* (Philadelphia), January 19, 1884, 1; Donnelly, *James Nutt*, 142. Quotation appears in *The Times*.

31. "James Nutt's Weak Mind," *The Patriot* (Harrisburg, PA), January 19, 1884, 1.

32. Donnelly, *James Nutt*, 142–50. For relevant Pennsylvania precedents regarding testimonial evidence of insanity, see John Henry Wigmore, *A Treatise on the System of Evidence in Trials at Common Law*, 4 vols. (Boston: Little, Brown, 1904), 3: 2574–75.

33. Donnelly, *James Nutt*, 142–50; "The Nutt Defense All In," *The Times* (Philadelphia), January 19, 1884, 1. Quotations appear in *James Nutt*, 149, 144, 146. Note that the term "unsound mind" was in the phrasing of Johnson's question, which the witness answered in the affirmative.

34. "Nutt's Trial Ended," *The Times* (Philadelphia), January 20, 1884, 1; "The Nutt Trial," *The Patriot* (Harrisburg, PA), January 21, 1884, 1.

35. Donnelly, *James Nutt*, 150–51. Quotation appears on 151.

36. Ibid., 151–53.

37. Ibid., 153–54. Quotation appears on page 153.

38. Ibid., 154.

39. Ibid., 154; "Nutt's Trial Ended," *The Times* (Philadelphia), January 20, 1884, 1.

40. "Nutt's Trial Ended," *The Times* (Philadelphia), January 20, 1884, 1.

41. "How Nutt and the Jury Spent Sunday," *The Times* (Philadelphia), January 21, 1884, 1.

Chapter 13

1. "In the Hands of the Jury," *The Times* (Philadelphia), January 22, 1884, 1; "The Lawyers Pleading," *The Patriot* (Harrisburg, PA), January 22, 1884, 1.

2. "Not Guilty," *Genius of Liberty* (Uniontown, PA), January 24, 1884, 1.

3. Ibid.; Edward J. Donnelly, *Trial of James Nutt for the Killing of N. L. Dukes at Uniontown, Fayette County, Pennsylvania, PA., June 13th, 1883: Containing a Complete History of the Dual Tragedy, Letters and Expert Testimony. Also, the Medical Expert Testimony, Verbatim; Speeches, Rulings, Charge of the Court, Points of Counsel, Portraits, etc.* (Pittsburgh: Stevenson & Foster, 1884), 155. Quotation appears in ibid.

4. Donnelly, *James Nutt*, 155; "Not Guilty," *Genius of Liberty* (Uniontown, PA), January 24, 1884, 1. Quotation appears in *James Nutt*.

5. Donnelly, *James Nutt*, 157–60. Quotations appear on pages 157 and 158.

6. Donnelly, *James Nutt*, 162–66. Quotation appears on page 166. For the audience applause, see "Not Guilty," *Genius of Liberty* (Uniontown, PA), January 24, 1884, 1.

7. Donnelly, *James Nutt*, 166; "The Nutt Jury Out," *Harrisburg Telegraph*, January 22, 1884, 1; Henry D. Jordan, "Daniel Wolsey Voorhees," *Mississippi Valley Historical Review* 6 (March 1920): 533.

8. Donnelly, *James Nutt*, 168.

9. Ibid., 169, 171; "Not Guilty," *Genius of Liberty* (Uniontown, PA), January 24, 1884, 1. Quotations appear in *James Nutt*.

10. Donnelly, *James Nutt*, 175–76.

11. Ibid., 176, 180.

12. "Not Guilty," *Genius of Liberty* (Uniontown, PA), January 24, 1884, 1; "The Nutt Jury Out," *Harrisburg Telegraph*, January 22, 1884, 1.

13. "Not Guilty," *Genius of Liberty* (Uniontown, PA), January 24, 1884, 1; Donnelly, *James Nutt*, 193–96, 208. Quotations appear in *James Nutt*, 193, 194.

14. Donnelly, *James Nutt*, 197–204; *Lizzie Nutt's Sad Experience: A Heart Broken, and a Family Plunged in Grief. Wreck and Ruin!* (Philadelphia: Barclay, 1886), 42. Quotations appear in *James Nutt*, 197, 202; *Sad Experience*, 42.

15. "Not Guilty," *Genius of Liberty* (Uniontown, PA), January 24, 1884, 1; Donnelly, *James Nutt*, 206–8, 210. Quotations appear in *James Nutt*, 210.

16. "Not Guilty," *Genius of Liberty* (Uniontown, PA), January 24, 1884, 1.

17. Donnelly, *James Nutt*, 181–82, 186–87. Quotations appear on pages 182 and 187.

18. Ibid., 187–88.

19. Ibid., 189–91.

20. Donnelly, *James Nutt*, 191, 192; "The Nutt Jury Out," *Harrisburg Telegraph*, January 22, 1884, 1. Quotations appear in *James Nutt*.

21. "In the Hands of the Jury," *The Times* (Philadelphia), January 22, 1884, 1.

22. Ibid.

23. "James Nutt Not Guilty," *The Times* (Philadelphia), January 23, 1884, 1; "Receiving the Verdict," *Harrisburg Telegraph*, January 23, 1884, 1.

24. "James Nutt Not Guilty," *The Times* (Philadelphia), January 23, 1884, 1; "A Welcome Verdict," *Inter Ocean* (Chicago), January 23, 1884, 5.

25. "A Welcome Verdict," *Inter Ocean* (Chicago), January 23, 1884, 5.

26. "James Nutt Not Guilty," *The Times* (Philadelphia), January 23, 1884, 1.

27. Ibid.; "The Temperature," *Pittsburgh Commercial-Gazette*, January 23, 1884, 4; "James Nutt Justified," *Harrisburg Telegraph*, January 22, 1884, 1; "Receiving the Verdict," *Harrisburg Telegraph*, January 23, 1884, 1. Quotations appear in ibid. and "Receiving the Verdict," *Harrisburg Telegraph*.

Chapter 14

1. "Not Guilty," *Genius of Liberty* (Uniontown, PA), January 24, 1884, 1; "A Welcome Verdict," *Inter Ocean* (Chicago), January 23, 1884, 5; "James Nutt Not Guilty," *The Times* (Philadelphia), January 23, 1884, 1. Quotation appears in *Inter Ocean*.

2. "James Nutt Not Guilty," *The Times* (Philadelphia), January 23, 1884, 1.

3. These remarks from Judge Stowe appear in both "Receiving the Verdict," *Harrisburg Telegraph*, January 23, 1884, 1; and "What the Judge Said," *Atlanta Constitution*, January 25, 1884, 1.

4. "Not Guilty," *Harrisburg Telegraph*, January 22, 1884, 4; "James Nutt Not Guilty," *The Times* (Philadelphia), January 23, 1884, 1.

5. "Receiving the Verdict," *Harrisburg Telegraph*, January 23, 1884, 1.

6. "Not Guilty," *Genius of Liberty* (Uniontown, PA), January 24, 1884, 1; "Acquitted," *Republican Standard*, January 24, 1884, 1, Historic Newspaper Collection, Pennsylvania Room, Uniontown Public Library; "Young Nutt At Home," *The Times* (Philadelphia), January 24, 1884, 1.

7. "Young Nutt At Home," *The Times* (Philadelphia), January 24, 1884, 1; "Acquitted," *Republican Standard*, January 24, 1884, 1, Historic Newspaper

Collection, Pennsylvania Room, Uniontown Public Library. Quotations appear in *Republican Standard*.

8. "James Nutt Released," *The Patriot* (Harrisburg, PA), January 24, 1884, 1.

9. "Young Nutt At Home," *The Times* (Philadelphia), January 24, 1884, 1; James Nutt Released," *The Patriot* (Harrisburg, PA), January 24, 1884, 1; "The Nutt Family at Home," *Harrisburg Telegraph*, January 24, 1884, 1. Quotations appear in *The Patriot* and *Harrisburg Telegraph*.

10. "The Nutt Family at Home," *Harrisburg Telegraph*, January 24, 1884, 1; Untitled, *Fort Wayne Sentinel* (IN), January 24, 1884, 2.

11. "The Nutt Family at Home," *Harrisburg Telegraph*, January 24, 1884, 1.

12. Quotations appear in "James Nutt a Free Man," *Wheeling Register* (WV), January 23, 1884, 2; Untitled, *Trenton Evening Times*, January 23, 1884, 2; "The Acquittal of Nutt," *New York Herald*, January 23, 1884, 4; "General Gossip," *Oshkosh Daily Northwestern* (WI), January 28, 1884, 2. See also untitled, *Parsons Daily Sun* (Parsons, KS), January 24, 1884, 2; "The Feeling on the Verdict," *Harrisburg Telegraph*, January 23, 1884, 2; the *Scranton Republican*'s editorial reprinted in "They Are All of One Opinion," *Harrisburg Telegraph*, January 26, 1884, 2; Untitled, *Wisconsin State Journal*, January 25, 1884 (Madison, WI), 4.

13. Quotations appear in Untitled, *Fort Wayne Daily News* (IN), January 23, 1884, 2; "A Just Judgment," *Courier-Journal* (Louisville, KY), January 23, 1884, 4; "The Nutt Verdict," *New Haven Evening Register*, January 23, 1884, 2. Examples of Democratic papers supporting James's acquittal include the Louisville *Courier-Journal*, *Indiana Democrat* (Indiana, PA), *Fort Wayne Daily News*, *New Haven Evening Register*, *The Times* (Philadelphia); examples of Republican endorsements of the verdict appear in *Indiana Weekly Messenger* (Indiana, PA), *Daily State Gazette* (Trenton), *Evening Critic* (Washington, DC), *Decatur Daily Republican* (IL), and *Jackson Daily Citizen* (MI).

14. Quotations appear in untitled, *Morning Oregonian*, January 24, 1884, 2; Untitled, *Evening Critic* (Washington, DC), January 23, 1884, 2; Untitled, *Cincinnati Commercial Gazette*, January 23, 1884, 4. Not every paper considered it problematic that James was found not guilty by reason of insanity. The Cleveland *Plain Dealer* considered the insanity plea "innocent subterfuge" rather than harmful—see untitled, *Plain Dealer* (Cleveland), January 23, 1884, 2. The Chicago *Inter Ocean* and Sacramento *Record-Union* are examples of the minority of newspapers that went

along, probably disingenuously, with the insanity plea—see the *Inter Ocean* editorial reprinted in "Another Way of Explaining It," *Harrisburg Telegraph*, January 25, 1884, 2; and untitled, *Record-Union* (Sacramento), January 23, 1884, 2.

15. "Acquittal of James Nutt," *Decatur Daily Republican* (IL), January 23, 1884, 2. See also "Emotional Insanity," *Boston Daily Advertiser*, January 23, 1884, 4; "A Puzzle for Jurors," *Jackson Daily Citizen* (MI), January 23, 1884, 2; "The Acquittal of Nutt," *New York Tribune*, January 23, 1884, 4.

16. "The Acquittal of Nutt," *New-York Times*, January 23, 1884, 4. See also "Weak and Silly Practices," *Indiana Herald* (Huntington, IN), January 30, 1884, 2; Untitled, *St. Albans Daily Messenger* (VT), January 23, 1884, 2.

Epilogue

1. "Fact and Fancy," *Parsons Weekly Sun* (KS), March 24, 1887, 8; Untitled, *Horton Headlight* (KS), January 17, 1895, 5; "Origin of Slang Word," *Salt Lake Tribune*, August 2, 1903, 8.

2. "The Weather," *Kansas City Star* (MO), February 5, 1895, 2; "James Nutt's Mad Crime," *Kansas City Star* (MO), February 7, 1895, 7; "Crazy from Drink," *San Francisco Chronicle*, February 6, 1895, 2; "A Horrible Crime," *Horton Headlight Commercial*, February 7, 1895, 4; "Attempted Murder!" *Horton Headlight*, February 7, 1895, 4.

3. "Bad for James Nutt," *Kansas City Star* (MO), February 11, 1895, 2; "Attempted Murder!" *Horton Headlight*, February 7, 1895, 4; "James Nutt's Mad Crime," *Kansas City Star* (MO), February 7, 1895, 7. Quotation appears in "James Nutt's Mad Crime," *Kansas City Star*.

4. "Diabolical," *Parsons Daily Sun* (KS), September 21, 1884, 1; "Atrocious Villainy," *Waterloo Press* (IN), September 25, 1884, 6; "Men Have Died for Her," *Inter Ocean* (Chicago), December 9, 1891, 1; "Mrs. Nutt Hears the News," *The Times* (Philadelphia), February 7, 1895, 1. For examples of national news coverage, see "Struggle for Life," *Logansport Reporter* (IN), February 6, 1895, 1; "News of the Day," *Alexandria Gazette* (VA), February 6, 1895, 2; "Horrible Tragedy," *Record-Union* (Sacramento), February 6, 1895, 1; "Nutt Not Badly Hurt," *Courier-Journal* (Louisville, KY), February, 7, 1895, 2; "Jim Nutt Not Dangerously Hurt," *Daily Chronicle* (Centralia, WA), February 7, 1895, 1; "Nutt Will Recover," *The Sun and the Erie County Independent* (NY), February 8, 1895, 2.

5. "Mrs. Payton May Recover," *Estherville Daily News* (IA), February 14, 1895, 2; "Jim Nutt Talks," *Harrisburg Telegraph*, April 18, 1895, 1.

6. "James Nutt on Trial," *Kansas City Star* (MO), May 11, 1895, 1; "Nutt Sheds Tears," *Wichita Daily Eagle* (KS), May 12, 1895, 1; "Nutt Murder Case," *Fort Wayne News* (IN), May 16, 1895, 2; "James Nutt Convicted," *Kansas City Star* (MO), May 16, 1885, 1; "Jim Nutt Gets 15 Years," *Evening Democrat* (Warren, PA), June 20, 1895, 1. Technically, there were two separate trials, one concerning each attempted murder charge—see "James Nutt Convicted," *Kansas City Star* (MO), May 16, 1885, 1.

Afterword

1. Both James McPherson and Lorien Foote acknowledge that honor played a role in the culture of the Union Army during the Civil War—see James McPherson, *For Cause and Comrades: Why Men Fought in the Civil War* (New York: Oxford University Press, 1997), 77–84, 168–70; Lorien Foote, *The Gentlemen and the Roughs: Violence, Honor, and Manhood in the Union Army* (New York: New York University Press, 2010), 6, 57, 73, 77–117. The Dukes–Nutt affair highlights the salience of the honor code outside the confines of the military in Northern society generally as well as honor's enduring influence decades after the guns fell silent at Appomattox.

2. One might argue for the family feud as a fourth type of honor killing, but the duel, lynch mob, and lone vigilante encompass the kinds of violence arising in the family feud.

3. Douglas W. Allen and Clyde G. Reed, "The Duel of Honor: Screening for Unobservable Social Capital," *American Law and Economics Review* 8 (Spring 2006): 83; and see generally John Lyde Wilson, *The Code of Honor; or Rules for the Government of Principals and Seconds in Duelling* (Charleston, SC: James Phinney, 1858).

4. Wilson, *The Code of Honor.*

5. Foote, *The Gentlemen and the Roughs*, 96; *Lizzie Nutt's Sad Experience: A Heart Broken, and a Family Plunged in Grief. Wreck and Ruin!* (Philadelphia: Barclay, 1886), 34, 42; "Fatal Impromptu Duel," *New-York Times*, December 25, 1882, 1. Quotations appear in *Sad Experience* and *New-York Times.*

6. On "retributive justice" as a "form of collective violence designed to redress violations against a particular understanding of what was socially right and wrong," see Kevin Kenny, *Making Sense of the Molly Maguires* (New York: Oxford University Press, 1998), 8.

7. Robert M. Ireland, "Insanity and the Unwritten Law," *American Journal of Legal History* 32 (April 1988): 158; Robert M. Ireland, "The

Libertine Must Die: Sexual Dishonor and the Unwritten Law in the Nineteenth-Century United States," *Journal of Social History* 23 (Autumn 1989): 31; "Thaw Insane; In Matteawan," *New York Times*, February 2, 1908, 1; "Thaw, Free, Flirts with the Old Life as Mother Waits," *New York Times*, July 17, 1915, 1.

8. Samuel Walker, *Popular Justice: A History of American Criminal Justice*, 2nd ed. (New York: Oxford University Press, 1998), 73, 81, 92, 100–2.

9. "Shame! Oh, Shame!!" *Republican Standard* (Uniontown, PA), March 15, 1883, 4; "Tampering with a Witness," *Republican Standard*, March 31, 1883, 4; "What Lizzie Nutt Says," *The Times* (Philadelphia), March 16, 1883, 1; Untitled, *Harrisburg Telegraph*, March 17, 1883, 4; "The Dukes Question," *The Patriot* (Harrisburg, PA), March 20, 1883, 1; "The Acquittal of Dukes," *The Times* (Philadelphia), March 15, 1883, 2. Quotations appear in "Shame! Oh, Shame!!" *Republican Standard*; "Tampering with a Witness," *Republican Standard*; *The Patriot*; "The Acquittal of Dukes," *The Times* (Philadelphia), March 15, 1883, 2.

10. Estelle B. Freedman and John D'Emilio, *Intimate Matters: A History of Sexuality in America* (New York: Harper & Row, 1988), 75; Karen Lystra, *Searching the Heart: Women, Men, and Romantic Love in Nineteenth-Century America* (New York: Oxford University Press, 1989), 106.

11. Jane E. Larson, "Women Understand So Little, They Call My Good Nature Deceit: A Feminist Rethinking of Seduction," *Columbia Law Review* 93 (March 1993): 382–87; Melissa Murray, "Marriage as Punishment," *Columbia Law Review* 112 (January 2012): 12–18; James Dunlop, *The General Laws of Pennsylvania, from the Year 1700, to April 1849*, 2nd ed. (Philadelphia: Johnson, 1849), 1012; *Penal Laws of Pennsylvania: Passed March 31, 1860* (Harrisburg, PA: Hamilton, 1860), 15; *Commonwealth v. McCarty*, 2 Clark 351 (PA 1844). See also Francis Wharton, *A Treatise on Criminal Law*, 9th ed. (Philadelphia: Kay & Brother, 1885), 2: 549. Quotation appears in *McCarty*.

12. Lystra, *Searching the Heart*, 119.

13. Freedman and D'Emilio, 57; Helen Lefkowitz Horowitz, *Rereading Sex: Battles over Sexual Knowledge and Suppression in Nineteenth Century America* (New York: Knopf, 2002), 8–11; "Shame! Oh, Shame!!" *Republican Standard* (Uniontown, PA), March 15, 1883, 4; Philadelphia *Times* reprinted in "Dirty Dukes," *Republican Standard* (Uniontown, PA), March 22, 1883, 2; "Dukes Found Not Guilty," *The Times* (Philadelphia), March 15, 1883, 1.

14. "The Avenger's Deed," *Harrisburg Telegraph*, June 15, 1883, 1.

15. Dukes Acquitted," *New York Herald*, March 15, 1883, 6; Untitled, *Worcester Daily Spy* (MA), June 15, 1883, 2; "Weak and Silly Practices," *Indiana Herald* (Huntington, IN), January 30, 1884, 2; Untitled, *Evening Star* (Washington, DC), June 14, 1883, 2; "The Acquittal of Nutt," *New-York Times*, January 23, 1884, 4.

16. To say that the rule of law is a key element of modernity is not to suggest that it is an invention of recent history. To be sure, the concept has a long past, dating back to classical antiquity—see Brian Z. Tamanaha, *On the Rule of Law: History, Politics, Theory* (Cambridge, UK: Cambridge University Press, 2004), 7.

17. *Sad Experience*, 41; Ayers, *Vengeance and Justice*, 234; Wyatt-Brown, *Southern Honor*, 364, 401, 437; *Poughkeepsie Eagle* reprinted in "Dirty Dukes," *Republican Standard*, March 22, 1883, 2; *Pittsburgh Commercial-Gazette* reprinted in "Dukes Shot Dead!" *Daily Republican* (Monongahela, PA), June 14, 1883, 1; Edward J. Donnelly, *Trial of James Nutt for the Killing of N. L. Dukes at Uniontown, Fayette County, Pennsylvania, PA., June 13th, 1883: Containing a Complete History of the Dual Tragedy, Letters and Expert Testimony. Also, the Medical Expert Testimony, Verbatim; Speeches, Rulings, Charge of the Court, Points of Counsel, Portraits, etc.* (Pittsburgh: Stevenson & Foster, 1884), 168. Quotations appear in *Sad Experience* and *James Nutt*.

18. Quotations appear in *Sad Experience*, 43–44; Donnelly, *James Nutt*, 29. The *Yale Law Journal* noted, "Trial lawyers have resorted to the plea of insanity to get before a jury all the circumstances of the so-called honor defense." To prevent the abuse of legal doctrines concerning insanity, the *Journal* recommended statutory reform to legalize honor killing: "It would seem that the proper solution of the problem lies in such legislative acceptance of the unwritten law"—see "Recognition of the Honor Defense under the Insanity Plea," *Yale Law Journal* 43 (March 1934): 810, 814. In the latter half of the nineteenth century, a few legislatures actually passed laws that allowed some forms of honor killing—see Ireland, "The Libertine Must Die": 40n8.

19. "Shame! Oh, Shame!!" *Republican Standard* (Uniontown, PA), March 15, 1883, 4; "Speech of Charles E. Boyle," *Genius of Liberty* (Uniontown, PA), April 5, 1883, 3.

20. Donnelly, *James Nutt*, 61, 63–64; 194. Quotation appears on page 64.

21. Adherents to the "Celtic thesis" could question the representativeness of the Dukes–Nutt affair for the North. Although Pennsylvania was

undoubtedly a Northern state, its southwestern corner, where Uniontown is situated, comprised the very Celtic settlers who populated the South and made honor a staple of Southern culture. Uniontown, they might say, is better understood as part of the American South—see McWhiney, *Cracker Culture: Celtic Ways in the Old South* (Tuscaloosa: University of Alabama Press, 1988), 12, 16.

The Dukes–Nutt episode, however, cannot be dismissed as the product of a Southern-oriented community in the North. For one, neither Nicholas Dukes nor Adam Nutt was of Celtic origin; Dukes was an Anglo from Ohio and Nutt a descendent of New Jersey Quakers. Furthermore, Uniontown's demographic composition was atypical of southwestern Pennsylvania—the town's Anglos outnumbered Celts by more than two to one. These numbers are derived using the 1880 census records and McWhiney's definition of Celtic (found on page 7 of *Cracker Culture*). Uniontown was approximately 54.9% Anglo-Saxon, 23.7% Celtic, and 21.3% other. And in an era when Republicans prevailed in the North and Democrats in the South, Uniontown had a Republican majority, further belying the notion that it was culturally Southern. Most important, the story of a father and brother willing to risk their lives for the honor of their family inspired a national outpouring of support that transcended the varieties of subcultures across the North and around the United States.

No quantitative study of honor killing yet exists that could establish whether the practice was less prevalent in the North than in the South, in either absolute or relative terms. In any event, numbers can be deceptive; a culture of honor can flourish even in a region with a low rate of honor-bound bloodshed. The mid-eighteenth century South, for instance, was enthralled with honor but saw few murders—see Randolph Roth, *American Homicide* (Cambridge, MA: Belknap Press of Harvard University Press, 2009), 13. The Gilded-Age North also valorized honor killings, perhaps without precipitating inordinate numbers of them. The historical value of the Dukes–Nutt affair is that it provides an opportunity to see the pervasive embrace of honor killing that raw numbers might otherwise mask. The press was quick to recognize honor killing as an accepted practice in all regions. As the *Buffalo Courier* wrote of the Kentucky congressman "Little Phil" Thompson (whom Voorhees defended in 1883 for slaying Walter Davis, his wife's seducer), "It is not likely that there is a single spot in the United States where he would be punished for killing Davis. The crime that he has committed involves a woman's virtue, and so far as we know that fact justifies a homicide from Maine to Texas." (*Buffalo Courier* reprinted in the *Courier-Journal*, Louisville, KY, May 10, 1883, 4.)

Another possible rebuttal to this book might point to Uniontown's rural location as evidence that the Dukes–Nutt affair was unrepresentative of a broad-based culture of honor. According to this reasoning, the honor code could be expected to endure in the undeveloped countryside while losing traction in modern urban centers. Yet the most strident endorsements of honor killing with respect to the Dukes–Nutt case appeared in the newspapers of America's leading cities including Cleveland, Washington, Chicago, Baltimore, Atlanta, and Cincinnati. Notably, it was James Nutt's counsel, prepared to champion honor, who wanted his trial moved to that paragon of urbanization, Pittsburgh. His prosecutors, set to argue for the rule of law, unsuccessfully petitioned for a rural change of venue. As David Patterson for the Commonwealth pointed out to Judge Willson, sympathy for the defendant was even stronger in Pittsburgh than in the countryside.

Given that honor's enduring cachet was partly a reaction to modernity, the resonance of honor in cities should come as little surprise. It was only natural that inhabitants of urban America—with its congestion, pollution, and stench—would have nostalgia for the countryside they left behind. Verdant suburbs, where a city's ruling class fled, embodied the desire to recreate the hinterlands in some form. Well into the twentieth century, urban planning in the United States was characterized not by an ambition to maximize the novel opportunities that cities afforded but by a reactionary impulse to disperse metropolitan populations into aggregations of towns—in short, to impose the logic of the country on the city; see Jane Jacobs, *The Death and Life of Great American Cities* (London: Jonathan Cape, 1962), 17–23. The values of the countryside, including the honor code, appealed to Americans whose concerns about the hazards of urbanization were not limited to landscapes.

INDEX

Page numbers in *italics* indicate illustrations.